Free Will and De
in Joseph Conrad's
Major Novels

Laurence Davie

Spring 2015

125

Internationale Forschungen zur
Allgemeinen und
Vergleichenden Literaturwissenschaft

In Verbindung mit

Norbert Bachleitner (Universität Wien), Dietrich Briesemeister (Friedrich Schiller-Universität Jena), Francis Claudon (Université Paris XII), Joachim Knape (Universität Tübingen), Klaus Ley (Johannes Gutenberg-Universität Mainz), John A. McCarthy (Vanderbilt University), Alfred Noe (Universität Wien), Manfred Pfister (Freie Universität Berlin), Sven H. Rossel (Universität Wien)

herausgegeben von

Alberto Martino
(Universität Wien)

Redaktion: Ernst Grabovszki

Anschrift der Redaktion:
Institut für Vergleichende Literaturwissenschaft, Berggasse 11/5, A-1090 Wien

Free Will and Determinism in Joseph Conrad's Major Novels

Ludwig Schnauder

Amsterdam - New York, NY 2009

Cover Image:
Joseph Conrad seated 1920" Beinecke Rare Book and Manuscript Library,
Yale University.

Cover design:
Pier Post

Le papier sur lequel le présent ouvrage est imprimé remplit les prescriptions
de "ISO 9706:1994, Information et documentation - Papier pour documents -
Prescriptions pour la permanence".

The paper on which this book is printed meets the requirements of " ISO
9706:1994, Information and documentation - Paper for documents - Requirements
for permanence".

Die Reihe „Internationale Forschungen zur Allgemeinen und Vergleichenden
Literaturwissenschaft" wird ab dem Jahr 2005 gemeinsam von Editions Rodopi,
Amsterdam – New York und dem Weidler Buchverlag, Berlin herausgegeben.
Die Veröffentlichungen in deutscher Sprache erscheinen im Weidler Buchverlag,
alle anderen bei Editions Rodopi.

From 2005 onward, the series „Internationale Forschungen zur Allgemeinen
und Vergleichenden Literaturwissenschaft" will appear as a joint publication by
Editions Rodopi, Amsterdam – New York and Weidler Buchverlag, Berlin. The
German editions will be published by Weidler Buchverlag, all other publications
by Editions Rodopi.

ISBN: 978-90-420-2616-2
E-Book ISBN: 978-90-420-2617-9
© Editions Rodopi B.V., Amsterdam - New York, NY 2009
Printed in The Netherlands

Contents

1. Introduction

In Joseph Conrad's novels the majority of protagonists fail in a more or less spectacular manner in what they attempt to achieve. Charles Gould in *Nostromo*, for instance, is not able to use the wealth of the San Tomé mine towards the good of his country but becomes its slave. Not least for this reason his wife Emilia is so disillusioned towards the end of the novel that she finds it hard to believe even in her charitable projects. In *Heart of Darkness* Kurtz, the would-be paragon of European civilisation, sets out into the Congo inspired by the imperialist mission but is transformed into a savage monster. Winnie and her mother in *The Secret Agent* sacrifice their lives to protect Stevie but only succeed in destroying him. The eponymous hero in *Lord Jim* wants to live up to his ideal of a gentleman-captain of the Merchant Marine but at the first sign of danger abandons his ship with hundreds of passengers on board to save his own life. The consequences of his deed haunt him for the rest of his short life and are among the causes that bring his reign in Patusan and his love for Pearl to an inglorious end. In *Under Western Eyes* Razumov's attempt to regain a measure of control over his life and identity by making a full confession to Natalia and the revolutionaries turns him into a cripple. In *Victory* Heyst withdraws to Samburan to safeguard his romance with Lena but cannot prevent the forces of evil from destroying his idyll. This list of failures suggests that Conrad's characters have little control over their lives. But what is it that exercises such power over them? Is it history, society, an economic system, flawed human nature, genetic inheritance, a particular character trait, a metaphysical entity, or the rule of arbitrary chance? Many critics have noted that Conrad's characters often appear helpless as against the forces arrayed against them, but no one has examined these powers systematically or attempted to rigorously address the central philosophical question which the figures' predicament raises: that of the freedom-of-the-will. This study attempts to remedy this neglect by discussing Conrad's novels not only in terms of the philosophical debate about the freedom-of-the-will problem but also in terms of the changing historical, economic, scientific, and literary discourses of the Victorian and Early-Modernist period in which the issue becomes manifest. In a paradigmatic analysis of *Heart of Darkness*, *Nostromo*, and *The Secret Agent* the freedom-of-the-will problem will be traced in certain recurring themes and dilemmas the characters have to face. Concomitant questions that also come into focus are the status of morality and moral responsibility, the human condition and possibilities of human conduct in a materialist-deterministic universe.

2. Free Will and Determinism: A Philosophical Introduction

2.1 Key theories in the Free Will and Determinism Debate

Free will and determinism is a perennial issue in philosophical debates and has been tackled in one way or another by almost all major thinkers. The problem is related, among others, to questions of cause and effect, of ethics and law, and of conceptions of the self. In philosophy we come across three major ways of thinking about the problem: libertarianism, hard determinism, and soft determinism. The terms "hard" and "soft" determinism were coined by William James in his essay "The Dilemma of Determinism" (1884). His terminology has persisted to this day although both libertarians and determinists largely discount the line of argument he put forward in favour of free will. The three theories can best be understood by analysing their respective positions with regard to the existence or non-existence of uncaused and free choices and to the relationship between free choices, moral responsibility, and determinism (cf. Double 201). Hard determinists are incompatibilists: they believe that free choices are incompatible with our choices being caused. Hard determinists hold that all our choices are caused and that therefore none of our choices are free. Consequently, we are never morally responsible. As Double puts it, "[w]hat is "hard" about hard determinism is its conclusion: no free will and no moral responsibility" (203). Many hard determinists express regret that they have to reach this verdict but accept it for the sake of consistency. The hard determinists' view that no one is ever free or morally responsible for anything has far-reaching consequences for how we view ourselves, our relationship to others, and the world at large. After all, holding that no one is truly morally responsible, would mean giving up all beliefs and practices that require moral responsibility for their justification. Criminals, for instance, could no longer be punished on the grounds that they deserve punishment but only for utilitarian reasons, such as deterring crime or rehabilitating criminals (cf. Double 204). Interpersonal attitudes such as love, friendship, gratitude, resentment, or indignation would have to be seen in a completely new light or given up altogether. The hard determinist position is elegantly summed up in

Jonathan Westphal's 'Master Argument' (cf. 136), which highlights the relationship between the various concepts and terms involved in the free will and determinism discussion. The hard determinist position is reached by accepting all the steps in the argument; the soft determinist and libertarian positions are reached by denying some of the steps:

(1) Every human action is an event.
(2) Every event has an explanation.
(3) Every human action has an explanation.
(4) Every explanation includes a cause.
(5) Every event has a cause.
(6) Every human action has a cause.
(7) If a human action has a cause, it is not free.
(8) No human action is free.

Soft determinists, like hard determinists, believe that all choices and therefore all actions are caused. Thus they accept the first six steps in the Master Argument. With regard to premise seven, however, they diverge from the hard determinists. Soft determinists believe that the fact that a choice and its resulting action are caused does not mean that they are not free. Therefore soft determinists are compatibilists. For them free will and moral responsibility are compatible with our choices being caused. According to Double, "[s]oft determinists claim to combine the best aspects of libertarianism and hard determinism" (204): they affirm free will as the libertarians do and believe that human beings are morally responsible for their acts; they, however, also believe that all choices are caused as the hard determinists do, thereby agreeing with most scientists. The soft determinists' main argumentative task is to disprove the incompatibilist claim that we cannot be morally responsible for caused choices (cf. Double 205). As soft determinists believe that we make both free and unfree choices they have to formulate criteria to distinguish between the two. One step towards this is a clarification of terms. As the soft determinist A.J. Ayer points out, the use of the word determinism is misleading as it "tends to suggest that one event is somehow in the power of another" (22). We form the mental picture of

> an unhappy effect trying vainly to escape from the clutches of an overmastering cause. But [...] the fact is simply that when an event of one type occurs, an event of another type occurs also, in a certain temporal or spatio-temporal relation to the first. The rest is only metaphor. And it is because of the metaphor, and not because of the fact, that we come to think that there is an antithesis between causality and freedom. (Ayer 22)

This antithesis is denied by soft determinists. They believe that freedom should not be contrasted with causality but with constraint. The soft determinist solution is therefore to accept that there are only caused actions and to distinguish among them between free and compelled ones. As Hospers explains, "[b]eing coerced is one form of causation, one way of being caused; all coerced acts are caused, but not all caused acts are coerced" (160). Jonathan Westphal gives the following example to highlight the soft determinist position:

> On the one hand, there is simple causation. Suppose, for example, a small boy is eating his soup. We can say that he is caused to eat his soup by his hunger. On the other hand, he can be made to eat his soup, or forced to eat, say by his mother [...]. This is more than causation. In the first case, says the compatibilist, the boy is eating freely, *because* he is not being coerced or forced. In the second case, he is not eating freely *because* he is being coerced or forced to eat. (138)

However, it is also possible to imagine a situation where the boy wants to eat his soup but is at the same time forced to eat it by his mother. To deal with such situations soft determinists add an extra requirement to their analysis, namely that – to stay with Westphal's example – the boy only eats freely "if he could have *not* eaten *if* he had not wanted to" (139). Therefore, when the boy is eating freely, he could have done otherwise if he had wanted to. The soft determinist analysis of a free choice can thus be formulated as follows: "S does *a*, S wants to do *a*, and S could have done otherwise if he or she had wanted" (Westphal 139). The point of this kind of analysis is to save the concept of moral responsibility: even though all our choices and their resulting actions are caused, we can still be held morally responsible for them if they are not coerced and if we could have done otherwise. This is, as it were, all the freedom that we need. As Hospers puts it, for soft determinists "[f]reedom exists only to the extent that determinism is true" (158).

One of the key issues that therefore divides compatibilists (soft determinists) from incompatibilists (hard determinists and libertarians) is the problem of how one should interpret expressions such as 'free to do otherwise', 'could have done otherwise', or 'his/her act was avoidable', which we use to mete out praise and punishment. Both compatibilists and incompatibilists seem to agree that people can be held morally responsible for their past actions only if they were able to do otherwise. Therefore, avoidability is a necessary condition of responsibility. Philosophers distinguish between two senses of 'avoidable', the categorical and the hypothetical sense:

> In the *categorical sense*, to say that an act is avoidable is to say that there were no antecedent conditions (causes) sufficient for its occurrence. In the *hypothetical sense*, to say that an act is avoidable is to say that *if* the actor had chosen (or, perhaps, intended) to do otherwise, he would have done otherwise (nothing would have stopped him). (Feinberg and Shafer-Landau 413-414)

Avoidability in the hypothetical sense is compatible with determinism and is employed by soft determinists. Avoidability in the categorical sense is not compatible with determinism and is used – for different ends – by hard determinists and libertarians. That soft determinists rely on a hypothetical analysis of freedom and avoidability is regarded by many philosophers as the theory's weakest point. Nevertheless, soft determinism is the best argued and most frequently held of the three theories under discussion and has been supported in the history of philosophy by Thomas Hobbes, John Locke, David Hume, J.S. Mill, Bertrand Russell, G.E. Moore, and many others. The challenge soft determinism issues to its opponents is not easy to meet:

> So long as you are choosing as you want [...] and as you reflectively think is best [...], what *more* could you want by way of free will? Do you want your desires, beliefs, and values *not* to cause your choices? Would you like to be in a situation where you want to choose X and end up choosing Y? How could the possibility that your choice might go awry *improve* your freedom? (Double 207)

These questions are particularly relevant to libertarianism, which is a form of indeterminism and therefore based on the belief that not all events in the universe are subject to causation. As Feinberg and Shafer-Landau point out, "[a]ll libertarians [...] are indeterminists (by definition), but not all indeterminists are libertarians" (413). It is conceivable to hold that all actions are uncaused and therefore occur by random chance. Such a view would be indeterminist but not libertarian. This position is usually neglected in the free will and determinism debate as it is regarded as irrational and nihilistic. Nevertheless, radical indeterminism, which was fuelled by developments in late nineteenth and early twentieth century science, has exerted a considerable attraction to philosophers such as Friedrich Nietzsche and Modernist writers such as Joseph Conrad. Radical indeterminism, like hard determinism, denies free will. It is arguably even more unpalatable than hard determinism as it implies that there is no conjunction between cause and effect and that we are subject to chaotic forces. Radical indeterminism has nothing in common with traditional libertarianism, which is characterised by moral conservatism and the upholding of humanist or Christian values. Libertarians believe that we sometimes choose freely and at those times – and *only* at those times – are morally responsible for our behaviour. Libertarians are incompatibilists in so far as they hold that caused choices cannot be free. They believe that we choose freely only when we make uncaused choices. As Double explains, a libertarian free choice is two-way in the following sense: "If we choose to do A, we could have chosen to do not A, and if we refrain from A, we could have chosen to do A, *given exactly the same circumstances*" (202). O'Connor adds that these circumstances must include both "(a) *internal* circumstances or the psychological and physical state of the agent, and (b) *external* circumstances or those features of the environment that are currently affecting him" (82). This last point is of prime importance in the debate between libertarians and determinists and refers back to the question of categorical and hypothetical avoidability discussed above. John Austin, a libertarian, gives the example of a golfer who misses a short putt and kicks himself because, with circumstances being exactly as they were, he could have holed his ball: "It is not that I would have holed it if conditions had been different. That might of course be so. But I am talking about conditions as they precisely were, and asserting that I could have holed it. There's the rub" (Austin quoted in Hospers 162). The determinist, of course, denies that under just those exact circumstances the golfer could have done otherwise. Something, either some external condition or some internal, mental condition, caused the difference. The determinist does not believe that the conditions could ever be exactly the same. Libertarians, on the other hand, hold that the exact circumstances are in principle repeatable and that the agent would be able to act differently due to the existence of free choices that are uncaused but not fortuitous. Because the exact circumstances are only repeatable in principle but not in practice the libertarian analysis of freedom is just as hypothetical as the soft determinist one.

Among libertarians there are two views as to how uncaused choices might occur (cf Double 202-203). 'Event-causation libertarianism' holds that "free choices occur in part due to our reason and in part due to uncaused events in the choosers' minds" (Double 202). These uncaused events might, for instance, be the unpredictable events uncovered by quantum physics. Such subatomic indeterminism might be amplified to makes choices in our brains indetermined. The question, of course, is whether this kind of indeterminism gives us the freedom that we want or whether it just leads to the kind of radical, nihilistic indeterminism described above. The second view as to uncaused, free choices is 'agent-theory libertarianism'. According to Watson this theory was developed because "the denial of determinism does not ensure, by itself, that *we* determine anything. So an incompatibilist who affirms freedom [...] must say what more is needed besides the absence of causal determination to get 'self-determination'" (9). This is why agent-theory libertarianism distinguishes between two kinds of causation: causation by events and causation by agents. As Double explains "[w]hereas event causation holds between two events (e.g., one mental event causing another), agent causation holds between a *thing* and an event (e.g., an agent and a mental event)" (203). In the case of human beings, the agent is the self: I believe that I am a self-moving being, a genuine originator of actions. My acts, although caused by me, are not the inevitable product of antecedent conditions. If they were, I would not be the agent but only the vehicle or instrumentality through which the causal chain proceeded. Determinists, of course, are not satisfied with this view because they do not believe that anything can be the cause of itself. In particular due to the rise and authority of scientific determinism, libertarians appear to be fighting for a lost cause.

2.2   Arguments for and against Determinism

Libertarians, soft determinists, and hard determinists believe that to decide whether we are free, we need to find out whether and how our choices and their resulting actions are caused. Although it is conceivable that all human choices are caused even if determinism is false, if it is true, then all human choices (along with all other events in the universe) are caused (cf. Double 211). For this reason the historical debate over the freedom-of-the-will-problem has focused on determinism in general. Before reviewing the arguments for and against determinism, three terms that frequently come up in the discussion should be clarified: fatalism, universal predictability, and chance.

Fatalism does not equal determinism. To say that an event was fated to happen is to say more than that it was causally determined. Fatalism implies that no matter which choices we make, they will have no influence on our lives. Our fate is sealed, regardless of how hard we try to escape it. Double compares fatalism to "the psychological concept of *learned helplessness*" (212) and according to Feinberg and Shafer-Landau it is "a doctrine with strange mystic overtones" (412). Whereas fatalism implies that our choices do not matter, determinism, especially the soft determinist variety, holds that they do. Our choices dictate how our lives shall be; it is just that our choices are caused. We should also bear in mind that determinism does not entail that we can predict the future. Determinism holds that every event is the necessary result of laws that govern all events and the condition of the universe immediately before an event. It might seem to follow that if someone were acquainted with all the laws of nature and had a complete knowledge of the condition of reality at any one moment, he would be in a position to predict the future. This train of thought is sometimes referred to as 'Laplace's Demon' as it was the eighteenth-century mathematician and philosopher Laplace who first formulated it (cf. Weatherford 55). However, the "one-big-clock view of the universe" (Ryle 123) is an illusion as prediction is an epistemological feat that we may or may not manage. As Double points out, "[m]any events that are determined are not predictable simply because they are complicated" (212). He gives the following example: if we drop a piece of chalk from a certain height we are not able to predict whether it will break or not, despite the fact that the chalk's breaking or not is determined. So the most we can say is that if determinism is true, then all events are *in principle* predictable but not necessarily *actually* predictable. Gilbert Ryle also claims that a "100 per cent total forecast" (145) is not only practically but also logically impossible: "Making a forecast is also part of the stream of events and it is logically impossible for it to include a forecast about its own effects. There is an inevitable unfinishedness attached to such predictions. I cannot overtake my own shadow, however fast I run" (145). The third term that needs to be clarified is chance. As in everyday life we often speak of events happening by chance, one could suppose that this is an argument for indeterminism. Determinists, however, point out that by chance we do not usually mean to say that the events referred to have no cause. Ryle (cf. 124) gives the following example: if I meet my brother 'by chance' on a station platform, this means that neither of us went there with the intention of meeting the other. It is a coincidence but it does not show that there was not a cause for my being there or for my brother's being there. According to Ryle,

> [t]here is a causal chain which led up to my being present on the station at that moment and so there is in the case of my brother. But the one series is quite independent of the other. [...] There can be no inference from the events that led up to the one [occurrence] to the events that led up to the other. (124)

Similarly, when biologists say that mutations occur 'by chance', this does not imply that mutations have no causes, only that their occurrence cannot be predicted because the causes are not known (cf. Hospers 157-158). Although 'chance' and 'randomness' are powerful concepts of great imaginative potential to which many creative artists have been attracted, it is nevertheless doubtful whether 'chance', scientifically speaking, ever means 'no cause at all'.

The strongest argument for determinism or universal causation is the progress of natural science. Although its history began much earlier, scientific determinism proper first gained strength during the rise of modern science in the sixteenth century and reached a first high point in the work of Descartes, Newton, and Laplace. By then mechanics, physics, and chemistry had become well-established sciences. In the following centuries, scientific determinism was extended to include biology and – most significantly – human beings as one began to see mankind as part of nature. Darwin's theory of evolution and Freud's theory of the human psyche provided further evidence for the existence of scientific determinism. Deterministic theories can, of course, not only be found within the natural sciences but also within sociology, economics, or history. As Hollis points out, however,

> [e]very social science is divided on the issue. For instance, the core of economics is taken by some to be a study of how economic agents rationally choose to allocate resources and by others as a study of the forces which shape the economy. Some sociologists portray us as creating our social world, whereas others make us its creatures. [...] Many historians tell a tale of influential, voluntary choices made at critical moments but others see that past as phases and movements, which sweep the actors along. (159-160)

Certainly, the further we move away from the 'hard sciences' such as physics or chemistry the less stringently determinism can be argued for. As McFee puts it, "the notion of causal necessity seems less convincing than when the causes are interpreted along lines suggested by physical sciences" (28). It is doubtful whether historical, sociological, or economic constraints can ever necessitate to the same degree as physical causes. However, even scientific determinism proper can be construed in a more or less deterministic way, depending on how the notion of causal laws is understood. Descartes, Newton, d'Holbach, and Laplace thought of nature as a machine that is governed by iron laws and forces. However, when science in the late nineteenth and early twentieth centuries subscribed to theories that accept an element of chance or indeterminism in nature, we come across 'softer' accounts of causality. Darwin's theory of evolution, for instance, which was earlier understood as implying a linear and strictly deterministic development of all life towards human perfectibility, was now interpreted as a directionless, random process with no ultimate goal. Similarly, Einstein's relativity theory and Heisenberg's uncertainty principle postulate that many events cannot be predicted exactly but only probabilistically. Whether the above-mentioned scientists were genuine indeterminsts, believing in a universe governed by chance and randomness is, however, doubtful. According to Ted Honderich their position can best be described as "*near-determinism*" (*How Free* 5), the belief that natural and physical processes are rule-governed but not to an exclusive extent.

Another 'softening' of the causal principle is due to more flexible ideas of cause and effect that go back to David Hume. The famous empiricist rejected the notion of iron, necessary laws and merely spoke of reliable patterns or 'constant conjunction'. He argued that the world that we learn about from experience consists of observable facts and regularities, which is all that science requires. The idea of causality becomes still more flexible if we regard it as barely more than an assumption of modern science. Causality is then regarded as something that we do not learn from the world but that we bring to it, something that we may adopt or abandon if we choose. As Hospers asks, "Why not consider the Causal Principle a kind of rule of the scientific game, a rule whose adoption makes the game more fruitful or yields some other desired result? If we adopt the rule we may be more encouraged to find causes" (150). This line of reasoning might, however, lead straight to William James's problematic doctrine of pragmatism. You simply believe in what seems the most workable thesis, without bothering about its truth or untruth. Although it may be refreshing to conceive of determinism as an assumption rather than an inescapable truth, this will leave both determinists and indeterminists dissatisfied.

More controversial than the general theory of determinism or universal causation is the thesis that all events *including* human choices are caused which, of course, has direct consequences for the existence or non-existence of free will. In support of the causation of human choices philosophers frequently employ the motive argument. It holds that conscious choices are always determined by our strongest motive, which is the result of various previous psychological states made up of our likes, dislikes, fears, hopes, beliefs, and values (cf. Double 215). What we commonly refer to as 'the will' – our ability to choose – is, as Double puts it, "pushed or pulled to choose as it does by the sum of the psychological states of the chooser" (215). The view of human behaviour that emerges from the motive argument is a gloomy one: none of our actions are free as they are all caused by motives that make us choose and act in particular ways. The determinist Gilbert Ryle does not refute the essential validity of the motive argument but believes that its implications for human life would not be so depressing if one used different metaphors. According to Ryle it is misleading to model the discussion of motives on "combustion engines" and to insinuate that "a motive is some sort of internal push, pull, pressure or build-up which issues in action" (136). Instead, Ryle advocates a soft determinist view. Normally we act in the way we want to act and are not helpless in our motives' clutches. It is only in special circumstances, for instance when we are under external or internal duress, that we are coerced to act against our grain. As Ryle says,

> [i]t is clear that the picture of wants as irresistible gales driving one in some direction has some basis, though not much because all the cases mentioned [by hard determinists] are exceptions and not the rule. In normal cases advice, the thoughts one thinks, etc. can make some difference and can make all the difference to what one does. (143-144)

Today the strongest arguments for the causation of human choices do not derive from the motive argument or psychological determinism but from neuroscience, which looks, as McFee puts it, at "the causal story "behind" the psychology" (48). Neuroscience, therefore, turns our attention once again towards physical determinism or, to be more precise, towards biophysical mechanisms. The evidence we have about the production of human behaviour indicates that it is caused by the central nervous system, in particular our brains. Neuroscience suggests that the brain operates according to electrical and chemical laws and that it functions just as deterministically as our other organs. If, as quantum theory claims, there is indeterminism at the level of the atoms, it does not seem to affect the functioning of the brain any more than it affects the working of any other organs. Richard Double (cf. 216) proposes the following syllogism in favour of our choices being subject to determinism:

> (1) Human behavior is a product of the brain.
> (2) The brain is a determined system.
> (3) Therefore, human behavior is determined.

Arguments that have been brought forward against this kind of determinism include, among others, mind-body dualism. Dualism, which goes back to René Descartes, is the belief that even though the body, being material, is subject to the mechanical laws of physics, people also possess non-physical minds or souls that make choices in indeterministic ways. However, there is no evidence that human beings possess non-physical minds and even if they did, it is doubtful whether these entities would behave indeterministically. Dualists also have to explain how a mind can be free while the body in which it is lodged is causally determined and subject to the laws of science. Similar to dualists, agent-theory libertarians have speculated that 'agents' – our 'selves' – are able to produce indeterministic choices. Again there is no evidence that agents in this sense exist and it is questionable whether something can be the cause of itself.

2.3   Arguments for and against Indeterminism

Indeterminism is simply the view that some events have no causes. Therefore, universal causation is denied. Arguments for indeterminism are often based on scientific theories that recognize the importance of randomness and chance in the universe, for instance the ones developed around the turn of the last century by evolutionists such as T.H. Huxley and physicists such as Einstein and Heisenberg. Libertarians have welcomed these theories as the most common objection to libertarianism is that it flies into the face of science. The following example will illustrate how libertarians have used the findings of quantum mechanics to bolster their position (cf. Trusted 56-57). Heisenberg's uncertainty principle implies that there are theoretical limitations to the possibility of simultaneously measuring the exact position and the exact velocity of a mechanical system or any part of such a system. Although the uncertainty principle applies to all events, it is significant only in relation to events concerning elementary particles that are subatomic in size and mass. One consequence of this principle is that it becomes impossible, not only in practice but also in principle, to predict the behaviour of elementary particles. Therefore, causal laws describing the characteristics of such particles can no longer be formulated. Another consequence is the identification of clearly defined classes of uncaused events, namely those occurring on a sub-atomic level. The argument of event-causation libertarians is that since we are all composed of such particles, all or most parts of human behaviour comprise such uncaused events. They believe that indeterminism within the atom may be amplified to contribute to uncaused choices in the brain at times of conflicting motivation. If this can be shown to happen, the consequence might be indeterminism in our choices. However, the objections not only to this particular argument but to the uncertainty principle in general are strong and numerous. First of all, Heisenberg's principle could simply be wrong. Many eminent physicists, such as Albert Einstein and Erwin Schrödinger, have refused to accept it. They argue that the unpredictability of certain quantum events is due to our lack of precise knowledge of what is happening and need not be an indicator of genuine indeterminism. Secondly, even if we admit that the uncertainty principle is correct and that subatomic events are indetermined, we still have to show how subatomic events in our brains could account for the much bigger electrical and chemical events that produce the nerve impulses that are responsible for our thoughts, choices, and actions. It is more likely that any indeterminacies that might occur inside the atom would cancel each other out rather than be amplified to affect macro-events. Thirdly, even if brain activity were indetermined due to amplified quantum indeterminacies, uncaused choices would probably not give us the kind of free will needed for moral responsibility. Uncaused choices would be random and not under our control. Thus they might actually be worse for our freedom than caused choices.

The second major argument for indeterminism and free choice has nothing to do with science and is based on our apparently intuitive feeling that we can choose freely and are morally responsible for our actions. This line of reasoning is often employed by libertarians with a Christian or humanist background. C.A. Campbell, for instance, argues that the self is the cause of our free choices and that the evidence for this lies in our own inner awareness of making moral choices. When we succumb to temptation we may be said to have been forced by our strongest desires into making that choice and thus the causal continuity is preserved. When we resist temptation, however, nothing compels us to choose as we do; therefore, we act freely and break the causal chain. As Campbell argues,

> Common Sense has here, in principle, hit upon the one and only defensible answer. Here, and here alone, so far as I can see, in the act of deciding whether to put forth or withhold the moral effort required to resist temptation and rise to duty, is to be found an act which is free in the sense required by moral responsibility; an act of which the self is sole author, and of which it is true to say that 'it could be' (or, after the event, 'could have been') 'otherwise.' (446)

Campbell's argument is problematic for a number of reasons. First of all, the only evidence we have for a 'self' is our intuition, which is unreliable. Furthermore, feeling morally responsible no more proves that we are morally responsible than feeling free proves that we are free. As Richard Double underlines,

> phenomenological feelings by themselves *never* provide evidence that things are the way we feel they are. [...] Feeling that we make uncaused choices does not provide evidence that we make uncaused choices, because we would feel as if we make uncaused choices even if our choices are caused. (217)

D.J. O'Connor adds that "Campbell limits the force of his own case unnecessarily by restricting free actions to those made in a situation of moral temptation" (86-87). Therefore, it is questionable whether Campbell can, as it were, 'save' enough freedom for a libertarian to be satisfied: if only actions done from duty are free, all the others would still be subject to causal necessity. So the determinist position would still be largely correct.

Subtler than Campbell's argumentation is Peter Strawson's. In his much discussed essays "Freedom and Resentment" he argues that because we cannot help acting as if we were free and morally responsible, there is simply no point in thinking we are not. He reasons that our normal reactions towards others, such as feelings of gratitude and resentment, which are intimately linked to our belief in moral responsibility, are not things that we could give up. For Strawson "the fact of our natural commitment to ordinary inter-personal attitudes [...] is part of the general framework of human life" (70). If we accepted determinism, our lives would have to be differently conceptualised. However, as our inter-personal attitudes are so central to our lives, we could not, in practice, cease to regard others in ways that presuppose these attitudes. For Strawson, therefore, determinism is irrelevant because, even if it were true, it would not be in our nature to act as though its logical consequences were true. What we should note is that Strawson does not dispute the possible truth of determinism. What he questions is the possibility of a general acceptance of determinism and all that would imply for the notion of moral responsibility. One of the problems of Strawson's argumentation is that the claim that persons cannot live without holding each other responsible cannot be proven. It is certainly possible to imagine a world where people live without the idea of moral responsibility.[1] Furthermore, the assertion that determinism is irrelevant because we could not believe in it anyway will not make the problem disappear and will leave us dissatisfied. We will continue to demand evidence either for the existence of determinism or for the existence of free will.

2.4   Free Will and Determinism in the history of philosophy

The modern, non-religious history of the free will and determinism debate can be said to have started with René Descartes (1596-1650). According to Roy Weatherford, Descartes

> stands as a fountainhead for the streams that divide into the great systems. Idealists claim him as a forbear for having demonstrated that our essential nature is mind, or spirit. Materialists see him as the first clear statement that all of physical nature is a network of systematic causation. (61)

Descartes divided the world into two substances: mind, whose freedom is limitless, and matter, which is subject to universal causation. For this reason both libertarians and determinists can refer to Descartes as a founder of their respective theories. With regard to determinism, Descartes' greatest achievement was to introduce a new concept of cause. In previous times a cause had been thought of as not just an earlier event but as an active and purposeful force. The fall of heavy objects, for instance, was explained by saying that they sought their proper place at the centre of the universe. However, Descartes, as Trusted explains, gave a new account of causation:

---

[1]   Double (cf. 219) mentions B.F. Skinner's novel *Walden Two* as an example. As we will see later, Joseph Conrad, too, shows in his fiction that some people live without feelings of moral responsibility or that a whole society may lack moral principles.

> Every physical event was the effect of some prior physical event [...] and would itself be the cause [...] of further physical events. The relation between physical events was governed absolutely by the laws of nature [...]. Thus the physical happenings in the universe could be described and explained in the same ways as the working of a machine – explanations were mechanistic. (31)

Descartes extended his mechanistic view to include animals – he believed they were automata – and the human body. Despite his belief that the physical body is subject to causation, he argued that human actions originate with a volition or choice made by the immaterial soul or mind. Since the latter is immaterial, it does not form part of the physical causal system and is not subject to the laws of nature. As Ilham Dilman points out it is "in this sense that for Descartes the will is self-determined and, therefore, free" (124). As we have already seen, the biggest drawback of Cartesian dualism is that it cannot satisfactorily explain the interaction between the two substances, mind and matter. Questions such as how it might be possible to perceive, to remember, or to think without a body and, in particular, without a brain remain unanswered. Descartes himself located the point of interaction between body and mind in the pineal gland but this did not even convince his contemporaries.

The British philosopher Thomas Hobbes (1588-1679) developed a similar view of universal causation as his contemporary Descartes. Indeed, Hobbes's materialism seems more consistent as he did not bother to account for an immaterial soul or mind. As Weatherford puts it, "[a]fter Hobbes it was possible to think of human beings as collections of material particles mechanically processing information. This revolution in human thought [...] is directly analogous to and of greater importance than the Copernican revolution" (49). Hobbes can also be regarded as the first of the great philosophers to propound the thesis of compatibilism, that is the belief that determinism and freedom do not exclude each other. In *Of Liberty and Necessity* he argues that "a *free agent* is he *that can do if he will*, and *forbear if he will*; and that *liberty* is *the absence of external impediments*" (quoted in Honderich, *Determinism* 88). Hobbes, therefore, does not contrast freedom with causation but with coercion and argues that we are only unfree when we are under constraint. Otherwise, as long as we identify with our actions and do what we want to do, we are free. In *Leviathan* Hobbes elaborates his position:

> *Liberty*, and *necessity* are consistent: as in the water, that hath not only *liberty*, but a *necessity* of descending by the channel; so likewise in the actions which men voluntarily do: which, because they proceed from their will, proceed from *liberty*; and yet because every act of man's will, and every desire, and inclination proceedeth from some cause, and that from another cause, in a continual chain, whose first link is in the hand of God the first of all

causes, proceed from *necessity*. So that to him that could see the connexion of those causes, the *necessity* of all men's voluntary actions, would appear manifest. (quoted in Honderich, *Determinism* 89)

This liberty or freedom is also sufficient for moral approval and disapproval. Thus Hobbes did not believe that the acceptance of determinism would affect moral responsibility.

The other great English empiricist with whom the tradition of compatibilism is associated is David Hume (1711-1776). As pointed out earlier, his view of causation was that the relationship between causes and effects is characterised not by necessity but by constant conjunction. It is, however, a mistake to conclude from his so-called regularity theory that he did not believe in universal causation or was not a determinist. The opposite is the case. With regard to Hume's compatibilism Ted Honderich points out that he "does not advance greatly beyond Hobbes in fundamental conceptions" but that his views on the matter have nevertheless "shaped, indeed governed, the tradition of Compatibilism" (*Determinism* 90). In his *Enquiry Concerning Human Understanding* Hume's line of reasoning is as follows:

For what is meant by liberty, when applied to voluntary actions? We cannot surely mean that actions have so little connexion with motives, inclinations, and circumstances, that one does not follow with a certain degree of uniformity from the other, and that one affords no inference by which we can conclude the existence of the other. [...] By liberty, then, we can only mean *a power of acting or not acting, according to the determinations of the will*: that is, if we choose to remain at rest, we may; if we choose to move, we also may. Now this hypothetical liberty is universally allowed to belong to every one who is not a prisoner and in chains. (quoted in Honderich, *Determinism* 91)

Hume, like Hobbes, goes on to argue that this liberty, which is wholly consistent with determinism, is all that is essential to moral approval and disapproval, to commendation and condemnation. He also claims that if constant conjunction of cause and effect were denied, the notion of moral responsibility could not be upheld. Where there is no determinism, people's actions are random and not under their control:

According to the principle, therefore, which denies necessity, and consequently causes, a man is as pure and untainted, after having committed the most horrid crime, as at the first moment of his birth, nor is his character anywise concerned in his actions, since they are not derived from it, and the wickedness of the one can never be used as a proof of the depravity of the other. (quoted in Honderich, *Determinism* 92)

Like Hume Immanuel Kant (1724-1804) argued in his *Critique of Pure Reason* that causality is necessary to the very possibility of experience (cf. Trusted 62-67 and Dilman 150-162). However, Kant was an incompatibilist and believed that determinism and free will exclude each other. In contrast to Hume, Kant identified causality with strict necessity and regarded it as a form of compulsion. From this he deduced that the will could not be free if we were completely part of the natural order. However, according to Kant, there is a duality about human beings. On the one hand we inevitably belong to nature or what he calls the phenomenal world. This is the reality we know through sense perception and this is where causality rules supreme. On the other hand we are also rational creatures and by virtue of this have the capacity to transcend what is natural in us. We have the ability to consider reasons for our actions, before acting as well as in retrospect, and to be moved by such considerations. There are therefore two aspects of the will. The heteronomous will is part of the phenomenal world and belongs to that part of ourselves that we know, namely our empirical ego. It is this will which is subject to causality, for instance to our passions and desires. The autonomous will, on the other hand, is part of the world of noumena – the so-called things-in-themselves – and belongs to the part of ourselves that we do not know, our transcendental ego. The autonomous will is absolutely free and freely chooses to follow the moral law laid down in the categorical imperative. If we were entirely rational beings, entirely of the noumenal world, then all our acts would be freely performed according to the moral law. If we were solely members of the phenomenal world our acts would be completely determined by our passions and desires. Because we are part of both worlds, moral conflicts between what is right and what is wrong arise. The concepts of obligation, of duty, and of moral responsibility are due to the interaction between the heteronomous and the autonomous will. As can be gleaned from even such a short summary, Kant's argumentation is highly abstract and most philosophers have found it difficult to conceive how his system could work in practice. As Jennifer Trusted summarizes, "[Kant's] suggestion of two worlds, and the arguments based on this, do not establish that human beings are free to choose how to act" (67).

John Stuart Mill (1806-1873), the most important Victorian philosopher, is well within the tradition of compatibilism and can be said to have continued and refined the line of thought developed by Hobbes and Hume (cf. Weatherford 82-86). As a utilitarian interested in legal and social reform it was essential for him to argue that human beings are not exempt from universal causation and that their actions follow inevitably from character and circumstances. He was at pains to emphasize that we can never, in any given circumstance, do other than we in fact do. Our awareness of our power to choose is an illusion and philosophical arguments based on this subjective feeling are invalid. What we are directly aware of is what is and not what will or can be. What we are able to do, we must learn by the doing of it. What we are then aware of in our consciousness is the having done it. On the other hand Mill also claimed that we could have done otherwise if we had wished to do so. This kind of freedom must, however, remain hypothetical as, in fact, we could not have done otherwise than we did. Nevertheless, this belief in a hypothetical freedom was all Mill needed to insist on the importance of ethics in general and of utilitarian reform in particular. Mill was adamant that determinism was distinct from fatalism and that our characters could – to some extent at least – be influenced by our wills:

> The true doctrine of the Causation of human actions maintains [...] that not only our conduct, but our character, is in part amenable to our will; that we can, by employing the proper means, improve our character; and that if our character is such that while it remains what it is, it necessitates us to do wrong, it will be just to apply motives which will necessitate us to strive for its improvement, and so emancipate ourselves from the other necessity. (*An Examination of Sir William Hamilton's Philosophy*, quoted in Trusted 42)

For Mill, the utilitarian, a justification of punishment and of the legal and social institutions associated with it, was of prime importance. We can justify punishment of others because it will causally shape their characters and therefore the actions that follow. The fact that human beings are subject to causation is therefore a prerequisite for punishment to be effective. If this were not so, there would be no justification for punishment in the utilitarian system:

> The question deemed to be so puzzling is how punishment can be justified if men's actions are determined by motives, among which motives punishment is one. A more difficult question would be how it can be justified if they are not so determined. Punishment proceeds on the assumption that the will is governed by motives. If punishment had no power of acting on the will, it would be illegitimate, however natural might be the inclination to inflict it. Just so far as the will is supposed free, that is, capable of acting *against* motives, punishment is disappointed of its object, and deprived of its justification. (*An Examination of Sir William Hamilton's Philosophy*, quoted in Weatherford 85)

Of course, there are cases when the will is not free, for instance when the cause of our action is external or internal compulsion, but this is an exception and not the rule. For Mill, just as for Hume and Hobbes before him, the kind of freedom required for morality is not only compatible with determinism but in fact presupposes and requires it.

Whereas the British philosophers advocated compatibilism, Arthur Schopenhauer (1788-1860) constructed a system of thought that is strictly incompatibilist and hard determinist. In his philosophy Schopenhauer brings together what Rüdiger Safranski calls "the three great affronts to human megalomania" (3): the cosmological affront – our world is just one of countless spheres in infinite space –, the biological affront – human beings are animals whose intelligence must compensate for a lack of instinct and for inadequate adaptation to the living world –, and the psychological affront – our conscious ego is not master in its own house.[2] The starting point of Schopenhauer's philosophy is the idea of 'the will', which he pictures as a dark, essentially hostile force, located at the centre of all things. In contrast to German idealist philosophers such as Fichte, Schelling, or Hegel, the Schopenhaueran will is "not the mind materializing itself but a blind, rankly growing, aimless, self-lacerating activity, with no clear direction towards anything meaningful" (Safranski 207). Reality is thus not pervaded by reason and rationality but by an all-powerful irrational force. The will, however, is not just something outside of ourselves but something we also experience internally, inside our living and breathing bodies. This is why Schopenhauer calls the will '*realissimum*'; it is the unifying point of all being. The will as experienced in our bodies is therefore the only reality we can be sure of and our only access to truth. Everything else, the world outside ourselves, is merely the representation of the will in our imagination and is therefore secondary, having the quality of an illusion. However, even the seeking of truth inside ourselves will lead us nowhere as the will has no truth and no meaning that can be discovered: "Being is nothing other than 'blind will', something vital but also opaque, not pointing to anything meant or intended. Its meaning lies in the fact that it has no meaning but merely is" (Safranski 209). Schopenhauer thus advocates a fundamental shift in epistemology which we will re-encounter in the thinking of the late nineteenth and early twentieth centuries. Reality can no longer be known by means of empiricism. It cannot be found in our surroundings but only inside ourselves. Thus the belief in a universal truth, which can be known by everyone, and in the power of the mind to discover it can no longer be upheld.

As Schopenhauer claims that we *are* will and that it is characterized by savagery, struggle, and unrest, we may not only feel alienated from a world which is ruled by an anarchic and irrational force but, as part of this force, also alienated from ourselves. However, we will only be seized by this kind of existential dread, if we, as it were, step out of our own body and regard it from the outside as representation, as an object among objects. Paradoxically, this ability to transfer oneself into the world of objects also offers a possible escape route from the otherwise utterly hopeless predicament of humankind. Normally, the will subjects us to constant, unthinking, painful servitude.

---

[2]   The last two "affronts" are most famously associated with Darwin's and Freud's theories but they were anticipated by Schopenhauer.

There are, however, moments in all our lives when "an external cause or inward disposition suddenly raises us out of the endless stream of willing, and snatches knowledge from the thraldom of the will" (Schopenhauer, quoted in Safranski 223). It is only in these trancelike and contemplative moments of insight that we experience something like peace: "[W]e are delivered from the miserable pressure of the will. We celebrate the Sabbath of the penal servitude of willing; the wheel of Ixion stands still" (Schopenhauer, quoted in Safranski 223). Once this "miserable pressure of the will" has been lifted we become free to view "the universal spectacle of the will" (Safranski 216) both with regard to ourselves and the world at large. Part of the spectacle which is revealed to us then is the movement of history. In complete contrast to the almost dogmatic belief in progress evinced by the majority of nineteenth century historians, Schopenhauer did not regard history as a goal-oriented and purposeful movement but as "a huge carnival of the unchanging same" (Safranski 232). Indeed, as Schopenhauer argued, if one has attained the contemplative state of mind described above one must discover

> that in the world it is the same as in the dramas of Gozzi, in all of which the same persons always appear with the same purpose and the same fate. The motives and incidents certainly are different in each piece, but the spirit of the incidents is the same. The persons of one piece know nothing of the events of another, in which, of course, they themselves performed. (quoted in Safranski 232-233)

History, therefore, constantly repeats itself: the will performs the same spectacle everywhere. The ultimate consequence of Schopenhauer's metaphysics of the will can only be a denial of the will. This can be achieved via a permanent state of rest or complete extinction of the will within us. Schopenhauer is here not recommending suicide but rather a complete withdrawal from and renunciation of life. In this conclusion to his view of the human condition Schopenhauer is, as in other aspects of his philosophy, influenced by Hinduism, which also regards asceticism as a higher ideal. That Schopenhauer's "mystique of denial" (Safranski 234) has a quasi-religious and cosmic flavour comes across in the famous words that conclude *The World as Will and Representation*:

> We freely acknowledge that what remains after the complete abolition of the will is, for all who are still full of will, assuredly nothing. But also conversely, to those in whom the will has turned and denied itself, this very real world of ours, with all its suns and galaxies, is – nothing. (quoted in Safranski 236)

Schopenhauer concerned himself explicitly with the freedom-of-the-will-problem and morality in two essays published in 1841 under the title *The*

Two Fundamental Problems of Ethics, Treated in Two Academic Prize Essays. The first of these was an answer to the set question, 'Can freedom of the will be proved from self-awareness?' Not surprisingly, his conclusion was that "[n]o matter how much one rummaged in one's self-awareness, one could not find freedom there but only the illusion of freedom" (Safranski 315). The problem, as Schopenhauer views it, is that the will is so primal to self-awareness that, strictly speaking, we only know what we want when we have already willed it, that is we only experience our will once it has become action. Schopenhauer discounts "intellectual will-intention[s]" as mere "deliberations of reason about what will be willed at some time, not real acts of will" (Safranski 225). Reason may supply motivations to the will but how the will reacts to them lies outside the power of reason. A decision therefore is not taken prior to an action in the sense of a causal link between decision and action, but the decision coincides with the action. This is also why we cannot discover who or what we are from our intentions, from our self-awareness, but only from the realized, 'embodied' pattern of our lives. The actions of our lives determine our identities. We are what we have willed. The will within us, however, is not something we can influence; it is something that is constantly changing and becoming. Schopenhauer thus argues against the freedom of the will and takes up an incompatibilist and hard determinist position. This is also reflected in his view of the human character:

> [Traditionally it is argued that] [f]reedom of the will [...] consists in man's being his own work in the light of knowledge. I, on the other hand, say that he is his own work prior to all knowledge, and knowledge is merely added to illuminate it. Therefore he cannot decide to be this or that; also he cannot become another person, but he *is* once for all, and subsequently knows *what* he is. With those other thinkers, he *wills* what he knows; with me he *knows* what he wills. (quoted in Safranski 225)

Even though our character is as immutable as a stone, we cannot discover its identity from the inside but only from the outside when we look at our actually realized actions. If we take this external view of ourselves as an object among objects, we will notice that there is a whole world of things and people that also act upon our will and move it in one direction or another. Schopenhauer regards the relationship between the environment and the individual will as a strictly causal one. Human beings act just like a billiard ball that is pushed across a table: "As little as a ball on a billiard table can move before receiving an impact, so little can a man get up from his chair before being drawn or driven by a motive. But then his getting up is as necessary and inevitable as the rolling of a ball after the impact" (quoted in

Dilman 167). Schopenhauer therefore does not only view the universe but human beings as well to be subject to iron necessity.

As Schopenhauer takes up a hard determinist position with regard to free will, the question of moral responsibility inevitably arises. How can I be morally responsible for an action that I have not freely willed? Surprisingly, Schopenhauer deduces the solution to this problem from his proposition that we are subject to the strictest causality:

> Having recognized, then, [...] as the result of the foregoing exposition, that man's action has not a particle of freedom, but is invariably under the dominion of strictest necessity, we are hereby led to the point at which we can grasp *true moral freedom*, which is of a higher species. (quoted in Safranski 317)

What Schopenhauer here refers to is our stubborn awareness of being the agents of our own actions and to the feeling of responsibility which necessarily arises from it, regardless of whether we have, in fact, freely willed these actions or not. As Schopenhauer says,

> [t]hanks to that awareness no one, not even a person totally convinced of the above demonstrated necessity governing our actions, would ever think of using that necessity as an excuse for an offence, or of shifting his responsibility on to those motivations, whose presence in fact made the action inevitable. (quoted in Safranski 317-318)

Even if attempts to shift the blame are made, the exoneration will not succeed because the feeling of responsibility cannot ultimately be suppressed.

Given Schopenhauer's understanding of free will and moral responsibility, it is not surprising that he is – just as Nietzsche later on – scathing in his criticism of conventional morality. In his second prize essay on morality Schopenhauer argues that traditional moral doctrines are – in a more or less disguised manner – theoretical justifications of egoism. Anyone performing 'good deeds' in the expectation of a reward in the beyond is not acting morally but egoistically, like a creditor granting a loan because he is speculating on a large interest to be gained later on. In contrast to Nietzsche, however, Schopenhauer does not dispense with morality altogether and believes in actions of genuine moral worth. These are actions "of voluntary justice, pure love of our neighbour and real nobility of soul" (quoted in Safranski 320). They occur against the natural urges of egoism and are not aimed, even by roundabout routes, at one's own advantage. Such actions spring from a quality that has a special place in Schopenhauer's philosophy: compassion. This is not something everyone possesses or which is at one's disposal all the time. Moments of compassion are rather like those of contemplation discussed earlier. The barrier between the ego and the non-ego is broken down and I share the sufferings of a fellow human being in a way in which I normally only feel my own suffering. Schopenhauer's ethics of compassion is, as Safranski calls it, "an ethics of 'nevertheless'" (321): without any backing from a belief in historical progress and against the background of a metaphysics of hopelessness, it advocates a spontaneity which aims at mitigating endless suffering in the full knowledge that, ultimately, suffering cannot be eliminated.

Given Schopenhauer's metaphysics, it is not surprising that his view of human relationships, of society, and of the state is also deeply pessimistic. His starting point is the individual who is locked in his own world, ruled by one mastering passion, egoism:

> [E]very individual [...] makes himself the centre of the world, and considers his own existence and well-being before everything else. In fact, from the natural standpoint, he is ready for this to sacrifice everything else; he is ready to annihilate the world, in order to maintain his own self, that drop in the ocean, a little longer. This disposition is *egoism*, which is essential to everything in nature. (quoted in Safranski 229)

Schopenhauer explains this disposition by postulating that it is only *within* ourselves that we experience the will as a reality. Everything else that lies outside ourselves, including other people, is given to us solely as an idea, as representation, and is therefore less real, less important than we are to ourselves. The will-dominated individual, therefore, cannot be anything but egoistical. Human society is therefore an aggregate of fierce egoists which would slide into anarchy if the state did not exercise restraining powers. The role of the state, in Schopenhauer's philosophy, is reduced to that of a defensive institution that is equipped with strong instruments of power to prevent the "*bellum omnium contra omnes*" (quoted in Safranski 229). The state's main task is not to improve its citizens – that would be a hopeless undertaking – but simply to protect individuals against themselves and against others. The state can thus at best couple collective egoism with collective self-interest.

As we have seen, society in Schopenhauer's view is a network of latent hostility, of reciprocal ill will. How is an individual who realizes this state of affairs to survive in such an environment, if he/she does not want to renounce all human contacts? Schopenhauer's advice is to keep a proper distance between oneself and society to avoid getting hurt or being destroyed altogether:

> [O]ne should learn to be lonely also in company, not communicate to others everything one thinks, nor take too literally what they say, but instead expect very little of them both

morally and intellectually, and remain indifferent to their opinions, so as not to lose one's equanimity. (quoted in Safranski 193)

Schopenhauer illustrates his advice with the famous parable of the porcupines which, because of their spines, have to keep a moderate distance from each other (cf. Safranski 336). As regards the questions of love and the relationship between the sexes Schopenhauer's position anticipates that of Darwin, Nietzsche, and Freud. Love, for Schopenhauer, is an illusion, a mere cover-up operation masking other and more basic urges. Schopenhauer argues that the will manifests itself in our bodies in varying strengths and that it is strongest in the genitals. This is where we are subject to the powers of the will in the most humiliating manner. The will – Darwin would later call it nature or evolution – is only interested in the propagation of the species. However, it disguises this purpose and 'sells' it to our consciousness and perception as the emotion of being in love. Our souls believe that they have found each other but, in fact, it is just our genitals that have sought each other out. Within society we have created myths around the emotion of love and the union between man and woman. However, in Schopenhauer's view the everyday manifestation of the marriage bond is more often than not "the plague of domesticity" (quoted in Safranski 226). Just as Nietzsche and his concept of the 'will to power' and in a similar manner to Sigmund Freud, Schopenhauer went on to demonstrate that our secret sexual urges are so strong that they can be found in spheres of life where one would not suspect their existence. In this respect, as in many others, Schopenhauer was far ahead of his time and laid the groundwork for theories and discoveries that were to dominate the late nineteenth and early twentieth centuries.

The philosophy of Friedrich Nietzsche (1844-1900) is in many ways a reaction to Schopenhauer's and we find many parallels and contrasts between them. Even more so than Schopenhauer's, Nietzsche's thinking exerted a formidable influence on the art of the *fin-de-siècle* and the early twentieth century. On the one hand Nietzsche is convinced of the soundness of Schopenhauer's conception of the world as a godless and irrational affair of ceaseless striving, contest, and suffering. On the other hand he does not agree with Schopenhauer's pessimistic and hopeless verdict as regards the worth of human existence and seeks ways of arriving at a different conclusion, one which would lead "to a new 'affirmation' and 'enhancement' of life" (Schacht 620). Most importantly, Nietzsche takes over the concept of the primacy of the will from Schopenhauer, but, as Hollingdale says, "the will to power is so different from Schopenhauer's will that the two principles have virtually nothing in common except the word 'will'" (67).

Before Nietzsche advanced his reinterpretation and re-evaluation of the world and of human life, he set himself the task to dismantle traditional Western concepts and values in as radical a manner as possible. One of the most famous slogans of Nietzsche's critique is 'God is dead'. This does not just refer to Christian belief but is meant to imply

> all that ever has been or ever could be subsumed in the name 'God', including all God-substitutes, other worlds, ultimate realities, things-in-themselves, noumenal planes and wills to live - the entire 'metaphysical need' of man and all its products. (Hollingdale 70)

Thus the formulation 'God is dead' also includes Schopenhauer's conception of the will which is a metaphysical postulate. For Nietzsche there is "no 'being' behind 'doing' [...], no 'will' behind 'willing'" (Hollingdale 182). He is a strict materialist, who recognizes only the world of phenomena and therefore claims that "appearance *is* reality" (quoted in Hollingdale 165).

As I pointed out earlier, Schopenhauer anticipated the insights of Darwin's theory of evolution. Nietzsche was in a position to actually incorporate the latter into his own interpretation of the world. Unlike the great majority of nineteenth century thinkers, Nietzsche has no illusions whatsoever as to the implications of Darwin's theory of evolution by means of natural selection. He is convinced that humankind has evolved in a purely naturalistic way through chance and accident. Furthermore, he sees no inherent order, directing agency, or meaningful progression towards a purposeful goal in evolution but just randomness and contingency. It is this radical understanding of Darwinism which informs Nietzsche's indetermininst view of the world and leads him to conclude that "[t]he total nature of the world [...] is [...] to all eternity chaos" (quoted in Hollingdale 73). Nietzsche believes that the concepts 'God' and 'humankind' as hitherto understood no longer exist and that the universe and the earth are without meaning. He considers it his task to come up with a new world-picture that takes Darwinism into account but is not nullified by it.

We will see in the next chapter that a problem of momentous import for all nineteenth century thinkers who concerned themselves with Darwin's theory was morality. How can traditional moral values be upheld once their divine sanction has evaporated? Most intellectuals opted for J.S. Mill's compatibilist solution: determinism allows for enough freedom to save the concept of moral responsibility. Nietzsche, however, was not convinced and accused nineteenth century rationalists of obtuseness and cowardice. Although they had rejected conventional religion, they were not prepared to face the radical consequences of this step. As Nietzsche asserted, "When one gives up Christian belief, one thereby deprives oneself of the *right* to

Christian morality" (quoted in Hollingdale 99). Inspired by Darwinism, the philosopher set out to dismantle traditional Western concepts of ethics. Hitherto the universally accepted idea had been that morals are something given, that they exist as part of the known world. However, according to Nietzsche, this is not so:

> When man gave a gender to all things he did not think he was playing, but that he had gained a deep insight: ... In the same way, man has connected everything with morals, and dressed the world in an *ethical significance*. One day this will have no more value than the belief in the masculinity or femininity of the sun has today. (quoted in Hollingdale 133)

Ethical significance, therefore, is simply something we read into the world but which, in fact, is not truly there. Morality is a custom that has grown out of a social or group instinct. Just as Darwin does in *The Expression of the Emotions in Man and Animals* (1872), Nietzsche analyses morality as a function and product of evolution and points out similarities between human and animal behaviour:

> The practices demanded in polite society: careful avoidance of the ridiculous, the offensive, the presumptuous; the suppression of one's virtues as well as of one's strongest inclinations; self-adaptation, self-deprecation, submission to order of rank – all this is to be found as social morality in a crude form even in the depths of the animal world [...]. [...] The beginnings of justice, as of prudence, moderation, bravery [...] are *animal*: a consequence of that drive which teaches us to seek food and elude the enemy [...]. It is not improper to describe the entire phenomenon of morality as animal. (quoted in Hollingdale 133)

Even though Nietzsche reveals morality to be merely a custom or social code which, for centuries, we have unquestioningly subscribed to, he nevertheless does not deny that despite all this we might still feel ourselves to be moral or immoral, possibly because these feelings have instinctual origins:

> I deny morality as I deny alchemy, that is, I deny their premises; but I do *not* deny that there have been alchemists who believed in these premises and acted according to them. I also deny immorality: *not* that countless people *feel* themselves to be immoral, but that there is any *true* reason so to feel. It goes without saying that I do not deny – unless I be a fool – that many actions called immoral ought to be avoided and resisted, or that many called moral ought to be done and encouraged – but I think the one should be encouraged and the other avoided *for other reasons than hitherto*. (quoted in Hollingdale 134)

This is similar to Schopenhauer's claim that even though we are not *truly* morally responsible for our actions, we nevertheless believe ourselves to be so. For Nietzsche *feeling* oneself to be moral or immoral is not good enough. Indeed, in Nietzsche's view, the categories moral/immoral, good/evil have lost their clear meanings. The distinction between them has become blurred as the fixed and divinely decreed standard formerly used to define these concepts has evaporated. The idea that 'good' and 'bad' are relative values, depending as to their meaning on one's point of view, one's time, and the social code one adheres to, became a cornerstone of Nietzsche's philosophy:

> All good motives ..., whatever exalted names we may give them, have grown up from the same roots as those we suppose are poisoned; between good and evil actions there is no difference of kind, but at most one of degree. Good actions are sublimated evil ones; evil actions are coarsened and brutalised good ones. (Nietzsche, quoted in Hollingdale 123)

Nietzsche sees his insight that we endow an essentially a-moral world with moral significance as just one example of the particularly Western penchant of ascribing certain shapes and forms to a universe which is essentially without structure, irrational, and indeterminist. Our sense impressions, which we believe to be conditioned by the outer world, are, in fact, conditioned by the inner world. Consequently, we are "always unconscious of the real activity of the outer world" (Nietzsche, quoted in Stevenson). Similar to Schopenhauer, Nietzsche thus undermines the belief in absolute truth and in the possibility of the human mind to uncover it. Language is another example of the way in which we impose particular categories on our surroundings. In this respect Nietzsche's critique anticipates not only the thoughts of Bergson, William James, and Saussure but, more generally, the crisis of language characteristic of Modernism. Because reality is ultimately unknowable and human consciousness can have no authentic contact with it, the idea that language can represent reality adequately is an illusion:

> [M]ankind set up in language a separate world beside the other world, a place it took to be so firmly set that, standing upon it, it could lift the rest of the world off its hinges and make itself master of it ... A great deal later – only now – it dawns on men that in their belief in language they have propagated a tremendous error. (quoted in Stevenson 184)

Although Nietzsche's critique of traditional Western beliefs is so radical that it tends towards nihilism, the philosopher's primary concern is, in fact, to overcome this nihilistic reaction and give the universe and human life new meaning. Nietzsche's starting point in his re-interpretation and re-evaluation is to regard the world in terms of a contest between forces determined by a 'will to power'. As Schacht explains,

> [i]n place of [the] cluster of traditional ontological categories and interpretations, he conceived of the world in terms of an interplay of forces without any inherent structure or final end, ceaselessly organizing and reorganizing themselves as the fundamental disposition he called 'will to power' gives rise to successive arrays of power relationships among them. (621)

This force dominates not only the universe but also human existence. Like Hobbes and Schopenhauer, Nietzsche believes individuals to be first and foremost egoists. In his writings, Nietzsche comes to the conclusion that virtually all human actions are to some degree motivated by the will to power. Should we have nothing left on which to exercise our will to power, we would even will our own destruction. As Nietzsche says, "man would rather will *nothingness* than *not* will" (quoted in Hollingdale 184). Nietzsche is, however, less concerned with the will to power as such but more in "the possibility that actions and sentiments not obviously connected with a desire for power are in fact prompted by it" (Hollingdale 121). Thus he claims

> that the weak and suffering may desire to arouse sympathy because this gives them the feeling they 'have at least one *form of power* despite their weakness: the *power to hurt* [...];[...]; that those who offer gratuitous advice do so with the aim of exerting power over him they advise [...]; [...]; that the acquisition of knowledge is accompanied by the feeling of pleasure because it is also accompanied by the feeling of enhanced power [...]; that truth is preferred to untruth because in the realm of thought '*power* and *fame* are hard to maintain on the basis of error or lies' [...]. (quoted in Hollingdale 122)

Not surprisingly, Nietzsche, like Schopenhauer before him, has no illusions about love. In his view, love is nothing but the desire to exercise the greatest possible degree of power over the loved person:

> One is surprised that this ferocious greed and injustice of sexual love should have been glorified and deified to such an extent at all times, that out of this love, indeed, the concept of love as the opposite of egoism should have been derived, when it is perhaps precisely the most unconstrained expression of egoism. (quoted in Hollingdale 142-143)

Nietzsche also tries to solve the freedom-of-the-will-problem by discussing it in terms of the will to power, thus removing it from the plane of abstract and often metaphysical philosophical discussion:

> Will is not only a complex of feeling and thinking, but above all an *emotion*: and in fact the emotion of command. What is called 'freedom of the will' is essentially the emotion of supremacy in respect of him who must obey: 'I am free, "he" must obey' – this consciousness adheres to every will. [...] ['F]reedom of the will' ... is the expression for that complex condition of joy of the person who wills, who commands and at the same time identifies himself with the executor of the command. (quoted in Hollingdale 183)

Nietzsche appears to argue that, as everyone feels the will to power and everyone has power over something or someone else, he/she will also possess a measure of free will. Beyond that there is no need to concern oneself with the problem. Nietzsche's analysis of the freedom of the will in terms of the will to power also leads him to the formulation of his most problematic concept, that of the *Übermensch* or super-man. He argues that by increasing our power we also increase our happiness and the freedom of our will. The greatest increase of power, therefore, brings the greatest freedom and the greatest happiness. That which demands the greatest power is the overcoming of oneself, the achievement of self-mastery. The happiest and freest person, therefore, is the one who has reached this goal and "has become who he is" (quoted in Hollingdale 162), a super-man. The overcoming of the self is not only the most desirable but also the most difficult task for a human being as the demands made of the super-man are exacting:

> Can you furnish yourself with your own good and evil and hang up your own will above yourself as a law? Can you be judge of yourself and an avenger of your law? ... you yourself will always be the worst enemy you can encounter; you yourself lie in wait for yourself in caves and forests. (Nietzsche, quoted in Hollingdale 162)

It appears that Nietzsche believed that the achievement of mastery over oneself is a prerequisite for the exercise of mastery over others. Furthermore, the qualities expected of the super-man are so demanding that he would destroy himself first before destroying others.

Next to the will to power and the super-man, the idea of eternal recurrence is the third central concept of Nietzsche's philosophy. Eternal recurrence is a consequence of Nietzsche's postulate that "appearance *is* reality" (Hollingdale 165) and that consequently there can be no breakthrough to a higher level of reality such as a world of metaphysics. Whereas the latter would be characterized by timelessness, the world to which we are bound exists *in* time and is conditioned by constant change. In Nietzsche's words, "reality is 'becoming' and never is" (Hollingdale 166). Consequently, our existence is temporal and unstable with a temporal infinity behind us and ahead of us. Although we can be sure that time is infinite, we cannot say with the same certainty that the number of possible forms in which our ever-changing reality appears is infinite as well. Nietzsche assumes that it is not. As time is infinite, the present state of reality must be a repetition of a previous state; all events must recur an endless number of times. The implications of this view for the movement of history are familiar from Schopenhauer's philosophy: history is not progressive but moves in a circle; it is the eternal recurrence of the unchanging same. According to Nietzsche, people who grasp this principle will be crushed by it unless they are able to attain a súpreme moment of existence for the sake of which they would be content to relive their whole lives. Here Nietzsche's philosophy comes full circle. The life to aim for is the life containing the greatest amount of happiness – and happiness, as we have seen, is the feeling that power increases, that an obstacle is overcome. The happiest man is the super-man, whose will to power has increased the most by overcoming the most. Such a person will not just affirm life but also misery and pain because he knows that the happiness he feels would not have been possible without the pain and misery he has known. As he will not be dismayed at the idea that the joy of his life will be repeated endlessly, neither will he flinch from the knowledge that its pain must be repeated too. In this way Nietzsche aimed to provide a re-interpretation and re-evaluation of the universe which he hoped would allow for a new affirmation and enhancement of life.

One of the most rigorous defenders of free will among twentieth century philosophers is Jean-Paul Sartre. Central to his philosophy is the notion that human freedom is absolute and unconditional. It is an inextricable part of human existence and as such cannot be limited, restricted, or lost. A consequence of this view is that we are always responsible for our actions even if we try to evade this responsibility. In this respect two of Sartre's most important statements are that "man makes himself" and that "in the end one is always responsible for what is made of one" (quoted in Solomon 812). Sartre's philosophy is clearly influenced by Cartesian dualism – the idea that the mind is free while the body is subject to strict causality – and Kant's notion of two realms of existence, the world of phenomena where universal causation holds sway and that of the noumena where this is not so. Similarly, Sartre distinguishes between consciousness – 'being-for-itself' – on the one hand, and the existence of mere things – 'being-in-itself' – on the other. Sartre therefore – like Descartes and Kant before him – sees humankind as different from the rest of nature. According to Sartre, consciousness is an activity; it is in constant motion and not subject to the rules of causality. It constitutes "a 'gap' between man and the world" (Dilman 192). Sartre argues that as conscious beings we are endowed with a unique form of existence which can be summed up as follows:

> (i) we have no positive being, our being or nature is not given to us from the outside, fixed independently of what we make of ourselves, and (ii) the environment or circumstances of our life do not impinge on us causally, but through what we make of them in our appraisals, through the significances we attribute to them. (Dilman 192)

In believing the human character to be undetermined by external causes Sartre stands in sharp contrast to Freud and Schopenhauer. In fact, Sartre argues that when we conceive of ourselves as fixed and settled – for instance, by virtue of a certain environment, certain circumstances, a certain social role, or a certain character we attribute to ourselves – we are in 'bad faith'. This is also the case when we deny authorship of and thus responsibility for our actions, seeing them instead as forced responses to situations which are not of our own making. Sartre knows that impediments to our freedom are ubiquitous in ordinary life but they are obstacles only because of our attitude towards them: "Human reality encounters resistances and obstacles which are not its own creation everywhere; but their character as resistances and obstacles comes from the capacity for free choice which defines human reality" (quoted in Dilman 195). There is in human life a constant, insoluble tension between what Sartre calls our 'facticity' – the body of facts we accumulate throughout our lives that are true of us – and our freedom. This implies that we have to contend with two conflicting forces: on the one hand we constantly try to define ourselves, to create a settled character for ourselves; on the other hand we are free and must use this freedom to envision new possibilities, reform ourselves, and reinterpret our facticity in the light of new projects and ambitions. For Sartre, however, freedom and the responsibility for our actions are not only gifts to be celebrated but also burdens. This is why Sartre speaks of freedom as something which is inescapable and to which we are condemned. Whatever we do in our lives is the result of choices we make or evade making. Even in the latter case it is still *us* who do the evading and therefore we are always responsible, whether we want to or not.

As a consclusion to this survey, I would like to ouline the positions of two contemporary philosophers, Ted Honderich and Thomas Nagel, who have drawn attention to the eminent role certain attitudes and perspectives play in the free will and determinism controversy. Honderich's two-volume *A Theory of Determinism: The Mind, Neuroscience, and Life-Hopes* (1988) has invigorated the debate and has been hailed by Roy Weatherford as "the most important book on the subject of determinism to appear in recent decades" (165). According to Honderich, compatibilism and incompatibilism are two sets of attitudinal responses to the theory of determinism. Compatibilism includes the central notion of voluntariness: as long as we are not coerced in our actions, we are free and morally responsible. Honderich calls this the response of intransigence: because we believe determinism to be consistent with free will, we assume that it does not substantially affect our day-to-day lives. Incompatibilism, on the other hand, includes the idea of human beings as originators, as genuine sources of new causal chains. This is held to be the prerequisite for moral responsibility and to be inconsistent with determinism. For Honderich, this is the response of dismay: determinism cannot be true, as it would destroy the belief in free will and moral agency. The philosopher's point is that "*both* compatibilists and incompatibilists have mistakenly taken their attitudes to consist in, require, or imply propositional facts about human beings or the world" (Weatherford 166). That is, both compatibilists and incompatibilists are guilty of having insisted on the truth of their respective position and of having claimed that if their position is right, the other must necessarily be wrong. Honderich's contribution to the controversy is to relocate the conflict in the realm of attitudes. He claims that neither of the two positions is based on actual facts and that to present them as such is a mistake. As both positions depend on attitudes, it is quite possible for the same person to hold both at once, which most people, in fact, do. It is important to emphasise that Honderich does not believe that determinism itself is attitudinal. Indeed, he regards determinism as a true theory of human nature. What is attitudinal, however, is our response to determinism and its possible truth, which falls into either of the two categories discussed above. Honderich argues that both are mistaken and that we should adopt a "response of affirmation" (*How Free* 126) instead. We should try

> by various strategies to accommodate ourselves to the situation we find ourselves in – accommodate ourselves to just what we can really possess if determinism is true, accommodate ourselves to the part of our lives that does not rest on the illusion of Free Will. (*How Free* 126; Honderich's italics)

Not surprisingly, Honderich is greatly concerned with the way the acceptance of determinism would change our lives. He is convinced that we would not only have to give up the view of ourselves as originators of uncaused actions as claimed by libertarians but that we would also have to adjust our outlook on life to a greater degree than compatibilists have traditionally claimed. As the acceptance of determinism would entail a reduced view of the scope of human agency, we would generally have to redefine our conception of moral responsibility. Honderich argues that there are only three ways in which a sense of responsibility can be upheld once the attitude of affirmation has been adopted: strict liability under the law, responsiveness to punishment, and responsibility arising from uncoerced intention (cf. Wheaterford 231). Consequently, in our relations with others, the response of affirmation would therefore include giving up feelings of resentment and the retributive aspect of punishment.

The notion of moral responsibility and human agency is also at the centre of Thomas Nagel's frequently anthologized essay "Moral Luck". Nagel is not concerned with proving or disproving determinism or with providing an outline of what the world would look like if determinism were accepted as a general truth. He points out that the degree to which we hold people responsible for their actions may simply depend on the perspective from which we view the action. The more impersonal our perspective is and the more we learn about the facts and circumstances involved in a certain action, the less we hold the agent responsible and the less he seems to be in control. The more personal and subjective our perspective is, the more we speak about an agent in terms of his intentions, his values, his selfhood, the more we hold him responsible for his actions. Nagel leaves this clash of perspectives unresolved but shows that we are in general less responsible for our actions than we suppose. Furthermore, we are frequently subject to moral luck, which he defines as follows: "Where a significant aspect of what someone does depends on factors beyond his control, yet we continue to treat him in that respect as an object of moral judgement, it can be called moral luck" (175). Nagel distinguishes between four ways in which our actions are subject to moral luck. There is first of all constitutive luck which refers to the kind of person we are, including our inclinations, our virtues and vices, our capacities, and our temperament. Nagel notes that people are always morally assessed for what they are like, irrespective of whether they can help being so or not. The second category is luck in our circumstances, which refers to the situations we find ourselves in, the things we are called upon to do, and the moral tests we have to face. This is particularly pertinent when we are engulfed by political or historical events, such as having to live under an oppressive regime or in times of war. The third category is luck in the way one's actions and projects turn out. More often than we commonly believe the outcome of certain actions determines what has actually been done. For instance, whether someone is prosecuted 'only' for drunk driving or for manslaughter may depend on the presence of a pedestrian at the point where the driver swerves off the road, something over which no one has any control. Nagel's fourth category refers to the thesis of universal causation including human choices, that is, the belief that our choices are the product of antecedent circumstances outside the will's control. According to Nagel, the result of consistently applying this deterministic and impersonal view of human action is that the "area of genuine agency, and therefore of legitimate moral judgement, seems to shrink [...] to an extensionless point" (183). Indeed, the idea of a responsible self dissolves as the result of focusing on the influence of what is not under our control. The self is, as Nagel puts it, "swallowed up by the order of mere events" (184). Nagel contrasts the external or impersonal perspective with an internal or subjective one:

> We are unable to view ourselves simply as portions of the world, and from inside we have a rough idea of the boundary between what is us and what is not, what we do and what happens to us, what is our personality and what is an accidental handicap. We apply the same essentially internal conception of the self to others. (185)

It is this internal view of ourselves that we apply to others when we pass moral judgement and hold people responsible for their actions. We extend to others the refusal to limit ourselves to external evaluation and accord others selves like our own. Inevitably, however, "this comes up against the brutal inclusion of humans and everything about them in a world from which they cannot be separated and of which they are nothing but contents. The external view forces itself on us at the same time that we resist it" (Nagel 185). By showing that the existence or non-existence of free will is more often than not a matter of perspective and by regarding compatibilism and incompatibilism as mere attitudes Thomas Nagel and Ted Honderich have respectively tried to break up entrenched position in the free will and determinism debate. Although their theories have certainly invigorated the discussion, they have as yet not been able to bridge the basic divide between the hard and soft determinists on the one hand and the libertarians on the other.

3. Free Will and Determinism in Nineteenth and Early Twentieth Century Britain

3.1 Victorian Compatibilism

The Victorian Age has variously been referred to as 'the age of science', 'the age of steam', 'the age of progress', or 'the age of improvement'. These keywords draw attention to the great Victorian successes in the areas of technology, economics, natural science, and international politics. What all of these achievements have in common and without which they would have been impossible is a certain approach to reality characterised by empiricism, materialism, and determinism. This world view has its roots in the discoveries of eighteenth century thinkers: materialist philosophers such as Thomas Hobbes, John Locke, and David Hume; social theorists such as Thomas Malthus; economists such as Adam Smith; or French scientists such as Condillac, La Mettrie, or Helvétius. In the early nineteenth century materialist thinking was continued by the utilitarians Jeremy Bentham and John Stuart Mill, by economic theorists such as David Ricardo, and, in the field of natural science, by the French evolutionists and zoologists Buffon, Saint-Hilaire, Cuvier, and Lamarck, whose findings inspired the geologist Charles Lyell and the evolutionists Robert Chambers and Charles Darwin. In very general terms, the materialist-empiricist world view can be described as the belief that human beings have access to a reality which can be observed, experienced, and, therefore, *known* in a similar manner by everyone. We can discover the laws according to which reality functions and use this knowledge to our advantage, for instance to exert a measure of control over our surroundings. Although the materialist interpretation of the universe was a fundamental source of Victorian confidence and prosperity, it inevitably clashed with the Christian-theological one and threw many Victorians into existential crises resulting in a loss of faith.

Although developments in economics and economic theory also contributed to the rise of a deterministic world view, it was in particular natural science which seemed to provide overwhelming evidence for the existence of a vast mechanism of cause and effect governing the universe. Among the many new discoveries in natural science it was without doubt

Charles Darwin's theory of evolution that had the most significance. Darwin was not the first person to think about evolution. The most important pre-Darwinian evolutionary theory had been formulated by Jean Baptiste Lamarck in his *Zoological Philosophy* (1809). Lamarckism had an enormous influence on the popular understanding of evolution both in the nineteenth and the early twentieth centuries and it is only in contrast to it that the radicalism of Darwinism becomes fully apparent. Lamarck held that the simplest forms of life had advanced gradually but inevitably along a scale or hierarchy of complexity until at length the human race had been formed. This idea of a necessary, goal-oriented, progressive process would become enormously influential throughout the nineteenth century because it could be reconciled with the overriding Victorian belief in progress. Lamarck thought that evolution worked by 'use-inheritance' or 'the inheritability of acquired characteristics'. He imagined that characteristics acquired during the lifetime of an organism are passed on to its descendants. His most famous example was that of a giraffe that stretches its neck to reach succulent leaves and, in the course of time, produces long-necked offspring as a result. Lamarck believed that the inheritance of acquired characteristics did not only apply to physical structures but to mental functions as well. As Bowler puts it, Lamarck believed that "[e]volution requires the conversion of learned mental habits into biologically imprinted behaviour patterns; in effect, instinct is unconscious memory inherited from previous generations" (*Darwin* 182). Even though Darwin did not take up the notion of use-inheritance, Lamarck's theory contributed to his conviction that all social instincts, including morality, have a biological origin. The most important idea that Darwin gleaned from Lamarck was that evolution *did* occur and that species were not fixed and unchanging. What both Lamarck and Darwin required for their theories to work was time. After all, evolutionary changes can only become effective after tens of thousands of years. Evidence for the existence of such massive time scales was uncovered by late eighteenth and early nineteenth century geologists. Their discoveries were also responsible for the first severe conflicts with the Church, which had until then claimed to be in sole possession of the truth with regard to the age of the earth. For two centuries people had believed Archbishop Ussher who had "calculated the generations recorded in the Bible back from the time of Jesus Christ to the time of Adam, concluding that the Creation had occurred in 4004 BC" (Gribbin and White 83). In the Victorian Age it was science that relegated to itself the position once held by the Church: to proclaim the truth about the universe and about humankind's place within it. In his *Principles of Geology* (1830) Charles Lyell refuted Archbishop Ussher's calcuations and claimed that all geological phenomena can be explained by natural processes that we still observe today and that operate over very long periods of time. This is all that is needed to account for the great changes that have occurred during the earth's history. Lyell not only proved that the earth is much older than believed hitherto but he also established Uniformitarianism as the guiding principle in geology. These two ideas formed the basis of Darwin's concept of evolution.

Another central notion of Darwin's theory is the struggle for survival leading to the survival of the fittest, which he derived from Thomas Malthus's *Essay on the Principle of Population* (1798). Malthus was intrigued by the way in which both animal and human populations have the tendency to increase at a geometric rate of growth. He, however, also observed that animal populations stay more or less constant. His answer to this paradox was that all populations are held in check by restraining influences, including the actions of predators, sickness, and, most importantly, the limited amount of food available. Populations, therefore, according to Malthus, expand only far enough to consume the resources available. What Darwin took over from the *Essay on the Principle of Population* was that

> the *majority* of all individuals, in the natural state, do not survive long enough to reproduce. Darwin wondered why some individuals, the minority, should survive and reproduce, while others did not. And he saw that the survivors would be the ones best suited to the way of life of that species – best fitted to their ecological niches [...]. (Gribbin and White 200)

Darwin was probably confirmed in this belief by the economic concept of the division of labour and specialisation in the industrial world, which had been developed by the free market theoreticians Adam Smith and David Ricardo. An industry can succeed only if a need is there or one can be created for it; if, in other words, an industry can fill a certain niche or can create one for itself. In a similar fashion Darwin reasoned that nature lends strength to those species that fit their niches. The actual struggle for survival then takes place between different individual members of the same species, competing for resources in the same ecological niche.

The main points of Darwin's theory of evolution as published in 1859 under the title *On the Origin of Species by Means of Natural Selection, or the Preservation of Favoured Races in the Struggle of Life* can be summarized as follows (cf. Gribbin and White 197-218 and Bowler, *Darwin* 12-14).[3] The two key elements are variation and selection. First, individuals in one

---

[3]   It should be emphasized that this summary reflects our contemporary understanding of Darwin's theory and not the nineteenth century one, which will be discussed later.

generation of a certain population reproduce to engender individuals that are not exact copies of their parents. There is, in a population, a variety of slightly different individuals in every generation. This variation – which is nowadays explained in terms of genetic differences – is more or less random and forms the raw material on which natural selection works. Selection, then, involves the preferential survival and reproduction of those individuals which, by chance, have inherited a variation that gives them an edge over their neighbours in coping with the local environment. These fitter or better adapted individuals survive and reproduce more readily than the others and their advantageous characteristics therefore increase in the next generation. Evolution thus works in two ways. First, it keeps an existing species perfectly adapted to its ecological niche, as long as the latter still exists. Second, by favouring individuals that carry an advantageous adaptive feature, evolution ensures that the latter spreads through the whole population so that the average character of the species changes. This process is speeded up when groups of individuals – through chance or necessity – become separated from one another and take up slightly different lifestyles. Ultimately, small changes in species produced in such a way lead to the large-scale developments that have characterized the appearance of new forms of life in the course of the earth's history.

The highest goal of evolution, however, is not just survival but also reproduction. An individual that survives long enough to find a mate, reproduce, and leave offspring can be termed an evolutionary success, an individual that leaves no offspring an evolutionary failure. Darwin indeed emphasizes that we should never forget "that every single organic being around us may be said to be striving to the utmost to increase in numbers," from which a "struggle for existence inevitably follows" (quoted in Gribbin and White 215). The view of nature, of human beings, and of the relationship between the two that emerges from *The Origin of Species* was shocking for most Victorians. While previously nature could be thought of as the manifestation and design of a good and benevolent God, now, as Desmond puts it, "[a] bloodthirsty leer crept over [its] face" (235). Darwin seemed to view nature as a battleground, in which individuals and species fight for their lives, where even the smallest piece of land is the scene of untold violence and suffering, and where the only aims are reproduction and survival at all costs. In a universe subject to such conditions, there can be no room for a benevolent God. There is only nature in the gruesome guise of Natural Selection, which is indifferent to all moral values and condemns all living beings to a life of instinctive cruelty, ending in purposeless death.

Another troubling question which *The Origin* inevitably raised was in how far evolution could also be applied to humankind. Even though Darwin did not explicitly say so, it was clear to most people that if he was correct, then humankind could only be one animal species among many others. Indeed, as soon as *The Origin* had been published, public debate centred on whether mankind was descended from the apes. In *The Origin* Darwin had only hinted that "[l]ight [would] be thrown on the origin of man and his history" (quoted in Bowler, *Darwin* 124). In 1871 he provided his own answer by publishing *The Descent of Man, and Selection in Relation to Sex*, in which he put humankind in its evolutionary place and established the apes as our evolutionary ancestors. He stated clearly that *all* features of human beings – even our social instincts – have evolved in accordance with the same natural laws that apply to all other forms of life on earth. Darwin thus administered another blow to the theological world view. Contrary to Christian belief humankind holds no special position within creation and is just another species among many others. Instead of being made in God's image, it now appeared that humankind had been made in an ape's image. The difference between human beings and animals, which had always seemed immeasurable, was all of a sudden reduced to almost nothing. Darwin, however, had more in store for his contemporaries. As the title of his book indicates, he was not only concerned with *The Descent of Man* but also with *Selection in Relation to Sex*. Darwin was at pains to show that sexual selection is a fundamental mechanism of evolution in order to be able to explain the existence of organs that display no apparently useful function. Darwin's well-known example is that of the beautiful tail of the peacock. It seems to serve no particular purpose and might be supposed a handicap as it impedes the bird's escape from predators. Darwin explained the evolution of this seemingly useless adornment as the result of sexual selection: all that is needed to produce the peacock's tail is for peahens to like it and for this preference to stay constant for a very long period of time. This reasoning directly contravened another element of Church doctrine, namely the argument from design, which held that "[s]eemingly useless beauty in nature hint[s] at the work of a Designer who [is] not only intelligent but [has] a highly developed aesthetic sense" (Gribbin and White 169). Once again the troubling question arose in how far Darwin's claims about sexual selection could be applied to humankind. Although Darwin could not be explicit in this respect, his writings clearly show that he placed human beings emphatically within nature and regarded them as subject to the same laws and processes. Indeed, Darwin provided further proof for the link between animals and humans in his next book *The Expression of the Emotions in Man and Animals*

(1872). Darwin showed that in many ways human beings react to stimuli in the same way that other animals, especially mammals, do. He took this as a clear sign of our animal ancestry. According to Bowler, Darwin thus accepted that "much of our unconscious behaviour is instinctive, programmed by evolution into the very structure of our brains" (*Darwin* 85). Darwin thus also touched upon the extremely sensitive topic of morality and how it had arisen. For centuries ethical values had been believed to be divinely sanctioned. Darwin, however, held that they were just another product of the inevitable workings of deterministic evolutionary forces and could be understood as the rationalization of our social instincts (cf. Bowler, *Darwin* 188-190). He argued that in animals that live in family groups, such as apes, evolution produces instincts that encourage cooperative behaviour and even a certain amount of self-sacrifice, which gives the group an advantage in the struggle for survival. The unsettling implication of this claim was that morality originates to an extent in selfishness. Humankind's moral sense then developed as the result of the interaction between these social instincts and growing intelligence. As our intellectual powers expanded, we managed to rationalize our instinctive feelings and set up certain external moral standards. Due to the increasing size of our societies, we were inevitably led to generalize the moral imperatives forced upon us by evolution and created religious and moral theories designed to promote ethical behaviour as an absolute good. Although Darwin's argumentation did by no means 'abolish' morality or question the validity of moral behaviour, this was how many people chose to understand it. They feared that once the divine sanctions of morality had been destroyed, morality would disappear and, as a consequence, society would disintegrate. This also explains why so many Victorian intellectuals were such fierce defenders of – in most cases – secular morality and exhorted their readership to recognize their duty towards their fellow human beings. Nevertheless, the question remained how morality could be insisted upon once its divine sanction had evaporated. Could a new morality really be derived from a mechanism such as natural selection, which functions according to unethical principles? Another question was whether human beings as products of natural selection could actually be expected to behave with more nobility than animals.

Although the Victorian were beset by these doubts and felt menaced by the determinist world science disclosed, they did not give in to despair. Due to their confident belief in hard work, duty, and self-restraint, they tried to fashion a new world view which combined elements of scientific materialism with remnants of the theological world picture, in particular the emphasis on human fellowship and the importance of morality. This compromise is frequently referred to as the Victorian Synthesis (cf. Bradbury, *British Novel* 7), which also comprises a compatibilist attitude towards the freedom-of-the-will problem. The Victorians believed not only in a world controlled by deterministic laws but also in control over one's destiny and in responsibility for one's actions. John Stuart Mill, as we have seen in the philosophical overview, was the most important proponent of this position in the Victorian Age. What supported the Victorians in their efforts to reconcile conflicting world views was their conviction of the existence of the truth and of the ability of the human mind to discover it. As Walter Houghton famously put it,

> [During the Victorian Age] doubt never reached the point of positive or terminal scepticism. It never involved a denial of the mind as a valid instrument of truth. [...] The Victorians might be, and often were, uncertain about what theory to accept or what faculty of the mind to rely on; but it never occurred to them to doubt their capacity to arrive at truth. (13-14)

John A. Lester indirectly confirms Houghton's argument by claiming that the *Late* Victorian period is distinguished from the Victorian Age proper by the denial of two fundamental axioms:

> The first axiom held that somewhere within or behind or beyond the world of observable experience there was an eternal and credible truth, a truth accordant to, at least consistent with, the human spirit and its aspirations. The second axiom held that man possessed a faculty capable of at least dimly perceiving that truth. (21)

The Victorians thus refused to be crushed by the loss of the Christian world view and found consolation in the hope that by trusting human rationality and intelligence human progress would be possible. It was indeed the idea of progress that became one the cornerstones of Victorian thought. As Peter J. Bowler points out (cf. *Evolution*, 96-97) the belief in a 'cumulative development' in an economic/materialist, historical/nationalist, biological/evolutionary sense was relatively recent and had only been made possible by the weakening of the Christian world view since the Enlightenment. Traditional Christianity had regarded man as a fallen creature, which had made thinking about progress inacceptable. Furthermore, the exaggerated respect for ancient Greece and Rome had made all later developments appear like degeneration. By the end of the eighteenth and the beginning of the nineteenth centuries a number of events took place that led to the breakthrough of the concept of progress. Many thinkers interpreted the French Revolution as the beginning of a new and progressive era. In the field of economics the Industrial Revolution brought about massive changes in the material lives of almost everyone. In Britain economists such as Adam Smith, Ricardo, and the utilitarians claimed that if one only did away with state intervention and other obstacles to laissez-faire economics, material and social progress would follow. Indeed, Britain's unprecedented economic and technological development seemed to provide undeniable evidence for such progress. Furthermore, the expansion of international trade brought with it increased contacts with non-European cultures, whose seeming backwardness could be regarded as further proof of the superiority of one's own culture. Finally, the many groundbreaking discoveries in the natural sciences led to increased confidence in humankind's ability to improve itself and its environment. Thus, as John Reed emphasizes, the idea of progress "developed slowly into the single most comfortable assumption of nineteenth-century Europe and America" (*Victorian Will* 86).

Not surprisingly, the idea of progress and the related tendency to formulate undeviating, universal laws true for all times can be found at the centre of the dominating systems of thought in the nineteenth century. Auguste Comte, for instance, adopted the law of progress as the driving force of his philosophy of Positivism, which was very influential in Victorian Britain. In his famous *Cours de Philosophie Positive* (1830-32) he argued that human nature is constituted in such a way that a progressive improvement of our understanding is inevitable. The historian Lord Macaulay "nam[ed] progress the key to history [and] located its culmination in the English people" (Reed, *Victorian Will* 89). In his essay "Sir James Mackintosh" he, for instance, claimed that the English had become

> the greatest and most highly civilised people that ever the world saw, have spread their dominion over every quarter of the globe ... have created a maritime power which would annihilate in a quarter of an hour the navies of Tyre, Athens, Carthage, Venice, and Genoa together, have carried the science of healing, the means of locomotion and correspondence, every mechanical art, every manufacture, every thing that promotes the convenience of life, to a perfection which our ancestors would have thought magical. [Therefore], the history of England is emphatically the history of progress. (quoted in Houghton 39)

Another influential Victorian historian was Henry Thomas Buckle, who, in his *History of Civilization in England*, sought to investigate the causes of progress by applying the methods of science and of statistical research. In contrast to Lord Macaulay or Thomas Carlyle he did not locate the driving force of history in individual 'great men' but in impersonal laws. For Buckle social phenomena were as regular as natural ones. The theory, however, that was most influential in confirming the idea of progress was Darwin's theory of evolution, whose central tenets have been discussed above. As Bowler points out, it is crucial to understand that the idea of progress had become prevalent *before* it became popular to account for the origin of man in terms of biological evolution. The progressive view of human society was a stimulus for, not a product of, the theory of organic evolution. Only later in the century, after the success of the Darwinian revolution in biology, were the two levels of progress synthesized into a comprehensive vision of universal development. (Bowler, *Evolution* 90-91)

The notion that evolution is necessarily progressive – that there is, in other words, a linear development from the lower to the higher or from the primitive to the sophisticated – is not really expressed in Darwin's theory but is simply how the Victorians chose to understand it. Darwin certainly contributed to this interpretation because he was anxious to imply that the mechanism of natural selection was, at least in the long run, beneficial and would push most species towards higher levels of development. In this way he could appeal to liberal thinkers who regarded evolution as a guarantor of social progress. As Houghton says, the ""myth of evolution" fitted so perfectly into the general atmosphere of Victorian progress that it was accepted without critical scrutiny" (38). The notion of a progressive evolution and all that was implied by it seems to have consoled the Victorians for the other negative implications of the scientific world view. The argument was that even though evolution left no room for a benevolent god, portrayed nature as a bloody battleground, saw human beings as descended from the apes, and questioned a divinely sanctioned morality, it had at least produced the human race as the 'crowning species', which it would continue to develop to perfection. The Victorians were confident that in the course of time they would discover the laws according to which evolution works and would learn how to influence human beings' fate. This would also give back to humankind a measure of free will and control. As John Reed says, "where progress was accepted, it was generally bound to some belief in the power of the human will to shape not only man's individual and communal destiny but the character of the material world itself' (*Victorian Will* 84).

The Victorian Synthesis and its concomitant compatibilism were, however, not just reflected in the philosophical and scientific writings of the period but also in its literary products, in particular the novel. For instance, the hallmark of Victorian fiction, realism, can be regarded as the direct product of the Victorians' world view. As Maurice Larkin argues,

[w]hat was fairly new – and what in some measure gave nineteenth-century Realism its capital 'R' – was its greater concern for material reality as a shaper of Man: a concern which invested the detail of daily existence with an active creative role in the lives of the novelist's main characters, instead of being largely a back-cloth to their activities. (2)

As we have seen above, this perception of reality often goes hand in hand with a compatibilist attitude towards free will and determinism. It is believed that the universe is subject to deterministic laws that can be described in scientific terms. Although we might not be able to change these laws, we can at least find out how they circumscribe our lives. Scope for free will lies in our private moral choices and actions, for which we are consequently fully responsible. Compatibilist Victorian authors such as George Eliot, in fact, regarded a deterministic world as a prerequisite for the existence of morality and free will: after all, if we could *not* rely on universal causation, we could not be held responsible for the consequences of our actions or learn from our mistakes. These beliefs are reflected in the characteristics of Victorian fiction. For instance, the overt, omniscient narrator so frequently used in nineteenth century novels is reminiscent of the Victorian scientist, historian, or sociologist who is absolutely certain that he knows the truth about the reality and the human beings he is describing. Like a god or like Laplace's Demon, he has all the causal factors pertaining to his fictional world at his command and can manipulate them as he wishes. The frequent narratorial comments and addresses to the reader are meant to lend additional authority to the fictional events. Characters and their actions can clearly be classified as either 'good' or 'bad'. Melodramatic elements and instances of poetic justice are introduced to drive home the narrator's moral point. The reality portrayed in Victorian fiction is always ordered, knowable, and subject to universal causation. On a structural level this is expressed by a strict adherence to the chronology of events: the story unfolds like a long chain of cause and effect. The past can explain the present and the present can foreshadow the future. The manner in which Victorian authors narrate their stories thus mirrors the nineteenth century view of history: a linear, logically ordered, meaningful process that moves towards a purposeful goal. The latter is indeed reflected in Victorian fiction's preference for closed endings: there is a brief summary of the characters' future fate and no questions are left open. The nineteenth century realist novel, therefore, can be said to reflect the world as imagined by the Victorians: it is controlled by the iron laws of causation and works according to a meaningful plan that entails the progress of creation towards perfection.

3.2   Late Victorian and Early Modernist Incompatibilism

Before delineating the general change in the intellectual atmosphere between the Victorian and the Late Victorian/Early Modernist period, I would like to return briefly to Friedrich Nietzsche as one of the most prominent and most explicit critics of the Victorian Synthesis described above. In an aphorism contained in *Twilight of the Idols* (1888) he, for instance, expressed his criticism as follows:

> They have got rid of the Christian God, and now feel obliged to cling all the more firmly to Christian morality: that is *English* consistency ... With us it is different. When one gives up Christian belief, one thereby deprives oneself of the *right* to Christian morality ... Christianity is a system, a consistently thought out and *complete* view of things. If one breaks out of it a fundamental idea, the belief in God, one thereby breaks the whole thing to pieces ... Christian morality is a command; its origin is transcendental ... it possesses truth only if God is truth – it stands or falls with the belief in God. – If the English really do think they know, of their own accord, 'intuitively', what is good and evil ... that itself is merely the *consequence* of the ascendancy of Christian evaluation. (quoted in Hollingdale 99)

Nietzsche thus accuses writers such as George Eliot and philosophers such as Ludwig Feuerbach or J.S. Mill of inconsistency with regard to the implications of a determinist world view. If one rejects the belief in God and holds the discoveries of science to be true, one cannot save the moral 'essence of Christianity' but has to reject that as well. Nietzsche also criticized two related concepts that often served nineteenth century thinkers as substitutes for the loss of religious faith: the idea that humankind is developing towards perfection and that nature is characterized by order and purpose so that invariable laws true for all times can be formulated. Nietzsche's criticism can be seen to inaugurate a process of disillusionment with Victorian ways of thinking and a loss of confidence and optimism that is characteristic of the late nineteenth century and the *fin-de-siècle*. When exactly this shift occurred is subject to debate. Walter Houghton locates the breakdown of the Victorian world view after 1870: "Victorianism was dying, and a new frame of mind was emerging, a *late* Victorian frame of mind, which pointed forward to the postwar temper of the 1920's" (xv). Newsome sums up the various positions as regards the end of Victorianism as follows:

> On the limits of the prosperous and relatively stable mid-Victorian period – the so-called 'Age of Equipoise' – historians differ, some placing the beginning of the late-Victorian age in 1867 (the Second Reform Bill), others choosing the early 1870s, with the onset of the 'Great Depression'. Certainly by 1880 there were sufficient indications that the Victorian age was moving into its 'flash Edwardian epilogue'. (7)

One aspect of this shift in the intellectual atmosphere was the loss of the ability to reconcile conflicting world views, such as the materialist-scientific and the theological one. As Bradbury says, "[i]t was in the late Victorian years that what historians have called the "Victorian synthesis" began to dissolve, and the cultural climate began to fragment" (*British Novel* 7). This fragmentation occurred in two stages. At first we come across an emphasis on determinism, which, in the field of literature, found its expression in Naturalism. Later on the focus shifted to near-determinism or indeterminism, which in various ways stimulated Modernism and went hand in hand with the foregrounding of subjectivism and solipsism. Determinism, near-determinism, and indeterminism were regarded by many as irreconcilable with free will, which contributed to the pervasive feelings of pessimism, uncertainty, and doubt characteristic of the period.

In the second half of the nineteenth century many people felt overwhelmed by the emergence of more and more evidence that human beings were completely determined by forces outside their control so that the scope for individual freedom and control seemed to dwindle to a nonentity. The literary movement of Naturalism, with proponents such as Zola, Hauptmann, Gissing, Moore, and Morrison, can be seen to reflect this change of perspective. The Naturalists regarded humankind as determined in particular by economic and biological forces. Maurice Larkin argues that economic determinism was foregrounded because "[i]ndustrial transformation was [...] a fact of life that impinged much more forcefully on the consciousness of the later Realists" (140). After all, the vast industrial wastelands and the endless vistas of slum dwellings mainly date from the latter half of the nineteenth century. Furthermore, the newspapers were full of reports on strikes, social unrest, and economic crises. Indeed, the last three decades of the century are often referred to as the era of the Great Depression when the increasing import of cheap food and raw materials from overseas led to severe economic problems all over Europe. There was also the influence of thinkers such as Karl Marx who asserted that the whole development of humankind and society depended primarily on economic factors. Karl Marx and Friedrich Engels had already published their *Communist Manifesto* in 1848; however, because of the turmoil of the continental revolutions it was taken little notice of at first and only became generally known in England in the 1880s. The fact that Marx recognized only *one* determining force in the universe shows that his philosophy is firmly rooted in the intellectual tradition of nineteenth century determinism. According to Marx, everything, from human behaviour to the movement of history, is subject to the iron law of economic determinism. Even our consciousness and intellectual life are not exempt from it. In *The Communist Manifesto* Marx and Engels pose the following rhetorical questions:

> Does it require deep intuition to comprehend that man's ideas, views and conceptions, in one word, man's consciousness, changes with every change in the conditions of his material existence, in his social relations and in his social life?
> What else does the history of ideas prove, than that intellectual production changes in character in proportion as material production is changed? (102)

Marx and Engels also claim that the current modes of production are controlled by the bourgeoisie and have emptied human relationships of all meaning: there is no longer any other "nexus between man and man than naked self-interest, than callous 'cash payment'" (82). Consequently, labourers have lost their individuality. They have become "a commodity, like every other article of commerce" and are reified as "an appendage of the machine" (87). The only solution to this state of affairs is the proletarian revolution, entailing the overthrow of the bourgeoisie and the abolition of all property. Marx believed that the revolution would occur inevitably, as a result of the universal and undeviating economic law that he had discovered. Like so many nineteenth century thinkers Marx also held that history is progressive and will lead to perfection. As A.J.P. Taylor explains,

> [t]he social conflicts which were the basis of his system would finally produce a synthesis where no conflicts were left, and history would come to an end. This synthesis was socialism, an ideal society or Utopia where everyone would be happy without conflict for ever more. (9)

In addition to emphasizing economic determinism, late nineteenth-century writers also took a more uncompromisingly scientific and biological view of human beings. Although earlier novelists such as George Eliot, Elizabeth Gaskell, or Charles Dickens had also paid attention to the formative influence of environmental and biological factors, their primary interest had been the delineation of individuals. In the Naturalist novel the emphasis was no longer on fully-fledged and easily recognisable characters but on the similarities between them. Thus the figures' social identity and their biological instincts were stressed. Like Marx's labourer under the conditions of bourgeois methods of production, the individual in the Naturalist novel was regarded as a product of evolutionary and environmental conditions. In *Le Roman Experimental* (1880) Zola summarized the aims of Naturalism as follows:

> [M]astery of the mechanism of human events: demonstration of the way in which intellectual and sensory processes, as explained to us by physiology, are conditioned by heredity and environment; and finally portrayal of the human being in the environment which he himself has made and alters daily, and in the midst of which he in his turn

undergoes continual transformation. And thus it is that we look to physiology for guidance, taking the isolated individual from the physiologist's hands in order to carry research further by solving scientifically the problem of how men behave once they become members of society. (quoted in Drew 311-312)

Although earlier writers such as George Eliot had also called for a close observation of nature based on the methods of science, they had combined this demand with the explicit aim to promote sympathy, tolerance, and altruism. In the quotation above these Christian or moral terms have completely disappeared. What has remained is the language of science and that of the laboratory. The Naturalist writer's task is to devise a conclusive series of reactions in a given experiment. Despite the differences between the earlier Victorian writers and the Naturalists, it has to be emphasised that the latter also make use of the realist, mimetic mode of their predecessors. They do not doubt the existence of a fixed and stable reality that can be known and therefore described in detail. Furthermore, although the Naturalist world view is more pessimistic and sombre than the mid-Victorian one, it is not despondent. As for many Naturalists the primary force that determines individuals is economic or materialist in nature, they hope that by modifying economic circumstances the plight and suffering of the poor and exploited can be alleviated.

This kind of optimism does not exist in the writings of another major writer of the period who is sometimes classed as a Naturalist, Thomas Hardy. His determinism is not only scientific and materialist but also metaphysical, influenced by Schopenhauer's philosophy of the will. In Hardy's novels the individual is not only determined by economic, social, and biological forces but also by the arbitrary, capricious workings of a metaphysical force which sometimes takes the shape of an evil god. In contrast to Modernist writers such as Conrad, Hardy's perspective of the universe and of humankind seems monolithic, like a closed system. According to Philip Drew, one of the assumptions that underpin Hardy's fictional world is that

[a]ll the Universe, including mankind, is one great machine, which is governed simply by its own state or its own inherent tendencies. Were things left at this one might suppose that Hardy implied a classical mechanical determinism [...], but he more often personifies the inevitable course of the world as Doom, or the Doomsters, or the Immanent Will. [...] Hardy [...] sometimes suggests that the Immanent Will moves along predetermined paths and sometimes that its 'designs' are simply matters of chance, 'crass causality' or 'purposeless propension' [...]. (246)

The 'Immanent Will' has not the slightest interest in human affairs. So indifferent is this force that it permits the most outrageous thwartings of human desires and aspirations. Sometimes it even appears to arrange coincidences and painful situations out of a malicious pleasure to torment an individual. In such a world there is no place for free will and consciousness seems to be a disease. Human beings have, at best, a choice in the manner in which they reach their inevitable destruction:

> If they struggle they regularly flounder deeper in the quicksand – so regularly that it seems inevitable – and the indifference or casual malevolence of the Immanent Will takes care that they realise that their sufferings are entailed by their own actions. Yet if they remain inert they will simply drift towards death and oblivion, and thus might as well be already dead. (Drew 247)

Hardy's characters need to show tenderness and compassion to vindicate their humanity; yet, paradoxically, the greater their sympathy for others, the more they will suffer. Human life, therefore, appears like a trap from which death is the only escape. Hardy's completely deterministic world view and the way he embodied it in his novels have come in for a lot of criticism. Walter Allen's view is representative:

> Hardy's chief weakness in plot arises from his view of causality. He is intent to show that the stars in their courses fight against the aspiring [...]. [...] We begin to feel that the author has aligned himself with the nature of things against his characters, that he is manipulating fate against them. [...] It is the one turn of the screw too many. (251)

Allen here echoes E.M. Forster, who claimed in *Aspects of the Novel* that Hardy "has emphasized causality more strongly than his medium permits" (93). It is revealing that these particular points of criticism have never been levelled against Conrad, even though in his novels the major characters also invariably fail and there seems to be little room for free will. Conrad certainly differs from Hardy in that his outlook on life, albeit pessimistic and sceptical, is not fatalistic. Conrad's universe is not a closed deterministic system but open, indeterministic, and ultimately unknowable. There is, furthermore, no room for a god or other metaphysical entity, be it benevolent or evil, and none for a fixed fate. Thomas Hardy therefore still belongs to the last phase of Victorianism, whereas Conrad already looks ahead to the Modernist period characterized by ambiguity, paradox, and janiformity.

As we have seen, late nineteenth century Naturalism was informed by strict scientific determinism. Mankind was seen as subject to fixed laws and to impersonal forces that left little room for free will. As James McFarlane points out, these views continued to survive well into the twentieth century, "sustained in large measure by the immense reserves of accumulated prestige" (75). However, even at a time when deterministic theories were still being formulated and literature inspired by scientific determinism was still being written, an epochal change in the natural sciences took place; away from determinism and strict causality towards indeterminism, relativity, and chance. This shift was most spectacular in physics and started in 1895 with Röntgen's discovery of the radioactive properties of uranium and the Curies' of radium (cf. Bullock 66 ff). This was followed by the discovery of electrons and isotopes and the development of a new model of the atom, which necessitated the reformulation of the classical theory of physics. The first step towards this was Max Planck's quantum theory of energy (1900), which was revised by Niels Bohr and Werner Heisenberg a few years later. Quantum physicists, faced with the problem of defining the nature of subatomic particles, "abandoned the classic common-sense distinction between mass and energy and accepted the existence of a wholly 'ambivalent' entity which was *both* wave *and* particle, and yet in a strict sense neither" (McFarlane 84-85). Einstein, who published his *Special Theory of Relativity* in 1905, argued that no physical law is entirely reliable and that the observer's position always influences the result which therefore becomes relative and contingent. He further claimed that space and time, instead of being the discrete and distinct dimensions they had always been taken to be, were in certain circumstances actually functions of each other. As Bullock puts it,

> in the twenty years between 1895 and 1915 the whole picture of the physical universe, which had appeared not only the most impressive but also the most secure achievement of scientific thought, was brought in question and the first bold attempts made to replace it by a new model. (66)

The implications of this new view of the universe were far-reaching. Pillars of Victorian thought, such as the belief in absolute, invariable laws based on universal causality, in the existence of a truth indivisible and one, and in the ability of the human mind to discover this truth, were overthrown. The new conceptions of matter and the universe that the physical sciences asked human beings to cope with were challenging indeed (cf. McFarlane 84-85). The revised laws of physics defied conventional logic and common sense; 'unscientific' notions such as a-logicality and a-causality demanded formal recognition. The uncertainty of probability replaced the sovereignty of precise knowledge and confident predictability. As scientific inquiry now concerned itself with astronomical and subatomic phenomena, the traditional notion of empirical observation was no longer applicable and it became evident "that the universe at these levels behaved in a different way from the commonsense world of everyday experience while the necessary questions could only be asked through highly speculative theory" (Bell 11).

Although contemporaries responded with great excitement to the theories put forward by early twentieth century physicists, their reaction was not usually one of relief at the lifting of the burden of a crushing determinism. On the contrary, as Lester argues, "[w]hat emerges clearly in the culture of this period is the conclusion that if deterministic materialism left no room for the human imagination and spirit, the new vistas of relativity offered little better" (37). After all, the two axioms that had helped the Victorians to overcome the shock of a deterministic and god-less universe – the existence of truth and the ability of the human mind to discover it – were now denied once and for all. In the chapter on Victorian compatibilism I quoted Walter Houghton, who maintains that in Victorian times "doubt never reached the point of positive or terminal scepticism" (13). In the course of the Late Victorian and Modernist periods doubt *did* reach that point. Truth became shadowy and fluctuating and the ability to perceive it seemed to be reduced to vanishing point. A typical reaction to these changes was the withdrawal into solipsism. As Lester describes it, the view of a world ruled by chance and flux "locked man within his own world of sense impressions, with no hope at all of a real or credible world behind sensed phenomena and, even if there were such a world, no means – not even the scientist's logic – which could perceive or envision it" (35). Worst of all was the suspicion that what lay behind the phenomena that *were* perceptible to human beings might be nothing at all: "[p]erhaps all the world man knew was blank and void at the heart" (Lester 32).

The fundamental reorientation of physics that occurred at the turn of the century was paralleled by a reinterpretation of Darwin's theory of evolution. This change was arguably not quite as radical as that in physics, but it nevertheless had far-reaching consequences, for instance for the Victorian belief in progress. Darwin's theory had initially been taken as proof of the idea of progressive development. According to this interpretation, the human race was the 'crowning type' of evolution and would develop further in its biological, mental, and moral characteristics towards perfection. Towards the end of the century, however, there occurred "a shift of primary interest from the Darwinian theory in general to a particular, almost "passing" element in that theory – *chance*" (Lester 46). Darwinians realized that "the individual variation upon which natural selection operates is essentially random: by itself it cannot force evolution along a particular path because its tendency is to spread out in all directions" (Bowler, *Darwin* 12-13). One of the first evolutionists to point this out explicitly was Darwin's formidable younger colleague T.H. Huxley (1825-1895), whom Adrian Desmond in his biography refers to as "the founder of the sceptical, scientific twentieth century" (xv). Huxley described evolution as an open-ended, non-progressive process ruled by randomness and chance. Evolution has no inbuilt direction or goal and develops in a haphazard manner. Even though laws can be formulated to describe it, they cannot tell us where evolution will lead to. Huxley, who was very much aware of the wider philosophical implications of his view of evolution, did not believe that this kind of near-determinism would give human beings more control over the universe. After all, if I am dealing with a completely deterministic system, there is hope that one day I might understand it completely. However, if there are random elements in the system, this hope is denied; the attainment of absolute truth becomes an illusion. Truth is, at best, relative and dependent on the circumstances of the moment. Huxley expressed this view – more typical of the *fin-de-siècle* than of the Victorian period – early in his career in an article that appeared in the *Westminster Review* in 1855. In language reminiscent of Conrad, Huxley claims that

> our knowledge is the knowledge of our time – that absolute truth is unattainable – that all our theories, however well founded, and however grand, are but myths, which enable us to grasp for a while that fragment of the incomprehensible universe which has presented itself, – to float thereby on the surface of the great abyss until some larger fragment come within our reach and the old is deserted for the new. (quoted in Desmond 672)

In this quote Huxley clearly moves towards the solipsistic view of the world which would become prevalent at the end of the century. Like Conrad in his letters and his novels, Huxley is also able to switch from solipsism – imagining the outside world as unreal and consciousness as the only reality that exists – to objectivism, viewing the universe as a machine and human beings as conscious automata. Adrian Desmond describes the scientist's shift between these viewpoints as follows:

> By 1874 Huxley was becoming more the scientific determinist, making one's feeling of 'Free Will' simply an emotional warmth which accompanies some compunction. Yet only three years earlier, in 1871, [he had admitted] that the world was as likely to be the mental construct of a conscious mind as an objective material entity [...]. (440-441)

At the end of his life, in his famous Romanes lecture "Evolution and Ethics" held at Oxford in 1893, Huxley again saw impermanence, change, and flux as the salient characteristics of the universe. The permanence we attribute to the environment that surrounds us and of which we form a part is an illusion created by the brevity of both our individual lives and humankind's existence on earth. As Huxley explains,

> the more we learn of the nature of things, the more evident is it that what we call rest is only unperceived activity; that seeming peace is silent but strenuous battle. In every part, at every moment, the state of the cosmos is the expression of a transitory adjustment of contending forces; a scene of strife, in which all the combatants fall in turn. What is true of each part is

true of the whole. [...] Thus the most obvious attribute of the cosmos is its impermanence. ("Evolution" 310-311)

Because Huxley views evolution as directionless and random, he rejects the belief in progress and human perfectibility. Although he argues that human beings are susceptible to improvement – especially via the means of education and the change of material circumstances –, he suggests at the conclusion of "Evolution and Ethics" that evolution might be cyclical and take a downward turn:

> The theory of evolution encourages no millennial anticipations. If, for millions of years, our globe has taken the upward road, yet, some time, the summit will be reached and the downward route will be commenced. [...] Moreover, the cosmic nature born with us and, to a large extent, necessary for our maintenance, is the outcome of millions of years of severe training, and it would be folly to imagine that a few centuries will suffice to subdue its masterfulness to purely ethical ends. (329)

Huxley here contributed to the fears of degeneration and atavism that became prevalent around the turn of the century. He believed that our hardly suppressed animal instincts might predominate again and that humankind might descend into barbarism. This downward route might be initiated by a change in environmental conditions as predicted, for instance, by the astronomer and physicist William Thomson, Lord Kelvin. Although Kelvin had already formulated his Second Law of Thermodynamics – also called the Law of Entropy – in the 1850s, its pessimistic implications appealed more to the imagination of the Late Victorians and Early Modernists. As Watts explains, the law maintained that "the amount of 'available' energy in the universe must gradually dwindle to nothing as heat flows from warmer into cooler masses until equalisation of temperatures prevails" (*Preface* 82-83). The most unsettling aspect of this law, however, was the notion that the sun, instead of shining inexhaustibly, would inevitably burn itself out so that the human race would become extinct amid icy darkness. In "Evolution and Ethics" Huxley took up this idea and claimed that if the earth were to cool, as Kelvin predicted, degeneration would set in and bring about "a population of more and more stunted and humbler organisms, until the "fittest" that survived might be nothing but lichens, diatoms, and such microscopic organisms as those which give red snow its colour" ("Evolution" 327). Although by the end of his life Huxley commanded great authority as a scientist, only a minority of his colleagues supported his claim that evolution is governed by randomness and chance. Indeed, the late nineteenth century saw what Julian Huxley calls the 'Eclipse of Darwinism' (cf. Bowler, *Darwin* 210). Instead of natural selection other mechanisms, such as the Lamarckian idea of the inheritance of acquired characteristics were favoured. Even though the belief in 'soft heredity' was being disproved by genetics, Lamarckism exercised an undiminished appeal to *fin-de-siècle* writers, scientists, and intellectuals. It informed among others the debates about 'nature' versus 'nurture', about the role of the state versus that of the individual, about degeneracy and perfectibility, and about the racial supremacy of Europeans and the inferiority of colonial subjects. Lamarckism was so popular because it allowed its adherents to believe in evolution as a purposeful, progressive process to which individuals can actively contribute. Furthermore, because of Lamarck's idea that certain behaviour patterns and mental faculties are learned habits which can be inherited as well, Lamarckians hoped that our social instincts, our moral behaviour, and our intelligence can be enhanced over the generations and that we have an influence on the development of the human race. They rejected Darwin's mechanism of natural selection because it implied a brutalized image of nature and because it denied humankind any hope of realizing noble aspirations, such as the generation of ever-higher mental states or the improvement of moral instincts. It is not surprising that Lamarckians also took a much more optimistic attitude towards education and cooperation than Darwinians. As believers in the importance of 'nurture', they held that progress for the human race "could best be promoted by a cooperative political system in which the best ideals of civilized man were implanted in each generation by state-controlled education" (Bowler, *Evolution* 227). Indeed, for Lamarckians, cooperation was not just a political programme but was seen as inherent in organic evolution. They saw the willingness to cooperate with each other and even to sacrifice oneself for others as the most successful evolutionary policy and as the essential stimulus for the growth of human civilization. They hoped that by taking the moral development of humankind into our own hands we could pass on enhanced moral values from one generation to the next. Charles Darwin had also argued that morality was a social instinct and that natural selection had promoted cooperative values among groups of animals. However, as he rejected the concept of use-inheritance and favoured 'hard heredity', he certainly did not believe that we could actively influence humankind's moral potential. According to Darwin, evolutionary developments occur extremely slowly so that changes in a species are only noticeable after thousands of years.

The re-emergence of Darwinism is connected with the focus on the problem of heredity, which paved the way for the new science of genetics (cf. Bowler, *Darwin* 213 ff). The British eugenicist Francis Galton and the German biologist August Weismann argued that heredity rigidly determines an individual's character and that there is no possibility of inheriting acquired characteristics. According to Weismann, the substance of heredity is located in the cell nucleus and is transmitted unchanged from one generation to the next. As a consequence, Weismann and later geneticists postulated that selection by the environment is the only factor that controls the flow of genes within populations. The latter exhibit random variability because a wide range of fixed hereditary factors circulates within them. They are combined and recombined in different, random ways due to individual matings. Selection then acts on the range of hereditable variation in the population, gradually shifting the range in the direction of increased fitness. These ideas were confirmed when, in the early years of the twentieth century, the botanists Carl Correns and Hugo De Vries rediscovered and confirmed the results of Gregor Mendel's breeding experiments with peas, which he had already published in 1865. They showed that hereditary factors are transmitted as distinct and absolutely fixed units that can be traced through several generations. The combination of genetics and Darwinism which emerged in this way and which is still the dominant paradigm in evolutionary thought today is referred to as the 'Modern Synthesis', named after Julian Huxley's 1942 study, *Evolution: The Modern Synthesis*. As Gribbin and White put it, "[i]f we had to draw the line somewhere, the publication of this book, 60 years after the death of Darwin, could be said to mark the moment when Darwinism finally became established as the best explanation of how evolution works" (294).

No matter whether turn-of-the-century thinkers advocated an extreme form of determinism or veered towards near-determinism or indeterminism, they shared a belief in the importance and power of impersonal forces at the expense of the significance of individual action. Within the disciplines of sociology and political philosophy we come across a similar movement: away from individualism towards collectivism. José Harris even refers to this change as the "thematic core of the period" (11). In nearly all branches of political and sociological thought there occurred "a shift from viewing society as an aggregation of private individuals to a vision of society as collective, public, evolutionary, and organic" (Harris 37). This shift was also reflected in a change in the relationship between the state and the individual. Whereas in Victorian times the predominant belief had been that individuals should make their own plans and should look to the state only for law and order, this now gave way to the idea that state and society were prior to individual citizens and were responsible for numerous aspects of their lives. Thus central government policies gradually encroached upon concerns of individuals which had hitherto been considered private and personal:

education and child care, health and medicine, sexual relations and fertility, immigration and employment, alcohol consumption and private morals. Among the reasons for this shift Harris (cf. 225) lists the increasing scale of urban life and productive processes; the rise of mass political organizations; the spread of compulsory education and of mass-circulation newspapers; and the sheer accumulation of statistical facts about society. There were also technological developments, such as the invention of the electric telegraph, the telephone, and the wireless, which facilitated the growth of central government and of state control over individual lives. Finally, we also have to take into account the influence of global economic and political developments such as imperialism. Even though Britain's economy remained one of strongest in the world, the country slowly lost its position as the undisputed leader among the industrial powers. Other countries, such as Germany, Belgium, and the United States, challenged not only Britain's economic supremacy but also its imperial hegemony. Even though the British Empire had reached its largest expansion by the turn of the century, there were fears that it was doomed and had, in fact, already started to crumble at the edges. Especially the military disasters of the Boer War (1899-1902) dealt a severe blow to imperial confidence, while at the same time jingoist propaganda increased. The fact that there were too few able-bodied recruits available for the South African War heightened anxiety as to the possible degeneration of the British race and led to the setting-up of the Interdepartmental Committee on Physical Deterioration and the creation of the cross-party 'national-efficiency movement' in the early years of the twentieth century. According to Harris, these two bodies launched an "all-out attack on the parochial, amateur, and libertarian traditions of British government and proposed widespread 'professional' restructuring of imperial government, social services, and national defence" (Harris 206). The move from individualism to collectivism and the concomitant growth of central government were therefore not only the result of changes within British society but were also linked to imperial expansion and defence.

In addition to technological, economic, and imperialist developments, evolutionary ideas, too, contributed to the foregrounding of collectivism. In fact, various models of 'social evolution' or 'Social Darwinism' were used as guidelines to social policies, to the duties of the state and the individual, to private and public morality and, most problematically, to imperialist policies in general and the relationship between the colonizers and the colonized in particular. The origins of Social Darwinism go back to Darwin's contemporary Herbert Spencer (cf. Bowler, *Darwin* 169-172 and Harris 225-226), who had developed his own view of evolution before the *Origin of*

Species was published. Spencer set out his account of evolution and natural selection not in the sphere of botany and zoology like Darwin but in sociology. He argued that both the selection of random variation and the preservation and inheritance of acquired characteristics must cooperate in the evolutionary process. Spencer thus revealed himself to be more of a Lamarckian than a Darwinian. In a series of writings on 'systematic sociology' Spencer attempted to show that human nature is not static but constantly evolving. Sociology should, therefore, concern itself with the establishment of the same kind of laws that we find in the physical sciences and should regard human societies as living organisms which are subject, like the rest of the natural world, to competition, selection, survival, and decay. To Spencer the purpose of struggle was not so much the weeding out of the unfit but the encouragement of individuals and larger social organisms to become fitter, in order to escape the suffering entailed in failure. He hoped that the efforts of human beings to cope with a constantly changing society would produce useful new characteristics, which could then be passed on to future generations. Without struggle there would be no pressure on individuals and societies to make adaptations. Evolutionary progress would therefore come to a standstill and degeneration, leading to extinction, would set in. Within this framework Spencer identified 'progressive' societies by the fact that, like higher organisms, their members practised a high degree of division of labour and functional specialization and were held together by a dense network of cooperation. This was only possible if a strong governing authority existed which ensured that evolutionary laws were observed. Spencer was convinced that if the element of struggle and competition between individuals and societies were enhanced, the outcome would be universal progress.

In contrast to Spencer, Charles Darwin held that changes in human nature only become noticeable after thousands of years of natural selection. Therefore, he did not believe that active policies pursued by the state or other bodies to further competition between individuals or to eliminate the unfit would have immediate effects. He believed that society should be left completely alone to take care of itself. In *The Descent of Man* he noted (cf. Bowler, *Darwin* 197) that the 'civilized' nations had circumvented the power of natural selection to eliminate the unfit by, for instance, introducing poor laws, medical care, and other ways of helping the unfortunate. He claimed that this might be harmful to the race as – by analogy – no breeder of domestic animals would allow his worst animals to reproduce. On the other hand he also pointed out that, as human beings, we possess social instincts built into us by natural selection which lead us to be charitable to the poor.

Furthermore, there was – according to Darwin – a tendency for the immoral to die without reproducing anyway so that there would be no need to resort to drastic measures. Although Darwin's argumentation was cautious and balanced, many of his followers interpreted this to mean that not interfering with society and not helping the unfit were ethical demands, as adhering to them would benefit the progress of the race.

T.H. Huxley put forward his own variant of Social Darwinism. Although he believed that the origin of morality should be located in the social instincts, he did not deduce that the struggle for survival that we observe in nature should be taken as a guideline to human ethics. For Huxley morality was an exclusively human quality, which had left its roots in the instincts behind. In fact, Huxley regarded the latter as "an amoral vestige to be repressed" (Desmond 564) and as something from which moral man should try to escape. Paradoxically, Huxley separated the realm of nature from the realm of morality *because* he embraced Darwinism to the full. As I have shown, Huxley understood evolution as a random, non-directed, and non-progressive process. It keeps life adapted to changing conditions but only at the cost of a vast amount of suffering and without moving towards a meaningful goal. As evolution is not even progressive in purely biological terms, it does not make sense to base hopes for a brighter future for humankind on its mechanisms. Because the process of evolution is meaningless and amoral, ethical values need to be located in the realm of the purely human. Huxley expressed this view in the already referred to Romanes lecture "Evolution and Ethics" of 1893. Huxley argues that human beings have reached their domineering position among all forms of life on earth by virtue of their success in the struggle for existence. Humankind has prevailed through qualities it shares with animals: "his exceptional physical organization; his cunning, his sociability, his curiosity, and his imitativeness; his ruthless and ferocious destructiveness" ("Evolution" 311-312). However, in proportion to the growth of humankind's social organization and civilization, these deeply ingrained qualities have become defects. According to Huxley, human beings would only be "too pleased to see "the ape and tiger die"" ("Evolution" 312). Unfortunately, however, they decline to suit man's convenience "and the unwelcome intrusion of these boon companions of his hot youth into the ranged existence of civil life adds pains and griefs, innumerable and immeasurably great, to those which the cosmic process necessarily brings on the mere animal" ("Evolution" 312). Huxley introduces a split in the universe: he separates what he calls "the cosmic process" from "the ethical process" or, in Desmond's words, "a wild zoological nature from our ethical existence" (598). Huxley identifies the cosmic process with the randomness and ruthlessness of evolution; with the struggle for survival and the survival of the fittest; and with the 'ape and tiger instincts' within human beings. The ethical process, on the other hand, Huxley associates with the essence of humanity, comprising morality and the achievements of civilization. Although moral values have their origin in the cosmic process as well, they have become divorced from it and are now in opposition to it. In Huxley's view human ethics have, therefore, been "evolved by natural selection to defy natural selection" (Desmond 598). Our moral standards are so essential precisely *because* "they go beyond nature to establish a sphere of activity that has become an integral part of our humanity" (Bowler, *Evolution* 244). In fact, our morality constitutes our humanity and this is why we have to struggle so hard to maintain it. Indeed, progress for humankind is only possible if we promote the ethical process at the expense of the cosmic process:

> [I]n place of ruthless self-assertion it demands self-restraint; in place of thrusting aside, or treading down, all competitors, it requires that the individual shall not merely respect, but shall help his fellows; its influence is directed, not so much to the survival of the fittest, as to the fitting of as many as possible to survive. It repudiates the gladiatorial theory of existence. ("Evolution" 327-328)

Even though Huxley was, in general, a sceptic and pessimist, he maintained that limited progress for humankind is possible, especially via the means of education and change of environment. Indeed, Huxley's own astonishing career was the best example of his claim that a human being is "susceptible of a vast amount of improvement, by education, by instruction, and by the application of his intelligence to the adaptation of the conditions of life to his higher needs" ("Prolegomena" 306). As Huxley denied the concept of human perfectibility, he was very critical of political solutions offering panaceas for social ills. Thus he, for instance, rejected Socialism on the Malthusian grounds that "[p]eace and plenty in a socialist arcadia would only increase the number of births and start the struggle for resources all over again" (Desmond 575). Huxley was also sceptical of the demands for a governmental eugenics programme, as this would mean taking the cosmic process as a model for human ethics. According to Huxley "there is no hope that mere human beings will ever possess enough intelligence to select the fittest" ("Prolegomena" 301-302). With regard to the debate about collectivism and the role of central government, Huxley opted for a powerful state that takes an active interest in and tries to regulate the affairs of its citizens. The state is not only responsible for the education, health, and living conditions of the individual but also for his/her morality. It is not only the individual's but also the state's duty to promote the ethical process and to fight the cosmic process, thereby preventing degeneration and the descent into barbarism.

The last model of social evolution I would like to discuss is that of the eugenics movement. Even though Spencer's, Darwin's, and even Huxley's views on government, society, and the individual are usually labelled Social Darwinism, Bowler points out that to be a true Darwinist in social affairs one would actually have "to insist that all aspects of personality are rigidly determined by heredity and that progress can only come about through the constant elimination of those individuals unfortunate enough to be born with inferior characteristics" (*Darwin* 199). According to these criteria, neither Spencer, nor Darwin, nor Huxley can be called Social Darwinists. The only Victorian evolutionist whose theory conforms to the above definition is Francis Galton, Darwin's cousin. He is best known as the founder of eugenics, whose central tenets he laid down in his *Hereditary Genius* of 1869. Galton believed that heredity was a much more rigid force than generally supposed and determined how parental characteristics are transmitted to the offspring. With regard to the 'nature' versus 'nurture' debate Galton and his followers therefore opted for the former. They rejected the claim by the Lamarckians but also, for different reasons, by Huxley that improved environmental conditions and education could have an extensive influence on character. Galton argued that because of the predominance of 'nature' people who inherit a bad character cannot be improved. Nothing can help them become 'better' persons and it is a waste of money and energy to even try. With regard to social policies we have seen that Darwin believed that society should best be left alone to develop according to evolutionary laws, whereas Spencer maintained that competition and struggle should be encouraged to force individuals and society to adapt to changing conditions. For Galton both views fell short of the mark. In his opinion laissez-faire social policies cannot prevent the laws of natural selection from being relaxed, as the least fit members of society are seldom left to die off completely. Galton therefore called for the state to play an active role in controlling the proportions of fit and unfit individuals. In other words, he proposed artificial selection. He termed this policy 'eugenics' and demanded measures to identify and institutionalise those physically and/or mentally inferior individuals who were a threat to the genetic future of the race. In the 1870s and 1880s Galton's views were largely ignored. Towards the turn-of-the-century, however, various factors contributed to the spread of his beliefs and the eugenics movement became a sizeable part of the intellectual and political scene, culminating in the foundation of the Eugenics Education

Society in 1907. One of these factors was the already mentioned rediscovery of Mendelian genetics, which proved Galton's belief in hard heredity. Another was the increased industrial competition and colonial rivalry between European powers, which encouraged the view that a struggle of survival was going on between nations and races. This raised the question whether one's own nation was fit enough to prevail in this struggle and which measures should be taken to make it fitter. In Britain fears of degeneration and decay seem to have been particularly prevalent, maybe because the country's industrial and imperialist supremacy had remained unchallenged for so long. Pseudo-scientific theories of degeneration, such as Max Nordau's and Lombroso's, were popular and widespread. The discussion focused in particular on the urban poor and on changing fertility patterns. This was grist to the mill of the eugenicists, as they regarded the slums of the big cities as breeding grounds of the worst kinds of human characteristics. In the aftermath of the Boer War the eugenicist cause received ambivalent support from the 1904 Interdepartmental Committee on Physical Degeneration. Even though the committee denied that the British population was in a state of irreversible physical and racial decline, it nevertheless emphasized that throughout urban Britain there was widespread physical unfitness, caused by poverty, malnutrition, environmental pollution, and bad personal habits. Furthermore, it called for state interference as, according to Harris, "the sheer scale of the problem and the resources required to deal with it now went far beyond the scope of even the largest local authorities" (Harris 206). A related anxiety that the eugenicists exploited was the general decline in fertility. The concern here was not just with quantity but also with quality. It appeared that the fertility decline was most pronounced among the rich and well educated, and that, therefore, "the poorest third of the nation was breeding and rearing two-thirds of the British race" (Harris 46). The eugenicists used these statistical findings to bolster their demand that 'superior' people – white-collar workers and middle-class professionals – should be encouraged to have more children, while the 'inferior' masses should be prevented from breeding, for instance, by sterilization or by segregation in disciplinary labour colonies. The greatest success of the eugenics campaign was the passing of the Mental Deficiency Act of 1913, which authorized the forcible institutionalisation of the feeble-minded. Nowadays, the eugenics movement is usually associated with the extreme right. However, in the early years of the twentieth century it was part of mainstream thought and even had supporters on the left (cf. Rose 135). Bernard Shaw, for example, insisted in *Man and Superman* that real social progress would be impossible unless steps were taken to breed a new type of human being and, in 1910, he "appalled even the Eugenics Education Society by recommending the gas chamber for social undesirables" (Rose 137). The socialist imperialist Karl Pearson became the first professor of eugenics at the University of London and his work interested Shaw, H.G. Wells, and Beatrice and Sidney Webb.

The survey of models of social evolution has shown that, with the exception of the eugenicists, evolutionists did not in general advocate active measures to eliminate the unfit within British society. It is pertinent, however, that they did not have any such qualms with regard to the colonies. In disregard of the implications of their own theories, all evolutionists were in agreement that non-white peoples belonged to 'inferior races' and that the Europeans therefore had the right to colonize, subjugate, or even exterminate them. The mere fact of imperial dominion had given credence to the superiority of the British and their institutions long before theories of social evolution appeared on the scene. Britain had, of course, already been a colonial power before Queen Victoria came to the throne in 1837 but during her reign and especially towards its end there was a change in attitude towards Empire: according to Newsome, it "became part of a political programme, and imperialism was born" (127). Newsome dates this change of mood from a speech by Benjamin Disraeli at Crystal Palace on 24 June 1872, in which the future prime minister exhorted the British to be "'proud of belonging to an Imperial country, and [...] to maintain, if they can, their empire'" (135). Disraeli further contributed to the rise of imperialism by gaining control of the Suez Canal in 1875 and by bestowing the title 'Empress of India' upon the Queen one year later. Imperialistic feelings reached a climax in 1897 when "[r]epresentatives of all the peoples and territories subjugated by the British, almost a quarter of the earth and its inhabitants, gathered in London to pay tribute to Queen Victoria on the sixtieth anniversary of her ascension to the throne" (Lindqvist, *Exterminate* 11). As Childs points out, imperialism was not only a system of power politics and economic exploitation but also "an ideology, a faith, fascinating intellectuals and writers, business men, soldiers, missionaries and politicians alike" (60). One of the most problematic aspects of this ideology was the way in which it was underpinned by a racist anthropology derived from evolutionary theories of the (mainly) Lamarckian kind. Ideas about race and national character had been prevalent in the early and mid-Victorian period as well but, as Harris points out, "they had only the sketchiest of roots in biological thought and were largely expressed in terms of constitutional tradition and political culture" (233). From the 1860s onwards, however, influenced by evolutionary theory, the concept of race as a medium of common cultural inheritance was gradually rivalled by and intermingled with a sense of race as a deterministic biological and anthropological force. The evolutionist who had the greatest influence here was Herbert Spencer. He argued that the development of the mind and of civilization went hand in hand. Whereas Spencer held Victorian industrial society to be the expression of the highest level of intelligence, he believed that non-industrialized communities were the products of an inferior or primitive mentality. Spencer's belief in natural selection and the struggle for survival allowed him to identify 'lower races' as evolutionary failures and to present their subjugation or even elimination as the consequence of a law of nature. Spencer's theory, which was largely Lamarckian in character, formed the basis of much nineteenth century anthropology. Thus, as Bowler points out, "[w]here Darwin saw biological evolution as a branching tree, the cultural evolutionists constructed a ladder of developmental stages which, they assumed, all races of mankind could ascend" (*Darwin* 192). Taking their cue from Spencer, anthropologists such as John Lubbock and Edward B. Tylor reserved the highest rung of the ladder for contemporary European society, which they saw as the goal towards which all other peoples were aspiring. Pre-industrial cultures were automatically assumed to have preserved the social structures that the Europeans had passed through in previous ages. In another analogy to evolution, they argued that 'primitive' peoples were 'living fossils' who had both culturally and mentally preserved an earlier evolutionary stage. So-called 'savages' were, therefore, relics of the ancestral form of humankind still surviving in out of the way parts of the world. James Hunt, the founder of the Anthropological Society, which, according to Desmond, was set up in 1863 "to measure and maximise racial differences" (320), went so far as to claim that the different peoples of the world were so many separate warring species. Furthermore, he maintained that black and white people were descended "from different 'species of apes'" (Desmond 320) and that the blacks were meant by evolution to be subservient to the whites. These examples illustrate to what problematic ends Lamarckism could be put when it was incorporated into late nineteenth century anthropological theories and imperialist ideology. As Bowler points out,

> a belief in the purposeful character of evolution could be combined with a ruthless attitude towards nature's failures. It was precisely because [according to the Lamarckians] evolution was designed to produce higher levels of mentality that it became necessary to eliminate those who did not keep up. (*Darwin* 195).

One should think that a strictly Darwinian view of human evolution would not lend itself so easily to an argumentation of this kind. However, in this respect Darwin himself was blind to the implications of his own theory. The idea of a progressive and hierarchical cultural evolution should have jarred with his non-progressive, branching concept. In *The Descent of Man* Darwin had said explicitly that intelligence or social organization were *not* decisive factors in the emergence of the human race but merely accidental by-products of a change in lifestyle and environment. Despite all this, Darwin was convinced that black people had lagged behind the whites in the development from the apes. He even went so far as to accept measurements according to which the average brain capacity of the white race was larger than that of other ethnic groups. Darwin equated a larger brain with a greater level of intelligence and therefore placed Europeans at the head of a hierarchy of racial types. Like most of his contemporaries, Darwin concluded that the Europeans were colonizing the world not just because they had superior technology but also because they were brighter than the other races and thus biologically superior. Towards the end of the nineteenth century it therefore became generally accepted that British ascendancy must be viewed in evolutionary terms and that, as an 'advanced' and 'progressive' nation, it was the country's duty "to promote rational organization among the backward and decayed" (Harris 230-231).

In my survey of the changes that led to the rise of incompatibilism I have so far focused mainly on theories which foreground impersonal forces that are external to human beings. However, around the turn of the century we also encounter a movement into the opposite direction: towards individualism, subjectivism, and solipsism. Among the philosophers and scientists that contributed most to this re-orientation were William James, Henri Bergson, and Sigmund Freud. In his *Principles of Psychology* (1890) James argued that the mind is not merely the mirror of external matter but has its own motions and structures for apprehending experience. By claiming that consciousness is not a chain of separate items but a constant flow of memories and impressions, he also contributed one of the key terms of Modernism, 'stream of consciousness' (cf. Stevenson 41). In *Time and Free Will* (1889) Bergson argued similarly to James that subjectivism is the only way in which we can know reality: "[F]acts and matter, which are the objects of discursive reason, are only the outer surface that has to be penetrated by *intuition* in order to achieve *a vision in depth of reality*" (quoted in Childs 48). Bergson here also employs the distinction between surface and deep structure that we have already encountered in the discussion of early twentieth century physics. The deep structure is more significant than the surface structure and can only be accessed via individual intuition. Bergson's best-known example of this contention is his distinction between clock-time and 'duration':

When I follow with my eyes on the dial of a clock the movement of the hands ... I do not measure duration ... Outside of me, in space, there is never more than a single position of the hand ... Within myself a process of organization or interpenetration of conscious states is going on, which constitutes true duration ... (quoted in Stevenson 107)

Bergson regarded the idea that time is a quantity that can be divided up into a succession of separate events as mistaken. The *true* experience of time takes place within each individual mind and cannot be measured according to the clock. 'Duration', therefore, is necessarily different for each individual. Bergson's concept of time also had repercussions for the representation of memory, which could no longer be regarded as a chronological sequence of events but as an evolving flow of mental states, where the past and the present coexist. As Stevenson summarizes, Bergson, together with Sigmund Freud, provided the impetus for the Modernist tendency "to move away from the rational, logical and deductive, in favour of the intuitive, the unconscious and the emotional" (Stevenson 109).

Just as Darwin did not 'invent' evolution, Freud did not 'invent' the unconscious. His theories became predominant because they were more stringently argued than others available at the time. Freud was a strict determinist and deeply indebted to nineteenth century rationalist thinking. Freud held that all psychological and mental phenomena, such as thoughts, feelings, and fantasies, are rigidly determined by the principle of cause and effect, even though much of that causation takes place in the unconscious. Addressing his audience in his *Introductory Lectures on Psycho-Analysis*, Freud claimed that the belief in freedom and choice, at least in the realm of psychology, is an illusion: "There is within you a deeply rooted belief in psychic freedom and choice ... [But] this belief is quite unscientific and ... must give ground before the claims of a determinism which governs even mental life" (quoted in Dilman 179). In his determinist view of human existence Freud was greatly influenced by Charles Darwin, who, as we have seen, believed that even highly complex behaviour can be traced to simple biological or instinctual origins. Freud, too, attempts, wherever possible, to reduce the psychological and emotional to the physical and organic. After all, as Storr points out, psychoanalytic theory is "an 'instinct' theory [and] primarily concerned with how the isolated individual finds or fails to find ways of discharging his instinctive impulses" (91). Freud not only sees aberrant mental behaviour but also dreams, slips of the tongue, fantasies, or artistic creations as the result of the repression of primitive instincts, especially sexual ones. Freud's determinism also informs central concepts of his system of thought, such as the tripartite division of the psyche into ego, id, and super-ego, and the rigid stages of childhood development. For Freud the divisions of personality are immutable structures. The ego is inevitably torn between the demands of the id and the super-ego so that freedom of action is hardly possible. Freud's view of individual character is equally deterministic and pessimistic. He believes that it is formed in decisive ways in the first four to six years of life, when we pass through the rigid stages of infantile sexual development. In our later lives we are determined by our childhood experiences, memories, and traumas. Our existence is ruled by attempts to defend ourselves from what we find painful; to compensate for what we feel we lack; to make amends for feelings of guilt; and to fight our childhood battles in our present lives. We are caught up in patterns of behaviour that we keep repeating. Despite Freud's determinism and pessimism, he did not, like Schopenhauer for instance, rest content with outlining a gloomy and hopeless view of human existence, but was concerned with finding ways to ameliorate our lot. Psychoanalysis and psychotherapy are meant to provide the means to access our unconscious and to help us understand the drives that determine our lives. Freud hoped that thereby we could come to grips with our inner constraints and would achieve greater autonomy and self-mastery in our lives. In this way Freud seems to have attributed at least a limited capacity for free choice and self-determination to individuals.

Given that Freud worked within the framework of nineteenth century science characterized by determinism, materialism, and rationalism, it is striking that the early twentieth century reception of his theories pointed into the opposite direction. Freudianism was understood as vindicating a concern with irrationality, contingency, a-logicality, and a-causality. The roots of this view lie in Freud's foregrounding of dreams and in his insistence that unconscious forces, of which we are largely ignorant, control our physical, mental, and linguistic behaviour. Dreams, in Freud's view, are disguised, hallucinatory fulfilments of repressed wishes and instincts. They are, like the id, chaotic and irrational. They ignore logic, syntax, and the accepted categories of time and space. Apart from dreams, slips of the tongue and the technique of free association used in psychotherapy can also provide clues to what is going on in the unconscious. As Storr points out, these ideas encouraged many people – in particular artists – "to experiment with the fortuitous and the irrational, to pay serious attention to their inner worlds of dream and day-dream, and to find significance in thoughts and images which they would previously have dismissed as absurd or illogical" (73). Freud's theories also strongly reinforced the pessimistic strain in early twentieth century culture. As I have pointed out, many intellectuals had withdrawn into subjectivity because they felt oppressed by the revelation of impersonal forces over which they felt they had no control. Freud now provided apparently incontrovertible scientific evidence that human beings are not even in control of their very own 'mental house' (cf. Storr 121). In Freud's model the ego is the seat of consciousness, reason, and common sense but it is, as Bantock explains, "a feeble thing, fighting for its life against the encroachments of the super-ego and the id" (20). This struck another devastating blow at man's sense of independence and his capability to make free choices.

As we have seen, Darwin regarded nature as a battlefield where a brutal struggle for survival takes place between organisms; Social Darwinists and anthropologists saw this struggle as going on between individuals, societies, and races; Marx postulated perpetual antagonism between social classes. For Freud, too, conflict was a fundamental principle of his world view but he located its origin in the mind of the individual, postulating a clash between the conscious and the unconscious, between the ego, the id, and the super-ego. This conflict is set in motion by the primal instincts that our mind tries to repress. While at the beginning of his career Freud only recognized the sexual instinct, he later on also accepted the existence of the death instinct, which is entirely independent of anything sexual. This discovery led him to construct a dualist scheme, in which all phenomena of mental life can be traced to a basic conflict between Eros and Thanatos. As Freud regarded psychoanalysis as a universal explanatory system, he did not restrict the conflict between the two instincts to the individual mind but believed it to determine the human species in general and social organisation in particular. This led Freud to describe civilizsation as

> a process in the service of Eros, whose purpose is to combine single human individuals, and after that families, then races, peoples and nations, into one great unity, the unity of mankind. But man's natural aggressive instinct, the hostility of each against all and all against each, oppose this programme of civilization. This aggressive instinct is the derivative and the main representative of the death instinct which we have found alongside of Eros and which shares world-dominion with it. And now, I think, the meaning of the evolution of civilization is no longer obscure to us. It must present the struggle between Eros and Death, between the instinct of life and the instinct of destruction as it works itself out in the human species. This struggle is what all life essentially consists of, and the evolution of civilization may therefore be simply described as the struggle for life of the human species. (quoted in Storr 53)

Civilization thus appears to be an embattled, fragile entity: while the love instinct supports and furthers it, the death instinct works towards its destruction. One should assume that Freud would be wholly on the side of civilization, regarding it as our most precious human achievement.

Surprisingly, however, Freud's view is ambivalent, regarding civilization "as the enemy of instinct and an instigator of repression" (Storr 69). To understand this perspective, it is necessary to recall that psychoanalytic theory is an instinct-theory: it is primarily concerned with how individuals find or fail to find ways of discharging their instinctive impulses. Thus, as Storr explains, it regards individuals as being thoroughly egoistic and

> relationships with other human beings [to have] value only in so far as they facilitate instinctual satisfaction. There is [in Freud's system of thought] no conception of friendship or other types of relationship as being valuable in themselves. All are considered 'aim-inhibited' substitutes for sexual relations. (91)

Civilization's main purpose can therefore only be to suppress our selfish drives. It does so not only from outside, via the individual's surroundings, but also from inside, via the super-ego. That Freud regarded civilization as oppressive and as provocative of neuroses also comes across in the following disturbing passage in which he imagines what life would be like without social and ethical restraints:

> We have spoken of the hostility to civilization which is produced by the pressure that civilization exercises, the renunciations of instinct which it demands. If one imagines its prohibitions lifted – if, then, one may take any woman one pleases as a sexual object, if one may without hesitation kill one's rival for her love or anyone else who stands in one's way, if, too, one can carry off any of the other man's belongings without asking leave – how splendid, what a string of satisfactions one's life would be! (quoted in Storr 90-91).

This paragraph may be – as Storr suggests – "ironically intended" (90), but it shows that Freud's view of humankind is sombre indeed: without the restrictions imposed by civilization, human beings – or *men* at least – would behave like criminals and would be reduced to the level of unreasoning animals. Most disturbingly, they would actually enjoy their new state of 'freedom'.

One final aspect of the movement towards subjectivism that should be highlighted is the new way of thinking about language. Among late-nineteenth century thinkers it was Friedrich Nietzsche who had first drawn attention to a discrepancy between language as an arbitrary ordering system and the reality it purports to represent. From a completely different perspective, Freud, too, showed that language could be treacherous. Slips of the tongue or trivial utterances may provide hints at what is going on in the unconscious. In psychotherapy sessions Freud encouraged his patients "to put into words without censorship whatever thoughts or phantasies spontaneously occurred to [them]" (Storr 30). This technique of free association was meant to open up a gateway to what is repressed in the unconscious. Freud's view of language has parallels to William James's concept of the 'stream-of-consciousness' and Bergson's idea of memory as a flow or flux of interpenetrating mental states. Bergson, indeed, regarded language as insufficient and inadequate to express true subjective experience: while words are fixed and static, the impressions of our individual consciousness are fluid and instable. Bergson even went so far as to claim that language produces two different selves: "One is the self which can be made to belong in language: defined, solidified, made visible, but falsified; the other running on deeply, continuously, but almost inaccessible, beyond reach of words" (Stevenson 183). The theories of Bergson, James, Freud, and Nietzsche thus questioned and redefined the nature and function of language. In the nineteenth century language had been held to be transparent, reliable, and, above all, meaningful. Just as the Victorians believed in the existence of truth and the ability of the mind to discover it, they also thought of language as a truthful mirror of the external world. This faith underpinned Victorian Realism. At the turn of the century, however, a gap opened up between words and their referents so that, as Stevenson puts it, "[l]anguage's innocence [was] lost" (Stevenson 184). Language did not only become detached from a reality it could no longer represent adequately but also from a mind whose movements it misrepresented by its inflexible aspects. Psychoanalysis showed that language was not under our control at all but tended to betray us by giving away our darkest secrets. This distrust of language was part of the epistemological shift towards subjectivism described above and led to the foregrounding of ambiguity, paradox, and miscommunication in Modernist writing.

4. Conrad and the Problem of Free Will

4.1 The Conradian world picture

In the history of Conradian criticism countless attempts have been made to define the writer's philosophy and to pin down his world view. Not only the sheer number of diverse, contradictory labels that have been attributed to Conrad is astonishing but also the fact that the writer and his work have managed to resist any pigeon-holing. But does Conrad actually have any coherent philosophy or consistent world view to offer in the first place? One of the earliest critics to voice such doubts was E.M. Forster. In his essay "The Pride of Mr Conrad," first published in 1921, he claimed that

> [w]hat is so elusive about him is that he is always promising to make some general philosophic statement about the universe, and then refraining with a gruff disclaimer. [...] [Conrad's work] suggest[s] that he is misty in the middle as well as at the edges, that the secret casket of his genius contains a vapour rather than a jewel; and that we need not try to write him down philosophically, because there is, in this particular direction, nothing to write. (396-397)

Maybe critics like Forster are asking too much of Conrad. Can we really demand of a writer that he should offer a consistent philosophy along with his fictional writings to, as it were, facilitate or channel the interpretation of the latter? With the exception of Jean-Paul Sartre, Albert Camus, and, possibly, Iris Murdoch, it is difficult to think of any recent writers who have been both successful philosophers and novelists. Certainly, Joseph Conrad viewed himself primarily as a writer of fiction and not as a philosopher. As he said in a letter written in 1911, "I have formulated no doctrine either for my own use or for the information of the world" (*CL4*: 457). On the other hand Conrad's interest in and knowledge of philosophy should not be underestimated. Throughout his fiction and his non-fiction there are numerous explicit and implicit references to certain philosophers and philosophical concerns. For instance, in his essay "The Crime of Partition" Conrad knowledgeably refers to Hegel and Nietzsche and there is John Galsworthy's well-known comment in his 1924 *Reminiscences of Conrad* that "[o]f philosophy he had read a good deal ... Schopenhauer used to give him satisfaction twenty years and more ago" (quoted in Spittles 150).

Although it cannot be shown that Conrad adhered to any particular philosophical system, his fiction demonstrates, as Spittels puts it, that he "was clearly aware of philosophic and ethical conflicts, and of the sources that had provoked them" (142-143). Even a negative judgment such as Forster's contains the implicit recognition that Conrad's works raise philosophical issues which are informed by contemporary debates. Conrad's fiction clearly addresses the latter but does not take up any entrenched positions or offer simple solutions.

A similar relationship exists between Conrad's fiction and science. Although, unlike H.G. Wells for instance, Conrad was not a trained scientist, scientific concepts and their philosophical implications also contribute to the thematic richness and complexity of his writing. Thus concepts derived from Darwinism lend themselves particularly well to an interpretation of Conrad's major novels. That the writer was aware of contemporary scientific ideas "in essence if not in detail" (Spittles 143) also comes across in his non-fiction. Conrad's essay "Turgenev," for instance, contains a sardonic comment on how "the infinite emotions of love [will be] replaced by the exact simplicity of perfected Eugenics" (46) and "The Ascending Effort" starts with an indirect quote from Francis Galton's work (cf. 72). When Conrad first encountered an X-ray machine at the home of the pioneer radiologist John McIntyre in 1898, he wrote a letter to Edward Garnett in which he expressed his excitement at the scientific principles involved and at the possibilities revealed by modern physics:

> [A]nd in the evening dinner, phonograph, X rays, talk about *the* secret of the universe and the nonexistence of, so called, matter. The secret of the universe is in the existence of horizontal waves whose varied vibrations are at the bottom of all states of consciousness. If the waves were vertical the universe would be different. This is a truism. But, don't you see, there is nothing in the world to prevent the simultaneous existence of vertical waves, of waves at any angles; in fact there are mathematical reasons for believing that such waves do exist. Therefore it follows that two universes may exist in the same place and in the same time – and not only two universes but an infinity of different universes – if by universe we mean a set of states of consciousness; and note, *all* (the universes) composed of the same matter, *all matter* being only that thing of inconceivable tenuity through which the various vibrations of waves (electricity, heat, sound, light etc.) are propagated, thus giving birth to our sensations – then emotions – then thought. (*CL* 2 94-95)

This letter provides direct evidence for Conrad's interest in and excitement at the discoveries of natural science. It is, however, also remarkable to observe how Conrad's imagination takes its starting point from principles of physics, uses them as a spring-board for philosophical speculations as to the nature of the universe, and finally transforms them into fantasy. Cedric Watts (cf. *Letters* 108) indeed speculates that the ideas contained in this letter may have formed the basis of *The Inheritors*, Conrad and Ford Madox Ford's attempt at writing science fiction.

Even though, therefore, a delineation of the Conradian world picture must take into account philosophical and scientific influences, it is not possible to whittle them down to just one source that could serve as the key to his work. Neither can we assign exclusive labels to Conrad, for instance that he was *either* a traditional conservative *or* a radical sceptic. Instead, to do justice to Conrad's complexity, we have to incorporate *both* these standpoints into an interpretation of his vision and works, without insisting on resolving the inherent contradictions. What we have to accept is that Conrad is – as he himself insists in a letter (cf. *CL* 2: 418) – *modern* and that therefore one of the essential characteristics of his thinking is the tendency towards paradox and ambiguity. As Cedric Watts emphasizes, "If any god presides over Conrad's best work, it is the god Janus. Janus is the two-headed god: he looks in opposite ways at the same time; he presides over paradox; and he is the patron of janiform texts" (*Preface* 7). Watts also insists that the recognition that Conrad's thinking and writing is informed by paradox and ambiguity should not be interpreted as uncertainty or "ideological fence-sitting;" it should rather be seen as "an uncompromising commitment to the actual complexities of human experience" (Watts, *Preface* 55). Although the janiformity at the heart of Conrad's vision cannot be resolved, we can at least attempt to circumscribe it by, for instance, looking at his autobiographical and cultural background, such as his childhood in Poland and his seafaring career.

Conrad's family belonged to the landowning gentry of a Poland that had more or less vanished from the map of Europe due to its annexation by Russia, Prussia, and Austria. Conrad's father, Apollo Korzeniowski, was involved in underground political activity to regain national independence, for which he was sentenced to exile by the Russian authorities. Together with his wife and the four-year-old Joseph he was sent to the remote town of Vologda, 300 miles from Moscow. After their return to Poland, Conrad's mother died in 1865 and his father four years later. Apollo's funeral turned into a patriotic demonstration with the eleven-year-old Conrad at the head of a procession of several thousand people. Already at a very early age Joseph Conrad thus knew from his own bitter experience many of the pessimistic themes which would later be so prominent in his writings: loneliness, suffering, and death; beleaguered solidarity; the frequently futile sacrifices exacted by political action; life under an autocratic regime; or the way the public and the private are intertwined. As Cedric Watts speculates (cf. *Preface* 53), these autobiographical experiences would also have attuned him to ambiguity and paradox. For instance, Conrad's father, by being loyal to Poland, became, in the eyes of the Russian occupiers, a subversive, law-breaking figure. Furthermore, Apollo's political involvement, his patriotism, and willingness to sacrifice his life for national independence, led to suffering not only for himself but also for his wife and son. In this way Conrad became aware of how loyalty to one cause may entail disloyalty or even betrayal to another. He also experienced at first hand the complexities of being in an imperialist situation. Born into the Polish gentry, Conrad knew how it felt to be among the elite of a given society. Yet, since the Poles were subjugated by Russia, Prussia, and Austria, he also knew what it was like being the underdog in an occupied country. Not only Conrad's narrative strategy of employing multiple perspectives in his later fiction may have its roots in these experiences but also his contradictory political outlook. It has often been noted that although Conrad sometimes voices very conservative opinions, such as the belief in a hierarchical and autocratic order of society, we also come across statements that seem left-wing, such as his pronounced critique of imperialism and capitalism. According to Cedric Watts, the paradox of Conrad's political views can be comprehended "when we see how strongly it relates to the values of a traditional land-owning gentry, and particularly to a gentry which, in the modern world, is denied its former political powers" (*Literary Life* 8). As the feudal-agrarian economy gave way to the mercantile-industrial economy, economic and political power tended to pass from the land-owning interests to business interests. For this reason it was "not entirely unusual for noblemen to espouse popular causes, seeking alliance with the socially low against the middle classes [...], or to offer criticisms of the middle-class outlook which resemble those offered by socialists" (Watts, *Preface* 57-58). Thus Conrad would always display a keen eye for the ways in which the ruthless acquisitiveness of individuals or of nations manifests itself and how this egoistic greed is often masked by grandiloquent phrases and slogans. A prime example is his 1905 essay "Autocracy and War," which takes as its starting point the Russo-Japanese war of that year. Although Conrad neglects no opportunity to attack Russia in vociferous terms, he also surveys the European political scene in general. The tone of his analysis is one of resignation, seeing war as the "principle condition" (108) of the present day:

> Never before has war received so much homage at the lips of men, and reigned with less disputed sway in their minds. It has harnessed science to its gun-carriages, it has enriched a few respectable manufacturers, scattered doles of food and raiment amongst a few thousand skilled workmen, devoured the first youth of whole generations, and reaped its harvest of countless corpses. (109)

According to Conrad, the main reason for the ubiquitous belligerence is materialist greed, of which he not only accuses individuals but also states, especially the young European democracies:

> Industrialism and commercialism – wearing high-sounding names in many languages (*Welt-politik* may serve for one instance) [...] – stand ready, almost eager, to appeal to the sword as soon as the globe of the earth has shrunk beneath our growing numbers by another ell or so. And democracy, which has elected to pin its faith to the supremacy of material interests, will have to fight their [sic] battles to the bitter end, on a mere pittance [...]. (107)

To the European nations, the "idea of ceasing to grow in territory, in strength, in wealth, in influence – in anything but wisdom and self-knowledge is odious [...] as the omen of the end" (109). In fact, Europe does no longer exist; there is just "an armed and trading continent, the home of slowly maturing economical [sic] contests for life and death, and of loudly proclaimed world-wide ambitions" (112). Especially Germany's policies prove "that no peace for the earth can be found in the expansion of material interests" (113). So is there no hope at all to break this vicious circle set in motion by the pursuit of materialism? Conrad suggests both practical and visionary solutions, even though, given his devastating analysis of contemporary politics and his pessimistic view of human nature, it is unlikely that he regards them as realisable. One way forward might be European and international solidarity and the creation of political bodies that would watch over "an international understanding for the delimitation of spheres of trade all over the world" (107). A long-term solution can, however, only be brought about by "the advent of Concord and Justice; an advent that, however delayed by the fatal worship of force and the errors of national selfishness, has been, and remains, the only possible goal of our progress" (96). The latter can therefore only be measured in moral terms and must have its roots in "a common conservative principle abstract enough to give the impulse, practical enough to form the rallying point of international action tending towards the restraint of particular ambition" (111). What this moral principle might be, however, Conrad does not reveal:

> Whether such a principle exists – who can say? If it does not, then it ought to be invented. A sage with a sense of humour and a heart of compassion should set about it without loss of time, and a solemn prophet full of words and fire ought to be given that task of preparing the minds. So far there is no trace of such a principle anywhere in sight [...]. (111)

In 1874 Conrad left Poland for Marseille to become a sailor, first in the French, then in the British Merchant Navy, in whose service he rose to the position of captain. There is little information as to what Conrad's feelings were on leaving his home country, but, as John Batchelor asserts, it seems clear from later evidence "that Conrad was very sensitive to the charge that he had deserted Poland" (22). In *A Personal Record* he comments on his decision a number of times. For instance, he admits that "in hours of solitude and retrospect" he catches himself

> meeting arguments and charges made thirty-five years ago by voices now for ever still; finding things to say that an assailed boy could not have found, simply because of the mysteriousness of his impulses to himself. I understood no more than the people who called upon me to explain myself. There was no precedent. I verily believe mine was the only case of a boy of my nationality and antecedents taking a, so to speak, standing jump out of his racial surroundings and associations. (121)

Conrad's use of the metaphor "standing jump" inevitably calls up comparisons to the jump of the eponymous hero in *Lord Jim*. The protagonist suffers from terrible feelings of guilt during the remainder of his short life for having deserted his ship and its passengers. Jim describes his jump to Marlow as if in that particular situation he had acted against his will and had succumbed to impulses over which he had no control. When he finds himself in the lifeboat, he is struck dumb by the fact that he has indeed jumped and at first tries to convince himself that it has not really happened. Conrad employs a similar strategy to justify his decision to go to sea. He talks about the "mysteriousness of his impulses," his lack of self-awareness and presents his choice as a spontaneous, instinctual, non-rational act. In an earlier chapter of *A Personal Record* Conrad defends himself against charges of desertion as follows:

> The part of the inexplicable should be allowed for in appraising the conduct of men in a world where no explanation is final. No charge of faithlessness ought to be lightly uttered. The appearances of this perishable life are deceptive like everything that falls under the judgment of our imperfect senses. The inner voice may remain true enough in its secret counsel. The fidelity to a special tradition may last through the events of an unrelated existence, following faithfully, too, the traced way of an inexplicable impulse. (35-36)

Even though it might outwardly appear as if Conrad has been disloyal to Poland by first going to sea and by later settling down in England as a writer, he has nevertheless inwardly remained committed to his original cultural heritage. In *Lord Jim* a similar predicament is elaborated. Jim cannot come to grips with the discrepancy between his private and his public life, between his heroic self-image and his actual deeds that tell a different story. In *A Personal Record* Conrad also often suggests that he has had little conscious control over how his life developed and that he cannot satisfactorily explain why he acted as he did. This is reinforced by the way he tells his life story in

A Personal Record, which is similar to the way *Lord Jim* is narrated: unchronologically and by association rather than by cause and effect.

Conrad's experiences at sea not only contributed to the formation of his world view but also provided ample material for his later fiction. In the late nineteenth century seafaring was still a very dangerous business and deaths by shipwreck were a daily occurrence. Various factors contributed to the risks that a sailor had to contend with (cf. Spittels 7-8): the inefficiency of land-based operators and the greed of some owners; the relative smallness and frequent unseaworthiness of sailing ships; and, most importantly, the unpredictability of the sea and the potential ferocity of weather conditions. A ship's crew only stood a chance in this unequal contest if it adhered to principles such as solidarity amongst its members, rigorous discipline, hard work, expert knowledge of a particular ship, and a willingness to sacrifice one's own life for a common cause. It is not difficult to see how the struggle of a small group of men on a ship with the vastness and uncontrollable power of the sea could be understood as a metaphor for the predicament of humankind facing a hostile and inhospitable universe. We not only come across this view in Conrad's sea stories, such as *The Nigger of the 'Narcissus', Typhoon,* or *The Shadow-Line,* but also in some of his essays. In "Well Done" of 1918, for instance, he describes the sea as

> uncertain, arbitrary, featureless, and violent. Except when helped by the varied majesty of the sky, there is something inane in its serenity and something stupid in its wrath, which is endless, boundless, persistent, and futile – a grey, hoary thing raging like an old ogre uncertain of its prey. Its very immensity is wearisome. [...] [It is the] greatest scene of potential terror, a devouring enigma of space. (184)

As the conflict with this hostile force does not take place under conditions of equality, it brings out humanity's courage, determination, and indomitability: "[O]ur lives have been nothing if not a continuous defiance [...]; a spiritual and material defiance carried on in our plucky cockleshells on and on beyond the successive provocations of your unreadable horizons" ("Well Done" 185). Therefore, '[t]he ship, this ship, our ship, the ship we serve, is the moral symbol of our life' ("Well Done" 188). However, if Conrad's view of the relationship between an individual or a group and the surrounding universe came down to nothing more than this, his vision and, consequently, his fiction would be schematic and banal. There would also be little point in analysing his position with regard to free will and determinism as it would be obvious anyway. Conrad was certainly aware that his demands for solidarity, discipline, service, fidelity, and work can only be made unambiguously in the literal context of a crew on a ship at sea where the variables that make up a particular situation can be clearly defined. This is underlined by the way

Conrad often contrasts the purity and simplicity of life at sea with the impurity and complexity of life on land. As he puts it in *The Nigger of the 'Narcissus'*, the latter "exists within the frontier of infamy and filth, within that border of dirt and hunger, of misery and dissipation, that comes down on all sides to the water's edge of the incorruptible ocean [...]" (6). Unlike many of his sea-stories, Conrad's land-tales thrive on paradox and ambiguity. Even though these narratives also uphold conservative, moral values, they are prone to be undermined by relentless scepticism and are revealed as illusions. Similar to Conrad's decision to leave Poland and become a sailor, his reasons for putting an end to his sea-career after sixteen years and for transforming himself into an English writer and country gentleman are not quite clear. The facts are that in 1894, at the age of 36, Conrad sent the typescript of his first novel, *Almayer's Folly*, to the publisher T. Fisher Unwin. In *A Personal Record* Conrad emphasises the accidental and unplanned manner in which he approached the writing of his first book:

> [M]y first novel was begun in idleness – a holiday task [...]. [...] It was not the outcome of a need – the famous need of self-expression which artists find in their search for motives. The necessity which impelled me was a hidden, obscure necessity, a completely masked and unaccountable phenomenon. [...] The conception of a planned book was entirely outside my mental range when I sat down to write; the ambition of being an author had never turned up amongst these gracious imaginary existences one creates fondly for oneself [...]: yet it stands clear as the sun at noonday that from the moment I had done blackening over the first manuscript page of "Almayer's Folly" [...] the die was cast. (68-69)

According to John Batchelor, Conrad is here slightly misleading his audience: given his early acquaintance with world literature and the fact that his father was a well-known author, "Conrad was, in a sense, born to the vocation of writer" (42). The passage also stands in contrast to Conrad's frequent demands, made in *A Personal Record* and otherwise, that a writer must approach his art with absolute seriousness, sobriety, and deliberateness. On the other hand the quote chimes with what Conrad frequently dramatizes in his novels: the lack of control we have over our lives and the discrepancy that often exists between our self-image and the way others see us. In *A Personal Record* Conrad also accounts for his decision to write in English in terms that suggest that he had little choice in the matter. As Conrad only learnt English in his early twenties and as his first foreign language was French, Conrad would have had various linguistic options to express himself artistically. However, in the "Author's Note" to *A Personal Record* he claims that

> English was for me neither a matter of choice nor adoption. The merest idea of choice had never entered my head. And as to adoption – well, yes, there was adoption; but it was I who

was adopted by the genius of the language, which directly I came out of the stammering
stage made me its own so completely that its very idioms I truly believe had a direct action
on my temperament and fashioned my still plastic character. (vii)

Even though Conrad achieved greatest mastery in his command of English
and despite his claims in the passage above, he remained, according to
Spittles, "generally aware of the alien nature of his rather curious relationship
with the English language" (23). In a letter written in 1898 he, for instance,
confesses to being "shy of my bad English" and refers to himself as a ""b – y
furriner"" (*CL2*: 16). Even in 1907, after having published, among others,
Heart of Darkness, *Lord Jim*, and *Nostromo*, he says that "English is still for
me a foreign language whose handling demands a fearful effort" (*CL3*: 401).
It has often been observed that there are many instances in Conrad's novels
where he seems to be thinking in Polish or French while writing in English.
In his correspondence he habitually switches between English and French,
even in one and the same letter. It is likely that what one might call Conrad's
linguistic hybridity contributed to his concern with the power but also the
inadequateness of words in his fiction. Although in the quote from *A
Personal Record* above Conrad asserts that his "character" and
"temperament" were shaped by the English language, there is evidence that
he did not regard his cultural identity as stable. In a well-known letter written
in 1903 he, for instance, claimed that even though "[b]oth at sea and on land
my point of view is English, [...] the conclusion should not be drawn that I
have become an Englishman. That is not the case. Homo duplex has in my
case more than one meaning" (*CL3*: 89). It seems that despite his marriage to
an Englishwoman and his success as an English writer, Conrad never lost his
foreignness and remained an isolated figure. As he declared in his "Author's
Note" to *A Personal Record*, "I have always felt myself looked upon
somewhat in the light of a phenomenon, a position which outside the circus
world cannot be regarded as desirable" (v). The reminiscences of his friends
and family also show that Conrad could "be taken for many things – an
English country gentleman, a French dandy, a 'dusky' Slav, even on occasion
for an 'Oriental' in his inscrutability" (Knowles 3). Conrad thus knew from
his own life what it is like to be assigned certain contradictory and
misleading labels, an experience that he would frequently fictionalize in his
novels. It seems that Conrad was not only *modern* in his writing but that as
"double man," "marginal man," or, even, "superfluous man" (cf. Knowles 3
and Watts, *Preface* 65ff) he could be said to have embodied modernity.

One of the most important friendships that Conrad formed during his life
in England was to the pioneer socialist and aristocrat R. B. Cunninghame
Graham. The letters Conrad wrote to his friend belong to the most candid and

revealing of his vast correspondence. They also provide an intimate insight into Conrad's thinking, as he is frequently concerned with defining the difference between his own and Graham's view of the universe and of humankind. For instance, Graham, as a socialist, believed that people could be improved by implementing political, economic, and educational reforms, whereas Conrad frequently expressed the opinion that, in its fundamentals, the human condition is irremediable. The following famous passage from a letter written in December 1897 must be understood in this context:

> There is a – let us say – a machine. It evolved itself (I am severely scientific) out of a chaos of scraps of iron and behold! – it knits. I am horrified at the horrible work and stand appalled. I feel it ought to embroider – but it goes on knitting. You come and say: "this is all right; it's only a question of the right kind of oil. Let us use this – for instance – celestial oil and the machine shall embroider a most beautiful design in purple and gold". Will it? Alas no. You cannot by any special lubrication make embroidery with a knitting machine. And the most withering thought is that the infamous thing has made itself; made itself without thought, without conscience, without foresight, without eyes, without heart. It is a tragic accident – and it has happened. You can't interfere with it. The last drop of bitterness is in the suspicion that you can't even smash it. [...]
> It knits us in and it knits us out. It has knitted time space, pain, death, corruption, despair and all the illusions – and nothing matters. I'll admit however that to look at the remorseless process is sometimes amusing. (*CL*1: 425)

What is immediately striking about the passage is Conrad's extreme pessimism. His perspective on the world is here reminiscent of the "iron-block view of the universe," a term William James coined to describe hard determinism (cf. 150). Conrad's metaphor of the knitting-machine can be read as standing for the universe and those impersonal forces which produce and condition human existence. The image has its roots in hard determinism in general and in Darwinian and economic determinism in particular. As we have seen in Chapter 2, the latter was very much in the foreground at that time, due to the rise of Marxism, the formation of the Labour Party, and large-scale industrial disputes. As the founder of the Scottish Labour Party, Cunninghame Graham participated vigorously in these debates. Conrad's metaphor, however, also suggests Darwinian determinism and an awareness of the contemporary interpretation of Darwin's theory of evolution. Conrad refers to the machine as having evolved itself by tragic accident. It is merciless, inhuman, and amoral in its workings. There is, furthermore, no hope for humankind ever to gain complete insight into the intricacies of the machinery and thus to change it in any way. This kind of reasoning is similar to the way evolutionists, such as Charles Darwin and T.H. Huxley, imagined the workings of Natural Selection in particular and evolution in general: as a random, non-progressive process without any higher goal or aim. In the context of his letter the function of Conrad's image of the knitting machine is to emphasize that, in contrast to Cunninghame Graham, he does not believe that humankind can be improved because its nature is fixed and unchangeable and because the control over the make-up and fate of the human species is not in our hands. In terms of the contemporary evolutionary debate this would have made Conrad a Darwinian and believer in 'nature,' while Graham, in his support of 'nurture,' would have been closer to the Lamarckian position.

In another letter to Graham written about three weeks later Conrad once again uses the metaphor of the machine as his starting point to argue against progress for humankind. However, the machine now no longer appears threatening in its mechanical solidity but has undergone a transformation:

> The machine is thinner than air and as evanescent as a flash of lightning. The attitude of cold unconcern is the only reasonable one. Of course reason is hateful – but why? Because it demonstrates [...] that we, living, are out of life – utterly out of it. The mysteries of a universe made of drops of fire and clods of mud do not concern us in the least. The fate of a humanity condemned ultimately to perish from cold is not worth troubling about. If you take it to heart it becomes an unendurable tragedy. If you believe in improvement you must weep, for the attained perfection must end in cold, darkness and silence. In a dispassionate view the ardour for reform, improvement for virtue, for knowledge, and even for beauty is only a vain sticking up for appearances as though one were anxious about the cut of one's clothes in a community of blind men. Life knows us not and we do not know life – we don't know even our own thoughts. Half the words we use have no meaning whatever and of the other half each man understands each word after the fashion of his own folly and conceit. Faith is a myth and beliefs shift like mists on the shore; thoughts vanish; words, once pronounced, die; and the memory of yesterday is as shadowy as the hope of to-morrow [...].
> (*CL2*: 16-17)

Conrad at first bolsters his argumentation against the susceptibility of humankind to improvement by referring to Lord Kelvin's law of entropy, which postulates that the amount of available energy in the universe will gradually dwindle to nothing and that the sun will inevitably burn itself out. Furthermore, due to the changes in environmental conditions, evolution will take a downward turn and humankind will degenerate. According to Conrad's provocative reasoning, a species that is "condemned ultimately to perish from cold" is "not really worth troubling about." Conrad then slowly shifts from an impersonal and determinist view – regarding human beings as subjected to inevitable evolutionary and physical processes – to a subjective and solipsist one, imagining the outside world as unreal and in constant flux, and the solitary consciousness as the only reality that exists. The various possible sources of this view have been examined in Chapter 2: the philosophies of Schopenhauer and Nietzsche, modern physics, evolutionary theory, and the emerging theories of the unconscious. In his letter Conrad also invokes the epistemological consequences of solipsism: as reality becomes unreal and elusive, the hope of discovering truth outside ourselves turns into an illusion. We therefore cannot "know life" and "beliefs shift like mists on the shore." However, our solitary consciousness cannot provide a reliable source of truth either because "we don't know even our own thoughts." Quite characteristically, Conrad combines his doubts as to the knowability of the world with linguistic scepticism: because there is no uniform reality but, at best, countless subjective ones, words have no clear referents any more and genuine communication is impossible. Although Conrad's combination of solipsistic and deterministic viewpoints in this letter might seem contradictory, we have seen, for instance with regard to T.H. Huxley and Freud, that frequently they are just two sides of the same coin.

As a letter to Graham from February 1899 illustrates, Conrad's pessimistic view of the universe and of the human condition also extends to human society and interpersonal relationships. Conrad takes his starting point from Graham's invitation to attend a meeting convened by the Social Democratic Federation in order to question the socialists' idealistic conceptions of fraternity and solidarity:

> International fraternity may be an object to strive for and, in sober truth, since it has Your [=Graham's] support I will try to think it serious, but that illusion imposes by its size alone. Franchement what would you think of an attempt to promote fraternity amongst people living in the same street. I don't even mention two neighbouring streets. Two ends of the same street. There is already as much fraternity as there can be – and thats [sic] very little and that very little is no good. What does fraternity mean. Abnegation – self-sacrifice means something. Fraternity means nothing unless the Cain-Abel business. Thats [sic] your true fraternity. (*CL2*: 159)

Conrad then moves on to contemplate human nature and society in general. As is usual with Conrad when he is particularly emotional or wants to give emphasis to his views, he switches to French. In translation the passage reads as follows: "Man is a vicious animal. His viciousness must be organised. Crime is a necessary condition of organised existence. Society is fundamentally criminal – or it would not exist. Selfishness preserves everything – absolutely everything – everything we hate and everything we love" (*CL* 2 160). The thinkers who provide a gloss for this passage are again Schopenhauer, Nietzsche, Freud, Darwin, and Huxley. As we have seen in the first two chapters, they all regard selfishness as the dominating, if not the defining quality of human beings. Just as Conrad does in the quotation above, the evolutionists locate the origins of our egoism in humankind's animal ancestry, even though they are in general not quite as pessimistic about organised society. Darwin and his followers believed that there *was* room for a certain amount of altruism and cooperation when it served the evolutionary interests of the species. The sheer magnitude of humankind's egoism that comes across in Conrad's letter recalls Schopenhauer, who claimed that for his well-being the individual is ready "to sacrifice everything else [, to] annihilate the world in order to maintain his own self, that drop in the ocean a little longer" (quoted in Safranski 229). Deducing that society is merely an aggregate of fierce egoists, Schopenhauer argued that the role of the state could not be to improve its citizens but only to restrain them; in other words, to protect individuals against themselves and each other. Judging from the letter quoted above, this was Conrad's position as well.

It is noticeable that in his correspondence with Graham, Conrad's view of human nature is consistently Darwinian. Like T.H. Huxley he, for instance, regards humankind's "ape and tiger instincts" as indomitable and ever ready to break the surface of our civilized veneer. The only quality that distinguishes us from animals is our consciousness. However, as the latter is just an accidental by-product of evolution and not a divine gift, it does not promote our nobility or virtue but, in fact, worsens our plight, as we become aware of our fallen state. As Conrad writes in another letter to Graham,

> [e]goism is good, and altruism is good, and fidelity to nature would be best of all, and systems could be built, and rules could be made – if we could only get rid of consciousness. What makes mankind tragic is not that they are the victims of nature, it is that they are conscious of it. To be part of the animal kingdom under the conditions of this earth is very well – but as soon as you know of your slavery the pain, the anger, the strife – the tragedy beings. We can't return to nature, since we can't change our place in it. Our refuge is in stupidity, in drunkenness of all kinds, in lies, in beliefs, in murder, thieving, reforming – in negation, in contempt – each man according to the promptings of his particular devil. There is no morality, no knowledge and no hope; there is only the consciousness of ourselves which drives us about a world that whether seen in a convex or a concave mirror is always but a vain and floating appearance. (*CL2*: 30)

Conrad here employs the trope of consciousness as a disease, which we also come across in Hardy's novels and in Schopenhauer's philosophy. A consequence of the belief that the function of consciousness is merely to aggravate human suffering is the suggestion that a primitive state of consciousness might be better than a sophisticated one. This line of reasoning, which Cedric Watts calls "anti-rational primitivism" (*Preface* 74), appears in various forms in Conrad's fiction. Its clearest expression in Conrad's letters can be found in his retort to Graham's request that Singleton of the *Nigger of the 'Narcissus'* – the archetype of the simple and reliable seaman – should have been granted an education:

Would you seriously, of malice prepense cultivate in that unconscious man the power to think. Then he would become conscious – and much smaller – and very unhappy. Now he is simple and great like an elemental force. Nothing can touch him but the curse of decay [...]. [...] Would you seriously wish to tell such a man: "Know thyself". Understand that thou art nothing, less than a shadow, more insignificant than a drop of water in the ocean, more fleeting than the illusion of a dream. Would you? (*CL*1: 423)

But how should we cope if we *do* have such knowledge and suffer from being conscious of the ineradicable blot on human nature? One solution that is frequently recommended in Conrad's novels is to adhere to the Carlylean work-ethic: to get a grip on surface reality by losing oneself in the effort, concentration, and discipline demanded by work and in the technical intricacies of one's chosen profession. Work, of course, is essentially action, in which, according to Conrad, "is to be found the illusion of a mastered destiny" ("Autocracy and War" 109). Whereas work is by definition meaningful and goal-oriented, action, defined as mere activity, is not necessarily so. Conrad sometimes suggests that people act for the sake of being active, without purpose or goal, simply to forget the plight of their existence. In his essay "Anatole France" Conrad claims that "only in the continuity of effort there is a refuge from despair [...]. Therefore he [=France] wishes us to believe and to hope, preserving in our activity the consoling illusion of power and intelligent purpose" (33-34). The frequently doubtful meaningfulness of human action and the precarious relationship between our ideals, our intentions, our actions and their consequences are important topics in Conrad's writings. He frequently suggests that ideals are just illusions. They may exist in the abstract but as soon as people try to realize them, they lose their pure form and are corrupted. As Conrad says in "Autocracy and War,"

it is the bitter fate of any idea to lose its royal form and power, to lose its "virtue" the moment it descends from its solitary throne to work its will among the people. It is a king whose destiny is never to know the obedience of his subjects except at the cost of degradation. (86)

The reasons why it is impossible to put ideals into practice without their being corrupted must be sought in the peculiarities of human nature and in the make-up of the universe. As we have seen, Conrad takes a largely Darwinian view of human nature and regards it as fundamentally flawed, in particular by the magnitude of our egoism. If the latter is indeed such an essential and indomitable part of our nature, it is very likely that all our strivings and values will be to some extent informed by it. This is what Conrad suggests in a letter from January 1898, in which he once again grapples with Graham's idealism: "Into the noblest cause men manage to put something of their baseness; [...]. Every cause is tainted: and you reject this one, espouse that other one as if one were evil and the other good while the same evil you hate is in both, but disguised in different words" (*CL2*: 25). Conrad's line of reasoning has a notable parallel in Nietzsche, who also bases his critique of Western values on a Darwinian view of the world. For Nietzsche the supreme expression of egoism is the will-to-power, which he reveals to inform virtually all human actions, sentiments, and values. Consequently, we can no longer distinguish between "purely" good and "purely" evil actions as both are the result of the will-to-power. Whether we regard something as good or bad depends on our perspective, the time we live in, and the socio-cultural code we adhere to. This is what Conrad, too, is driving at in the letter quoted above. Whereas Nietzsche, however, sees egoism or the will-to-power as something positive, as a sign of an individual's vitality, Conrad interprets it negatively, as evidence of the blight on human nature and, consequently, on all human efforts. In "Autocracy and War" he, for instance, insists that "eagle-eyed wisdom alone cannot take the lead of human action, which in its nature must for ever remain short-sighted" (111). The problem with human action is that we can never foresee its consequences, which will always be different from what we had originally envisaged. Whether our deeds are deemed good or bad by the world is also not within our control. No wonder then that ideals become fleeting illusions as soon as we try to realize them. This already depressing state of affairs may be aggravated by the nature of the universe. If the latter is indeed, as Conrad says, an inhuman machine with absolute power which "knits us in and knits us out," then any apparently purposeful action may appear meaningless. As Cedric Watts comments, "[i]f humans [are] predetermined beings, the puppets of causality, in a universe devoid of God, of responsiveness, of ultimate purpose, [human actions are] all, in a sense, quixotic: futile and deranged, the sense of effective action being only an illusion" (*Preface* 71). In such a world the causal links between our ideals, our intentions, our actions and their consequences are broken and our deeds appear to be cruel mockeries of what we, in good faith, originally set out to do. It is only occasionally that Conrad's world view reaches such extremes of pessimism. Nevertheless, the discrepancy between our original intentions and the actual consequences of our actions is an important Conradian theme and raises the question of moral responsibility. How can we be responsible for something that we have not consciously willed? Ideally, it should be as Conrad demands in his "Author's Note" to *Chance*: "[I]t is only for their intentions that men can be held responsible. The ultimate effects of whatever they do are far beyond their control" (x). Conrad, however, was aware that, in everyday life, we usually *do* feel responsible for the effects of our actions and/or are held responsible for them by our surroundings, even if we know that we have not consciously intended them. Conrad shares this paradoxical view of human responsibility with Schopenhauer and T.H. Huxley. In a letter written to Marguerite Poradowska in 1891 Conrad claims that "[e]ach act of life is final, and inevitably produces its consequences despite all the weeping and gnashing of teeth, and the sorrow of feeble souls who suffer the terror that seizes them when confronted by the results of their own actions" (*CL1*: 95; translated from French). Conrad clearly recognizes that it is only our actually realized actions that can be subject to moral responsibility. It is they that are visible to the public eye and that ultimately define our identity in our own eyes and in those of others. In his fiction Conrad frequently dramatizes the conflict between the identity we would like to have and the identity that is contributed to us due to our actions and their consequences.

Conrad's paradoxical attitude to moral responsibility is mirrored in his general view of morality. As the letters to Graham quoted above indicate, Conrad seems to have believed with many other thinkers influenced by Darwinism that divinely sanctioned and everlasting ethical standards, according to which morality and immorality, goodness, and badness can be measured, have evaporated or have at least become ambiguous. Indeed, in *A Personal Record* Conrad asserts that

> [t]he ethical view of the universe involves us at last in so many cruel and absurd contradictions, where the last vestiges of faith, hope, charity, and even of reason itself, seem ready to perish, that I have come to suspect that the aim of creation cannot be ethical at all. I would fondly believe that its object is purely spectacular [...]. (92)

This analysis is surprisingly similar to Nietzsche's critique of traditional concepts of morality. The philosopher, for instance, claimed that "man has connected everything with morals, and dressed the world in an *ethical significance*" (quoted in Hollingdale 133), meaning that ethics is something we merely read into the world but which, in fact, is not truly there. Although Conrad seems to have shared this view he continued to uphold traditional moral principles throughout his fictional and non-fictional writings. This apparent contradiction can be understood with the helps of another reference to Nietzsche, who continued his critique of the ethical view of the universe in the following manner:

> I deny morality as I deny alchemy, that is, I deny their premises; but I do *not* deny that there have been alchemists who believed in these premises and acted according to them. I also deny immorality: *not* that countless people *feel* themselves to be immoral, but that there is any *true* reason so to feel. (quoted in Hollingdale 134)

This is similar to saying that I *feel* responsible and/or that I am held responsible for the effects of my actions, even though I know that I have not consciously willed them. Conrad, too, claims in one of his letters to Graham that "[i]t is impossible to know anything tho' it is possible to believe a thing or two" (*CL*1: 370). In his essay "Alphonse Daudet" he says that "[a] gift from the dead [...] almost makes one believe in a benevolent scheme of creation. *And some kind of belief is very necessary*" (20; my italics). According to this reasoning, Conrad's concept of morality might be explained as follows. The grounds for moral principles can no longer be sought in divine, absolute decrees, or in an ethical view of the universe but exclusively in our understanding of what it means to be human. Morality, in addition to consciousness, is the only thing that distinguishes us from animals. If we want to remain human, we therefore have to insist on moral principles. Consciousness is instrumental here because only if we are aware of the ferocity of our "ape and tiger instincts" can we appreciate the importance of moral behaviour. However, because Conrad is convinced of the validity of the materialist-scientific world view, he also knows that there are certain situations in which moral concepts become paradoxical and ethical standards relative. Nevertheless, this does not, in principle, devalue moral values because they are, despite their occasional ambiguity, the only guarantors of our humanity. Jacques Berthoud puts forward a similar explanation of Conard's concept of morality when he argues that Conrad's "rejection of the 'ethical universe' in favour of the 'spectacular universe' has *moral* consequences" (*Conrad* 9). He thereby takes his cue from the paragraph from *A Personal Record* already quoted above, which continues as follows:

> Those visions [of a spectacular universe] are a moral end in themselves. [...] And the unwearied self-forgetful attention to every phase of the living universe reflected in our consciousness may be our appointed task on this earth[:] [...] to bear true testimony to the visible wonder, the haunting terror, the infinite passion and the illimitable serenity; to the supreme law and the abiding mystery of the sublime spectacle. (92)

According to Berthoud, therefore, moral action for Conrad "is not justifiable in terms of abstract principle or revealed dogma, but in terms of imaginative understanding" (*Conrad* 9).

This insight provides a direct link to Conrad's view of the role of the writer and of the nature of his craft, which he usually describes in moral terms. Given the radical scepticism that emerges from Conrad's correspondence with Graham, it is poignant that otherwise Conrad always defends himself from accusations that he is promoting a despairing or cynical view of the world. In his essay "Poland Revisited" he, for instance, emphasises that "from the charge of cynicism I have always shrunk instinctively. It is like a charge of being blind in one eye, a moral disablement, a sort of disgraceful calamity that must be carried off with a jaunty bearing – a sort of thing I am not capable of" (143). In "Books" he even argues that pessimism is detrimental to artistic endeavour:

> What one feels so hopelessly barren in declared pessimism is just its arrogance. It seems as if the discovery made by many men at various times that there is much evil in the world were a source of proud and unholy joy unto some of the modern writers. That frame of mind is not the proper one in which to approach seriously the art of fiction. It gives an author [...] an elated sense of his own superiority. And there is nothing more dangerous than such an elation to that absolute loyalty towards his feelings and sensations an author should keep hold of in his most exalted moments of creation. (8-9)

What Conrad demands of the writer is sympathetic and moral imagination, coupled with a devotion to truthfulness. Sympathy and compassion arise from an insight into the plight of humankind. According to Conrad, one reason why human beings deserve admiration is their stubborn unwillingness to surrender to an inhospitable universe and to the knowledge of their own blighted nature:

> For mankind is delightful in its pride, its assurance, and its indomitable tenacity. It will sleep on the battlefield among its own dead, in the manner of an army having won a barren victory. It will not know when it is beaten. And perhaps it is right in that quality. ("Henry James" 14)

It is indeed humankind's "capacity for suffering which makes man august in the eyes of men" ("A Familiar Preface" xviii) and which calls forth our pity and respect. The writer should therefore pay humankind an "undemonstrative tribute of a sigh which is not a sob, and of a smile which is not a grin" ("A Familiar Preface" xxi). Conrad thus turns both against Victorian sentimentalism and Modernist detachment. As he asserts in his essay "Certain Aspects of the Admirable Inquiry into the Loss of the *Titanic*,"

> I am not a soft-headed, humanitarian faddist. I have been ordered in my time to do dangerous work; I have ordered others to do dangerous work; I have never ordered a man to do any work I was not prepared to do myself. I attach no exaggerated value to human life. But I know it has a value for which the most generous contributions to [charitable] funds cannot pay. And they cannot pay for it, because people, even of the third class [...], are not cattle. Death has its sting. (247)

Although Conrad commends moral values in his writings, he eschews moral didacticism. A case in point is the way he treats the concept of solidarity, which is another element of his notion of the sympathetic imagination. In his famous "Preface" to *The Nigger of the 'Narcissus'*, which is usually regarded as his artistic manifesto, he comments on the role of the writer:

> He speaks to our capacity for delight and wonder, to the sense of mystery surrounding our lives; to our sense of pity, and beauty, and pain; to the latent feeling of fellowship with all creation – and to the subtle but invincible conviction of solidarity that knits together the loneliness of innumerable hearts, to the solidarity in dreams, in joy, in sorrow, in aspirations, in illusions, in hope, in fear, which binds men to each other, which binds together all humanity – the dead to the living and the living to the unborn. (viii)

At first glance Conrad's insistence on the "feeling of fellowship with all creation," on the "conviction of solidarity" and on the idea that the past is implicit in the present and has effects on the future is reminiscent of Victorian moral realism. A more careful reading, however, reveals these parallels to be deceptive: the "feeling of fellowship" is only "latent" and the solidarity Conrad seems to have in mind is of an intellectual rather than a practical nature, obtaining between isolated people who are united in their disillusioned experience of life. Indeed, in *A Personal Record*, the idea of fellowship that a writer is supposed to promote through his fiction appears to have dwindled to an overcoming of solipsism: "What is it that Novalis says? "It is certain my conviction gains infinitely the moment another soul will believe in it." And what is a novel if not a conviction of our fellow-men's existence strong enough to take upon itself a form of imagined life clearer than reality [...]" (15). The quote suggests that it is only through fiction that the existence of other people becomes real to us. This is a far cry from the robustness of Victorian moral realism as exemplified by writers such as George Eliot.

As we have seen, an important moral demand that Conrad makes of the writer and his craft is sympathetic imagination, which comprises a sense of fellowship. Another requirement is truthfulness. As Conrad says in *A Personal Record*, the "first virtue" of the novelist "is the exact understanding of the limits traced by the reality *of his time* to the play of *his invention*" (95; my italics). We should note here the implication that reality is relative to the time in which we live and the perspective from which we see it. A prerequisite of truthfulness is sincerity and "that sobriety of interior life, that asceticism of sentiment, in which alone the naked form of truth, *such as one conceives it, such as one feels it*, can be rendered without shame" (*A Personal Record* 111-112; my italics). Again we find here the suggestion that truth is subjective and depends on one's viewpoint. Conrad emphasizes this by claiming that "[o]nly in men's imagination does every truth find an effective and undeniable existence" (*A Personal Record* 25). According to

Conrad's "Preface" to *The Nigger of the 'Narcissus'*, the resulting work of art based on this definition of truthfulness should be

> a single-minded attempt to render the highest kind of justice to the visible universe, by bringing to light the truth, manifold and one, underlying its every aspect. It is an attempt to find in its forms, in its colours, in its light, in its shadows, in the aspects of matter and in the facts of life what of each is fundamental, what is enduring and essential – their one illuminating and convincing quality – the very truth of their existence. (vii)

The artist thus becomes a seer whose supreme aim is to reveal the truth as it appears to him. That this is how Conrad views his *own* role is emphasised in his famous apostrophe to the reader: "My task which I am trying to achieve is, by the power of the written word to make you hear, to make you feel – it is, before all, to make you *see*." ("Preface" x). Of highest importance to Conrad is not just the revelation of truth to the reader but also the manner in which this is done. The artist must strive for a "complete, unswerving devotion to the perfect blending of form and substance" (ix) and therefore "cannot be faithful to any one of the temporary formulas of his craft. The enduring part of them – the truth which each only imperfectly veils – should abide with him as the most precious of his possessions [...]" ("Preface" x). That is to say, the author must find an individual style in which to express the truth as he sees it. Conrad puts so much emphasis on form because the truth that he is trying to reveal is not plain to see. It can no longer be arrived at by a description of surface reality and the accumulation of details as in Victorian realism. Truth is no longer held to be indivisible and one, to be sought by empirical means in the world surrounding us, but it has become elusive, multiform, opaque, and subjective. This view is reflected in Conrad's description of the writing process in his essay "Henry James":

> [T]he creative art of a writer of fiction may be compared to rescue work carried out in darkness against cross gusts of wind swaying the action of a great multitude. It is rescue work, this snatching of vanishing phases of turbulence [...] out of the native obscurity into a light where the struggling forms may be seen, seized upon, endowed with the only possible form of permanence in this world of relative values – the permanence of memory. (13)

The writer then holds up this rescued fragment of life "before all eyes and in the light of a sincere mood. It is to show its vibration, its colour, its form; and through its movement, its form, and its colour, reveal the substance of its truth [...]." ("Preface" x). Conrad here combines the terms and concepts of Impressionism with a Victorian insistence on the truthfulness and moral sincerity of fiction, which shows that he indeed refused to be tied down by any "temporary formulas of his craft." In addition to seer and moral agent, Conrad also wants the novelist to be a chronicler of human experience. After all, as he claims in "Henry James," "[f]iction is history, human history, or it is nothing" (17). However, whereas conventional historiography is informed by "documents, and the reading of print and handwriting – on second-hand impressions," fiction is based "on the reality of forms and the observation of social phenomena" ("Henry James" 17). For this reason, Conrad concludes, "fiction is nearer truth" ("Henry James" 17).

Through his belief in the intrinsic value of literature Conrad therefore manages to overcome, at least temporarily, his deep-seated scepticism, to give back significance to human experience, and to infuse moral concepts with new substance. In the visionary paragraph which concludes his essay on Henry James, he voices the hope that the creative imagination might even survive the apocalypse of entropy:

> When the last aqueduct shall have crumbled to pieces, the last airship fallen to the ground, the last blade of grass have died upon a dying earth, man, indomitable by his training in resistance to misery and pain, shall set this undiminished light of his eyes against the feeble glow of the sun. The artistic faculty, of which each of us has a minute grain, may find its voice in some individual of that last group, gifted with a power of expression and courageous enough to interpret the ultimate experience of mankind in terms of his temperament, in terms of art. ("Henry James" 13-14)

4.2   Conrad's position in the Free Will and Determinism Debate

In Conrad's non-fictional work we come across only two short passages that might be interpreted as direct references to the free will and determinism debate. Both of them occur in *A Personal Record*. In his "Familiar Preface" Conrad declares that "the proper wisdom is to will what the gods will without, perhaps, being certain what their will is – or even if they have a will of their own. And in this matter of life and art it is not the Why that matters so much to our happiness as the How" (xxi). The suggestion here is that, in general, our capacity for free choice or control over our lives is very limited and that we fare better if we simply resign ourselves to this state of affairs without trying to get to the bottom of it. Revealingly, Conrad even doubts that "the gods"[4] themselves "have a will of their own," implying that they might be controlled by someone/something else. It seems unlikely that human beings would ever be in a position to discover the truth about this latter entity which is, as it were, at a second remove from human existence. The second reference to free will and determinism in *A Personal Record* occurs in Conrad's account of his first meeting with Charles Almayer, who inspired his first novel, *Almayer's Folly*. Conrad presents Almayer's invitation to dine with him on shore as an important link in the mysterious chain of cause and effect that led to his becoming a writer:

> At the moment of stepping over the gangway he checked himself, though, to give me a mumbled invitation to dine at his house that evening with my captain, an invitation which I accepted. I don't think it could have been possible for me to refuse.
> *I like the worthy folk who will talk to you of the exercise of free will "at any rate for practical purposes." Free, is it? For practical purposes! Bosh! How could I have refused to dine with that man?* I did not refuse simply because I could not refuse. Curiosity, a healthy desire for a change of cooking, common civility, the talk and the smiles of the previous twenty days, every condition of my existence at that moment and place made irresistibly for acceptance; and, crowning all that, there was the ignorance, the ignorance, I say, the fatal want of foreknowledge to counter-balance these imperative conditions of the problem. A refusal would have appeared perverse and insane. Nobody unless a surly lunatic would have refused. But if I had not got to know Almayer pretty well it is almost certain there would never have been a line of mine in print. (86-87; my italics)

What is revealing about this passage is, first of all, the inevitability which Conrad attributes to his decision. His detailing of the circumstances of the situation suggests that it was *they* that determined his choice and not his own will. As has been noted, this is a perspective on his life which Conrad employs throughout *A Personal Record*. Even more remarkable is that in the italicised lines Conrad displays an awareness of the contemporary debate about free will and determinism. It was William James, the founder of the philosophy of pragmatism, who, in his essay "The Dilemma of Determinism," suggested that even though the existence of free will cannot be proven, we should nevertheless believe in it for practical purposes. Conrad, apparently, was not convinced by this line of reasoning. The passage above could mean *either* that Conrad found so much evidence in his own life against free will that he could not even bring himself to believe in it for practical purposes or that he wanted a firmer base for the concept of free will than Jamesian pragmatism. In general, of course, both quotes from *A*

---

[4]   Although it is not quite clear what Conrad means by the term "gods," it seems certain that no genuinely religious meaning is intended. As Watts emphatically asserts, to Conrad "the heavens, once thought to be benevolent to humans, are empty" (*Preface* 46).

Personal Record are too slight in substance to base upon them a hypothesis regarding Conrad's position on free will and determinism. Nevertheless, what the quotes above *do* demonstrate – and this is sufficient for the kind of approach I have chosen in this study – is that Conrad was aware of the discussion concerning free will and determinism.

If we attempt to narrow down Conrad's position in the freedom of the will debate by referring to the various theories discussed in the previous chapters, it can be safely established that Conrad was not a compatibilist, as would have been characteristic of the Victorian Age, but an incompatibilist, typical of the Late Victorian/Early Modernist period. There is in Conrad's world picture as described above and in his fictional works an unresolved tension between a moral view of human affairs, which presupposes the existence of some degree of free will, and a determinist or, possibly, indeterminist perspective informed by Darwinism, which denies it. Mid-Victorian writers such as George Eliot could still reconcile these two world views by, for instance, promoting belief in an empirically knowable, basically benevolent truth at the heart of the universe which our minds can discover and from which we can benefit. In her novels Eliot gave expression to compatibilism by, for instance, representing society as a harmonious whole, by suggesting that human beings can come to a new understanding with nature, and by using metaphors expressive of organicism such as the web or the river. In Conrad's novels, on the other hand, we find an emphasis on pervasive discord, chaos, paradox, existential isolation, and failure, which suggests an unbridgeable gap between a yearning for harmony, meaning, free choice, and control over our actions on the one hand and the existence of powerful impersonal forces on the other which impose severe limits on our lives.

In philosophical terms, the compatibilist or soft determinist position can be summed up as follows: even though all our choices and their resulting actions are caused, we can still be held morally responsible for them *if* they are not coerced and *if* we could have done otherwise than we did. Free choice, therefore, exists under certain conditions and, in fact, requires determinism. If we relate this position to an analysis of Conrad's novels we could, for instance, ask whether characters such as Kurtz, Jim, Charles Gould, Winnie Verloc, or Razumov are coerced in their actions or whether they could have done otherwise. The problem with such a question is that the answer must remain purely hypothetical. Of course, it is possible to argue that Kurtz need not have gone to the Congo, that Winnie Verloc need not have killed her husband, that Jim need not have jumped from the *Patna*, that Razumov need not have betrayed Haldin, or that Charles Gould need not have started the silver mine. This is, however, pure speculation, as it simply did not happen this way.[5] The characters have to live with the consequences of their actions even though they might be different from what they had originally intended. As Conrad says in a letter quoted earlier, "[e]ach act of life is final, and inevitably produces its consequences despite all the weeping and gnashing of teeth" (*CL1*: 95). In his novels he indeed shows that the characters referred to above feel responsible for their actions to varying extents; some, such as Jim, indeed suffer from the burden of responsibility all their lives. As, according to the soft determinist position, feeling morally responsible presupposes having taken a free choice, one could assume that the decisions taken by Conrad's characters were not coerced in any way. However, if we look more closely at the circumstances of their choices and take into account psychological, historical, materialist, or Darwinian forces, as Conrad clearly wishes us to, the decisions no longer appear free at all. What Conrad thus shows is that his characters feel responsible for their actions, even though there are no true reasons for doing so. One of the best examples is Dr Monygham in *Nostromo*, who, despite having been coerced to inform on his friends under torture, feels guilty and worthless because of this forced betrayal. We can conclude that for the reasons mentioned above the soft determinist or compatibilist position is not one we can ascribe either to Conrad's vision or his work.

Within the incompatibilist approach to free will and determinism there are basically two contrasting positions: hard determinism and libertarianism. The former holds that there is no free will and only constraining necessity; the latter denies universal causation and defends free will. Because libertarians often employ arguments based on notions of a naturally given or innate morality, one could assume that this position might be applicable to Conrad's work as well, which is, after all, emphatically concerned with moral questions. One of these arguments takes its starting point from introspection: because we intuitively feel that we are morally responsible for our actions, it follows that free, uncaused choices exist. As we have already seen above, this argumentation cannot be applied to Conrad and his work. Although he certainly shows that his protagonists feel responsible for their actions, it is doubtful whether they were in fact free in their choices. What can be argued, however, is that the characters in Conrad's novels that possess moral potential, act according to moral principles, or follow an ethical code of conduct, appear freer and more human than those that have no moral awareness. The latter, such as Kurtz, the Pilgrims, General Montero, Sotillo,

---

[5]   As we have seen in Chapter 1, it is generally recognized that the weakest point of the soft determinist position is precisely its hypothetical analysis of freedom.

Gentleman Brown or the Professor, appear to be determined by their instincts and passions to a much greater extent than others, such as Monygham, Mrs Gould, or Marlow, who resist the lure of material interests and the concomitant greed and rapacity. On the surface this observation seems to tie in with the reasoning of the Christian libertarian C.A. Campbell, who has formulated a variant of the argument from introspection. Campbell holds that only when we manage to consciously resist temptation, do we act freely and break the causal chain. This argument, of course, only has genuine value in a theological framework, which Conrad without doubt rejected. Indeed, in his fiction Conrad frequently suggests that even though it may *appear* that the characters that act on moral principles are freer than others, this is just an illusion. Conrad thus implicitly aligns himself with those critics of the Campbell position who argue that feeling morally responsible no more proves that we are *in fact* morally responsible than feeling free proves that we actually are free. The third and last variant of the argument from introspection refers to human nature. Philosophers such as Peter Strawson or Isaiah Berlin have argued that human beings simply could not help acting as if they were free and morally responsible, even if determinism were true. This cannot be Conrad's position either. He not only portrays characters that feel morally responsible without having any true reasons for doing so but also shows others that seem to have either no or only a perverted sense of responsibility. It can also be argued that the kind of society Conrad delineates in *Nostromo, The Secret Agent*, or *Heart of Darkness* is basically without morality as most of its members are motivated only by self-interest. Libertarians sometimes also use scientific indeterminism derived from quantum physics or evolutionary theory to argue against universal causation and for the existence of free will. However, as has frequently been pointed out, it is doubtful whether scientific indeterminism can provide the freedom that libertarians wish us to possess. For many people, a universe ruled by randomness and chance implies that we have even less control than in a deterministic universe, which is at least predictable and ordered. Conrad, as will be argued in more detail below, certainly does not use indeterminism to argue for free will as the libertarians do but, on the contrary, uses it to suggest that the universe is chaotic and that notions of individual control are illusions.

Whereas libertarianism is therefore not a position applicable to Conrad, the case is different with the second theory within the incompatibilist tradition, hard determinism. This is the belief that we are completely controlled by certain constraining forces, be they scientific, economic or metaphysical. There is no room for free will and none for moral responsibility based on free choice. A metaphor frequently used to describe the hard determinist perspective is that of the machine, which, indeed, Conrad, too, employs in the famous letter to Graham quoted earlier. As we will see later on, Conrad's fictional representation of the world and of human affairs also often lends itself to an analysis in strictly deterministic terms. To be a full-fledged hard determinist, however, entails believing in either a metaphysical entity whose powers are absolute or in the total and exceptionless rule of universal causation. Conrad neither took a metaphysical view of the universe nor put his trust in Laplace's Demon, that is hope that due to universal causation we would one day achieve total knowledge of the universe. Indeed, throughout his work, Conrad is extremely sceptical as regards the knowability of the world and the possibility of discovering any rational order in it. In his novels he emphasises again and again that we do not even know ourselves and the people who are closest to us. Sources of these epistemological doubts are, among others, the implications of contemporary scientific near-determinism. If we accept randomness as part of the universe, we can no longer hope to discover the ultimate truth about it. Although it is possible to describe the forces that shape the world and human life, the way these forces interact, the exact extent to which each of them determines us and in which direction they push us is unknowable because subject to chance. Ted Honderich has termed this position near-determinism because it postulates indeterminist elements in an overtly determinist system. As we have seen, near-determinism is associated not only with early twentieth century physics but also with evolutionary theories as put forward, for example, by T.H. Huxley.

Huxley's theories are not only exemplary of turn-of-the-century near-determinism based on Darwinism but can also help to delinate Conrad's position in the freedom-of-the-will debate. Similar to the knitting machine in Conrad's letter to Graham, evolution is for Huxley a remorseless, inhuman, and amoral system that keeps life adapted to changing conditions at the cost of a vast amount of suffering and without moving towards a meaningful goal. As a sceptic and pessimist Huxley does not interpret his recognition of indeterministic elements in an otherwise strictly deterministic universe as a gain but as a loss of control. Although evolution can be described with the help of deterministic laws, they must – due to the presence of chance – remain hypothetical and temporary. The Victorian belief of discovering everlasting truth becomes an illusion. At best, truth is relative and dependent on the circumstances of the moment. Huxley's views on morality and on the plight and duties of human beings as expressed in "Evolution and Ethics" can also be used as a model to elucidate Conrad's. As explained in Chapter 2,

Huxley splits the universe into two parts, the "cosmic" and the "ethical" process. Whereas the cosmic process is identified with the randomness and ruthlessness of evolution, the ethical process is associated with moral values and civilization. It is within the latter that Huxley locates the essence of humanity. He argues that even though morality has its origin in the cosmic process, it has become divorced from it and is now in opposition to it. Humanity can only survive if it ceaselessly promotes the ethical process at the expense of the cosmic process. Not surprisingly, Huxley's views are, like Conrad's, fraught with paradoxes. For instance, we are, on the one hand, part of nature and subject to its mechanisms; on the other hand, because the latter are inhuman and amoral, we feel alienated not just from nature but from ourselves as well. This paradox can also be found in Conrad's novels, for instance, in Stein's famous speech on "how to be" in *Lord Jim*. Huxley also held that it is not by design but by cosmic accident that evolution has endowed us with consciousness and a high level of intelligence. Paradoxcially, however, this endowment is not just a gift but also a bane, for instance when we become aware of the brutal, meaningless, and amoral workings of the universe to which we are subjected. The consciousness-as-a-disease trope to which this insight contributed is also used in Conrad's letters and appears in the guise of anti-rational primitivism in his fiction. Because we are part of nature and determined by materialist forces to an overwhelming extent, we are not free in our choices and therefore – theoretically at least – not fully responsible for our actions. However, we have to act *as if* we were free and responsible as this constitutes our humanity. From this it follows that when we act ethically, we act against the laws of nature and against that which we are part of. For this reason ethical action and moral principles are ideals which we have to aspire to but which are not always realizable. Some people might also succumb to their "ape and tiger" instincts more easily than others because they possess less moral potential. Huxley draws attention to this in a letter written in November 1892, in which he describes the moral sense as

> a very complex affair – dependent in part upon associations of pleasure and pain, approbation and disapprobation formed by education in early youth, but in part also on an innate sense of moral beauty and ugliness [...] which is possessed by some people in great strength, while some are totally devoid of it. (quoted in Reed, "Huxley" 33)

If we act without moral principles we act inhumanely because we give free reign to our animal instincts. On the other hand, in strictly evolutionary terms, an amoral action may sometimes be the more successful one because it is in tune with the laws of the struggle for survival and the survival of the fittest, which we are also subject to. Conversely, acting morally may make us more fully human but in certain situations ethical behaviour might actually be to our disadvantage. In his novels Conrad, too, shows how characters that possess high moral awareness appear more human and freer than others that have no sense of responsibility and are completely controlled by their instincts. On the other hand he also creates situations in which ethical standards appear ambiguous and illusory.

In my examination of the applicability of the various free will and determinism theories to Conrad's vision, we have so far come across two that seem to chime with it. The first one is hard determinism combined with scepticism as regards our ability to discover the truth about ourselves and the world. The second is near-determinism: although the forces that determine us can be identified and described, there is also an element of chance and randomness to be reckoned with. A third and final position which should be added is radical indeterminism, which we have, for instance, come across in Nietzsche's philosophy: all certainties are gone; the world appears to be completely chaotic; all action seems purposeless and human existence absurd. This more or less nihilistic position goes hand in hand with solipsism, which holds that everything outside us is unreal so that the only source of knowledge is our isolated consciousness. As we will see, there are certain situations in Conrad's novels for which only radical indeterminism can account. In general, however, Conrad's stance in the free will and determinism debate veers between the three positions mentioned above. They cannot always be separated clearly from each other, nor can they be fused to form a completely consistent philosophical position. An element of contradiction and paradox will always remain.

5. *Heart of Darkness* and the Empire Machine

5.1   The frame tale and Marlow's preamble

The frame-narrator's prologue and Marlow's preamble to his narration proper introduce the narrative's seminal themes and establish its intricate pattern of parallels, contrasts, and cross-references. *Heart of Darkness* opens with a view of the Thames estuary from the cruising yawl *Nellie*, on which five old friends have gathered. Although the focus seems to be on the tranquil beauty of the sunset scenery and the affection between the men on board, appearances are deceptive. There is darkness "above Gravesend, and farther back still seemed condensed into a mournful gloom, brooding motionless over the biggest, and the greatest, town on earth" (HD 45). It is noticeable that the phrase "brooding gloom" is repeated five times within the first seven paragraphs of the tale, thus creating the sense of waiting for something ominous and sinister to happen. The darkness, which emanates primarily from London, is so intense and pernicious that the frame narrator imagines the setting sun "without rays and without heat, as if about to go out suddenly, stricken to death by the touch of that gloom brooding over a crowd of men." (HD 46). As we have seen in Chapter 2, solar death and the subsequent extinction of the human species were predicted by Lord Kelvin's Second Law of Thermodynamics, which contributed to the apocalyptic and pessimistic strain in *fin-de-siècle* literature. In *Heart of Darkness* this is the first use of what Cedric Watts has termed "dwarfing perspective: [...] a viewpoint that offers a reductive, dwarfing view of human activities" (*Heart* 71). The gigantic time-scales of cosmic evolution, which the reference evokes, point to the brevity of humankind's existence and make its struggles seem absurd and futile. It is remarkable that the frame narrator links the image of solar death to the gloom that emanates from London, as if the city were somehow responsible for the doom of the human race. Indeed, one paragraph later the town, which at first appeared to be "the biggest, and the greatest [...] on earth" (HD 45), has become "monstrous [...] marked ominously on the sky, a brooding gloom in sunshine, a lurid glare under the stars" (HD 48). In paragraph three the narrator confessed to finding it hard to believe that the "Director of Companies [...,] our captain and host," did not work "out there in the luminous estuary, but behind him, within the brooding gloom" (HD 45) that is London. Again appearances are deceptive: the director only "*resembles* a pilot, which to a seaman is trustworthiness personified" (HD 45; my italics); in fact, he is, like the lawyer and the accountant, a City businessman. But what could be suspicious about working "within the brooding gloom" of London? One reason might lie in the contrast Conrad frequently invokes between a corrupt and duplicitous land-life and a pure and honest sea-life. More subtle reasons only reveal themselves if we look at the parallels between the frame and the framed narrative of *Heart of Darkness*. The characters Marlow will encounter in the course of his journey are, with the exception of Kurtz, also only referred to by their functional titles: the doctor, the chief accountant, the general manager, the brickmaker, or the pilgrims. Therefore the Director of Companies on the *Nellie* anticipates the director of the "Company for trade" (HD 52) who interviews Marlow in Brussels and the yachting accountant prepares us for the chief accountant Marlow will come across at the Company Station. The connection between frame and framed tale is reinforced when the accountant on the *Nellie* takes out "a box of dominoes and [toys] architecturally with the bones" (HD 46). As Adams explains, "the use of the word 'bones' reminds us that, prior to mass-production, dominoes were often made of ebony inlaid with bone or ivory, and that bone and ivory were for centuries mistakenly believed to be the same substance" (8). Ivory, of course, is a key term in *Heart of Darkness*: it is, in Goonetilleke's words, the "actual raw wealth which private individuals, colonial companies and imperial powers covet, as well as a symbolic centre for their self-aggrandising motives" (69). The reference to "bones" also introduces the theme of death and waste of human life and anticipates Marlow's description of the remains of his predecessor Fresleven just a few pages later: "[T]he grass growing through his ribs was tall enough to hide his *bones*" (HD 54; my italics). One of the functions of what Watts has called the "tentacular" (*Heart* 2) relationship between frame and framed tale of *Heart of Darkness* is to show that, as businessmen and capitalists, the friends on board the *Nellie* are implicated in the imperialist exploitation of Africa. One of the centres of this empire of business was London and this might explain why the "brooding gloom" is so intense above the town. As Fleishman explains, there is in *Heart of Darkness* "a general rejection not only of colonial society but also of the economic system on which it is based: the capitalist economy of the home countries" (*Conrad's Politics* 12). Indeed, the many references to the entanglements of Britain and the British in the exploitation of Africa could be regarded as a sub-theme of *Heart of Darkness*. In addition to the setting of the frame tale, there are the many

British products Marlow comes across in Africa: the textiles used to barter with the natives; the weapons such as the "loaded Martini-Henry leaning in a corner" (HD 109) of Marlow's pilot-house; or the book on seamanship Marlow discovers in the Harlequin's hut (cf. HD 99). Other references to Britain include the map of the carved-up Africa in Brussels, on which Marlow notices with satisfaction "a vast amount of red" (HD 55) signifying British territories; Kurtz's partly English education and heritage (cf. HD 117); and the "English half-caste clerk" (HD 90) whom Kurtz employs. Marlow himself is of course also English. Brian Spittles, finally, has drawn attention to the similarities in profession, class, and outlook of Marlow's listeners on board the *Nellie* and the first readers of the tale in the largely conservative, traditionalist *Blackwood's Magazine*. The effect is that "the involvement of the audience of characters [in imperialist exploitation] is implicitly projected onto the readership. The reader too is implicated in the rape of Africa" (Spittles 80).

Another direct allusion to Britain's imperialist activities is the frame narrator's paean to the River Thames. This celebration of the river and the service it has done to "the race that peopled its banks" (HD 46) is, according to Watts, "one of the most accomplished "false starts" in literature" (*Heart* 39); Hampson refers to it as a "'reader trap'" (Introduction xxix). The imperialist rhetoric in which the passage is couched seems to be addressed explicitly to the tale's first readers described above. Its function is to lull them into a false sense of security, encouraging them to expect a conventional tale of empire and adventure. If we look at the grandiloquent vocabulary of the passage – "venerable," "august," "reverence," "the great spirit of the past," "knights," "bearers of a spark from the sacred fire" (HD 47) – we clearly recognize the stereotypes of imperialist ideology and rhetoric. The intertextual references evoked by these lines are not only to the adventure fiction of writers such as G. A. Henty, Rider Haggard, Robert Louis Stevenson, Conan Doyle, John Buchan, or Rudyard Kipling, but also to Victorian historiography. As we have seen in Chapter 2, nineteenth century historians, such as Lord Macaulay or H.T. Buckle, saw history in general and British history in particular as a grand narrative, a "gigantic tale" (HD 47), as the frame narrator puts it, of inevitable progress, consisting of adventures, conquests, and explorations by men such as Drake, Franklin, Livingston, or Stanley. As Fothergill says, the passage invites the reader of *Heart of Darkness* "to accept not just an adventure story but [...] a way of looking at history which embodies an ideological frame of reference we would now call imperialist or colonialist" (18). The frame narrator's confidence and optimism is, however, famously undercut by Marlow's laconic assertion that "this also [...] has been one of the dark places of the earth" (HD 48). By referring to the Roman Conquest Marlow turns the primary narrator's perspective on its head. All of a sudden, *Britain* appears to be a place of darkness and the British as ignorant 'savages' who are colonized by a superior race. They are no longer the perpetrators of grandiose historic acts but their victims. Although this reversal of referents is stunning by its sheer abruptness, Marlow's suggested parallel between the Roman and the British Empire and between the ancient Britons and contemporary 'savages' was nothing out of the ordinary. As Griffith has pointed out, the analogy derives from the "'comparative method' that dominated Victorian anthropology" (110). He quotes the English anthropologist James Prichard, who claimed that "the ancient Britons were very much on a level with the New Zealanders or Tahitians of the present day, or perhaps not very superior to the Australians" (110). This, of course, did not imply that *contemporary* Britons could be compared in any way to colonial subjects. After all, turn-of-the-century anthropology was dominated by Lamarckism and therefore postulated a strict hierarchy between races and cultures. By applying the standards of material and even ethical development, anthropologists believed to be able to determine the place of a certain people on a progressive scale. To compare ancient Britons to present-day colonial subjects simply meant that one condescended to grant them the capacity of improvement. It is important to see that Marlow's cultural relativism is more radical than that. He starts out by saying, "I was thinking of very old times, when the Romans first came here, nineteen hundred years ago" (HD 49). For a Lamarckian, believing in use-inheritance, this time period, spanning innumerable generations, would certainly be sufficient to explain fundamental biological differences between 'superior' and 'inferior' races. For a Darwinian, on the other hand, who believes that millions of years are needed to account for evolutionary changes, the Roman Conquest would only have taken place "the other day" (HD 49), as Marlow indeed says. Although Marlow cannot be called a conscious Darwinian – he often employs the Lamarckian paradigm as well –, this is nevertheless a position that he frequently moves towards. The following passage that continues his speech may serve as another example: "Light came out of this river since – you say Knights? Yes; but it is like a running blaze on a plain, like a flash of lightning in the clouds. We live in the flicker – may it last as long as the old earth keeps rolling! But darkness was here yesterday" (HD 49). A consequence of the evolutionary perspective that Marlow takes here is the suggestion that the differences between the Europeans and the Africans are – at least on a biological or racial level – negligible. Another implication is that if the development of British civilization has occurred in such a radically foreshortened period of time ("But darkness was here yesterday"), then, of course, the reverse process, degeneration, might be just as rapid ("We live in the flicker –"). Just as the Roman Empire had its heyday and passed away, the British one might be doomed as well. In this way Marlow juxtaposes an evolutionary or Huxleyan view of history that emphasizes change and impermanence to the primary narrator's Victorian concept of history as a linear, irreversible progress towards perfection.

Marlow proceeds by asking his audience to imagine two Romans, the first "a commander of a fine [...] trireme in the Mediterranean" (HD 49) who is ordered to go up the Thames; the second "a decent young citizen in a toga" who gets sent to "some inland post" in order to "mend his fortune" (HD 50). A first-time reader of *Heart of Darkness* will perhaps only note Marlow's skill in recreating this lively vignette of the two Romans and will smile at their struggle with the savagery of ancient Britain. A reader who comes to the novel a second time might, however, notice that these character sketches are like "the dumbshow which used to precede certain early Elizabethan plays, giving a forecast of the action" (Williams, quoted in Tredell 24). Thus the trireme-commander's experience on the Thames foreshadows Marlow's on the Congo River, while the young citizen's in "some inland post" (HD 50) anticipates Kurtz's at the Inner Station. Just as Marlow has to cope with a "battered, twisted, ruined, tin-pot steamboat" (HD 85) on a river difficult to navigate, the Roman commander is in charge of a ship "about as rigid as a concertina" surrounded by a landscape consisting of "[s]and-banks, marshes, forests, savages" (HD 49). The military camps "lost in a wilderness, like a needle in a bundle of hay" (HD 49) call up the desolation of the stations along the Congo; the constant presence of death "skulking in the air, in the water, in the bush" (HD 49) is something Marlow, too, will be confronted with. Similar to Kurtz, the "decent young citizen in a toga" is isolated in the wilderness and feels that "utter savagery [...] [has] closed round him" (HD 50). Also like Kurtz, he experiences the "fascination of the abomination" and is overwhelmed by a mixture of contradictory passions: "[T]he growing regrets, the longing to escape, the powerless disgust, the surrender, the hate" (HD 50). Marlow in this way draws a parallel between the imperialist experiences of two Romans and two contemporary Englishmen[6] that supplements his earlier comparison between the Roman and the British Empire.

---

[6]   Kurtz has been partly educated in England and his mother is half-English.

As he continues, however, Marlow seems concerned with finding differences between British and Roman imperialism, possibly with the intention to lull a pro-imperialist audience into a false sense of security. At first he invokes the work ethic and the late Victorian cult of efficiency as backbones of successful colonialism and argues that this is what the Romans lacked: "They were no colonists; their administration was merely a squeeze, and nothing more, I suspect" (HD 50). The Romans were mere "conquerors" and

> for that you want only brute force – nothing to boast of, when you have it, since your strength is just an accident arising from the weakness of others. They grabbed what they could get for the sake of what was to be got. It was just robbery with violence, aggravated murder on a great scale, and men going at it blind [...]. (HD 50).

What is striking about the first sentence of this paragraph is the way Marlow explains the superiority of a certain people in Darwinian terms. It is not that one nation has been chosen by providence or destiny to rule over another or that its pre-eminence is due to particular intellectual, moral, cultural, or racial characteristics; what imperial dominance boils down to is the basic biological factor of physical strength. However, that is not the only determinant; even more influential is accident or chance. It is the latter that decides who comes out on top in the struggle for survival. The next two sentences make the reader wonder whether Marlow is still talking about the Romans as the terms he uses anticipate the behaviour of the pilgrims he will encounter in the Congo. Does Marlow, therefore, imply that "robbery with violence, aggravated murder on a great scale" is what *all* imperialism comes down to? This suspicion is strengthened by Marlow's following statement, which he puts in such a general way that it is surely applicable to any imperialist situation: "The conquest of the earth, which mostly means the taking it away from those who have a different complexion or slightly flatter noses than ourselves, is not a pretty thing when you look into it too much" (HD 51). As we start wondering whether Marlow means to say that this is also Britain's true justification for imperialism, he changes tack and tells us that "[w]hat redeems it is the idea only. An idea at the back of it; not a sentimental pretence but an idea; and an unselfish belief in the idea – something you can set up, and bow down before, and offer a sacrifice to...." (HD 51). It seems that just as Marlow is about to open up fissures in imperialist ideology and to begin, as Edward Said has put it, "to actively comprehend how the [empire] machine works" (27), he becomes afraid of his own insight and returns to the fold of ideology by invoking "idea worship," the "modern version of idol worship" (Brantlinger, "Victorians and Africans" 76). However, Marlow's curious phrasing and sudden breaking off show that ideology does not, as it were, determine his mind-set completely. As Robert Hampson argues, "Marlow's assertion of the redeeming 'idea' behind imperialism leads him into figurative language which subverts the idea he has been asserting" (Introduction xxx). This is because he realizes the implications of the image he has employed. As Watts points out, Marlow's evocation of the "redeeming idea" anticipates Kurtz, "the one-time idealist who [becomes] for the natives literally what "the idea" is supposed to be for good imperialists" (Watts, *Heart* 45), namely something to "bow down before, and offer a sacrifice to." That it is Kurtz who is already on Marlow's mind also becomes clear from the casual and indirect reference to him a few lines later (cf. HD 51). The example is typical of the way Marlow, throughout his narrative, struggles with imperialist ideology, sometimes subverting it, sometimes employing its stereotypes to describe his African experience.

5.2   Marlow's decision to go to Africa and his appointment

Among Marlow's more prosaic motives to go to Africa are his need for a job and money. He admits to having become quite desperate because "the ships wouldn't even look at me" (HD 52). Another motive is his childhood passion for maps and unexplored regions, which is rekindled by a map of Africa he sees in a shop-window. The force with which the idea of the Congo River takes hold of Marlow is indeed remarkable: "[I]t fascinated me as a snake would a bird – a silly little bird" (HD 52). The snake/bird image anticipates the powerlessness Marlow will experience in the course of his journey in general and *vis-à-vis* the African environment in particular. Marlow is not, as it were, a snake charmer but, on the contrary, *is* charmed and – in a manner reminiscent of Kurtz – nearly swallowed up by the reptile. The biblical connotations of the simile also remind us of the Fall and the loss of innocence: by agreeing to work for the "Company for trade on that river" (HD 52), Marlow will become part of the empire machine and, to an extent, guilty of its crimes. His desire to go to Africa grows so strong that he feels "[he] must get there by hook or by crook" and admits that "the notion drove [him]" (HD 53). Marlow, however, does not manage to get the job by his own efforts but has to rely on his aunt's influence. In this way, as Hampson puts it, Marlow's "assumptions about power and gender are undermined," which emphasizes Marlow's increasing "unease at the experience of his own powerlessness" (Introduction xxxvi).

The story of the Danish captain Fresleven's death, which ensures Marlow's appointment, anticipates the mixture of absurdity and horror surrounding the incidents Marlow will witness in Africa. Quite typical is the linking of a trivial or negligible cause with a disproportionate effect: a "misunderstanding about some hens" (HD 53) leads to the murder of Fresleven, which again inspires mad terror in the natives, who desert their village never to return. What is also striking is the degree to which Marlow identifies himself with Fresleven. He not only describes himself as having "stepped into his shoes" (HD 54) but also goes to look for his predecessor's remains in Africa. This incident foreshadows Marlow's frequent struggles to hold on to his own identity in the course of his journey.

Before starting on his trip Marlow has to present himself for an interview at the Company's headquarters located in an unnamed continental city[7] that reminds him of "a whited sepulchre" (HD 55). This is a term used by Christ in St Matthew's Gospel to describe those who are not what they seem (cf. Hampson, Notes 130). One of the implications of Marlow's metaphor is that the beauty of the city's buildings and streets and the wealth of its inhabitants are based on the riches extracted by brutal force from the colonies. The idea that the "sepulchral city" (HD 152) is hiding a dark, horrifying secret is reinforced by the way Marlow notices a "dead silence" in the "deserted" (HD 55) street in which the Company building is located and by his comparison of the latter to "a house in a city of the dead" (HD 57). What happens within the Company's offices is even more unsettling. According to Ian Watt, Marlow is "being initiated into the most universal and fateful of modern society's rites of passage – the process whereby the individual confronts a vast bureaucracy to get a job from it" (*Conrad* 193). This process consists of "a sequence of routinised human contacts" (Watt, *Conrad* 193) carried out by people who seem devoid of any individuality. The secretary who beckons Marlow into the director's "sanctuary" (HD 56) is described only in terms of "a white-haired secretarial head [...] wearing a compassionate expression" and "a skinny forefinger" (HD 56). The "great man himself" appears to Marlow only as a "pale plumpness in a frock coat" (HD 56). The interview is so short that Marlow does not even remember whether they shook hands. Most conspicuous are the receptionists, "[t]wo women, one fat and the other slim, [sitting] on straw-bottomed chairs, knitting black wool" (HD 55). The task of the younger one is to introduce the people who are arriving. The way she walks "straight at" (HD 55) Marlow without saying a word or ceasing to

---

[7]   The headquarters of Leopold II's *Société Anonyme Belge* were located in Brussels.

knit, makes her appear to him like a "somnambulist" (HD 55) or automaton. The older one is characterized by the way she looks with "swift and indifferent placidity" (HD 56) and with "unconcerned wisdom" (HD 57) at the job applicants, many of whom never "saw her again – not half, by a long way" (HD 57). Marlow's emphasis on the "uncanny and fateful" (HD 57) aura of the two knitters has led many critics to compare them to the Fates of Greek legend, Clotho and Lachesis, who spin the thread of each man's life until it is cut by Atropos. That the receptionists are said to be "guarding the door of Darkness" (HD 57) also evokes memories of the Sibyl in Virgil's *Aeneid*, who guards the door to the Underworld. On a more materialist level, Ian Watt, quoting Max Weber, sees them as products of "that modern bureaucratic administration [which] brings with it "the dominance of a spirit of formalistic impersonality"" (*Conrad* 194). Both readings emphasize Marlow's awareness that from now on it is no longer *he* who controls his life but impersonal forces of a materialist or possibly even metaphysical nature. His ominous feeling that he has been "let into some conspiracy" (HD 56) which no one deigns to explain to him is compounded by the ensuing visit to the Company doctor.

The doctor expresses a special interest in Marlow's racial background, inquires into possible madness in his family and finally asks him "with a certain eagerness whether [he] would let him measure [his] head" (HD 57). Although the doctor does not explain in detail, he hints at "a little theory which you Messieurs who go out there must help me prove" (HD 58). This he regards as his "share in the advantages my country shall reap from the possession of such a magnificent dependency" (HD 58). That his seemingly objective scientific interest is explicitly tied to the profits of colonization draws our attention to the way science, too, is implicated in imperialism. The doctor's methods of examination show that he is an adherent of the pseudo-science of craniology, that is, he is interested in measuring his patients' skulls in the hope of establishing permanent and measurable race differences, which could be used to justify the colonization of 'inferior peoples'. That the doctor, however, also refers to madness and says that it would be "interesting for science to watch the mental changes of individuals, on the spot [in Africa]" (HD 58), reveals that his "little theory" is also concerned with a possible correlation between foreign environment, physiognomy, race, and mental health. Griffith (cf. 131ff.) relates this interest to the contemporary anthropological idea of 'acclimatization' and the related discussion as to which members of the white race would prosper best in tropical climates. In his notorious book *Hereditary Genius* the eugenicist Francis Galton, for instance, had called for the collection of empirical data on adaptability in order to "assure ourselves as to the possibility of any variety of white men to work, to thrive, and to continue their race in the broad regions of the tropics" (quoted in Griffith 132). The doctor's examination certainly makes sense in this light: he is, as Griffith puts it, "concerned with gathering accurate data to further the kind of research that will perpetuate Galton's colonial agenda" (132). Marlow's increasing irritation is not only due to the doctor's intrusive questions but also to his awareness that he is forced to participate in questionable experiments. Marlow realizes that he is being reduced to a specimen for pseudo-scientific analysis. As Fothergill puts it, the incident reveals that

> no sooner does [Marlow] enter the employment of the Company, than he becomes complicit in its processes and structures, but less as a controlling subject than an *object* of them. Marlow, the detached observer, is now also observed; aware [...] of his own potential reification, his 'alienation'. (33)

Whereas the examination scene reveals the implication of science in the imperialist project, the farewell visit to Marlow's aunt draws our attention to the concomitant rhetoric. Again Marlow has certain roles and identities thrust upon him that make him feel uncomfortable and not in control of the situation. First of all, his aunt tells him that she has represented him to "the wife of [a] high dignitary" in the Company Administration as an exceptional and gifted creature – a piece of good fortune for the Company – a man you don't get hold of every day" (HD 59). This recommendation, which reaches the Congo before Marlow does, will later lead the pilgrims to associate him with Kurtz as another member of the "new gang – the gang of virtue" (HD 79). The aunt then launches into a stream of imperialist rhetoric and attributes certain ideological roles to Marlow: he is now "one of the Workers, with a capital" and "an emissary of light, something like a lower sort of apostle" (HD 59). What the aunt invokes here is the work ethic, which had been turned into an *ersatz*-religion and was used as a justification for imperialism. The way the aunt behaves and speaks like a fanatical "arm-chair missionary" (Fothergill 34) shows how somewhat naïve women like her or the Intended unthinkingly contribute to the imperialist cause: they form the façade behind which men such as the manager or Kurtz can go about their 'work'. The incident is also a powerful example of the way imperialist ideology determined the mind-set of ordinary people. As Owen Knowles has pointed out, "for most of these speakers such rhetoric is a reflexive act: they are not, on the whole, individuals seeking to use hyperbole to disguise an unsavoury truth, but inert victims and instruments of linguistic coercion" (Introduction xvii). Although Marlow distances himself from his aunt's rhetoric by hinting "that the Company was run for profit" (HD 59), his position is fraught with contradictions. As Fothergill points out, "he differentiates and disassociates himself from colonialism's ideological manifestations at the very moment he is engaging with it himself" (34). No wonder that he feels like an "impostor" (HD 60). Although he is not the man his employers believe him to be, he is nevertheless playing a willing part in what Adams calls "the Company charade, while being under no illusions as to the nature and implications of that charade" (23).

5.3 Marlow's journey to Africa and his arrival at the Outer Station

When Marlow starts on his voyage he feels "as though, instead of going to the centre of a continent, I were about to set off for the centre of the earth" (HD 60). As he travels along the African coast in a French steamer, Marlow realizes that he is being initiated into a reality where traditional ordering systems and concepts of causation become ambiguous, indeterminate, or are simply not applicable. He also has his first impressions of imperialism 'in practice':

> We pounded along, stopped, landed soldiers; went on, landed custom-house clerks to levy toll [...]; landed more soldiers – to take care of the custom-house clerks, presumably. Some, I heard, got drowned in the surf; but whether they did or not, nobody seemed particularly to care. They were just flung out there, and on we went. (HD 60-61)

What is noticeable about the passage is the impersonal and mechanical repetitiveness of the process, which is totally indifferent to individual lives. We also become aware that the victims of colonization are not only the natives but also the colonizers themselves. As Anthony Fothergill points out, imperialism is made to appear like "a destructive machine [which] owes no more allegiance to its creator and agents than to its most obvious victims" (40). Typical of Marlow's observations of African reality is also the way he contrasts the activity of landing soldiers and custom-house clerks to the environment in which they will be active: in "settlements some centuries old, and still no bigger than pin-heads on the untouched expanse of their background" and in "what looked like a God-forsaken wilderness, with a tin shed and a flag-pole lost in it" (HD 60). By thus combining what Watts calls a "dwarfing perspective" (*Heart* 4) with a "frustrating context" (*Heart* 5) the colonial activities appear absurd, futile, and purposeless. Marlow uses similar stylistic techniques in the well-known passage describing the French man-of-war, senselessly shelling the bush (cf. HD 61-62), which many critics regard as symbolic of Marlow's general view of the ineffectuality, indeed the insanity of the colonial project in Africa.

Marlow's first observations of imperialism are confirmed by what he witnesses at the Outer and Central Stations. There his focus is more exclusively than later in his narrative on colonial practice, on the discrepancy between imperialist ideology and what is actually going on. One of the justifications for imperialism was that white Europeans would bring progress to the colonized regions, which meant – on the most basic level – economic development. Since, according to imperialist reasoning, the natives were too inefficient and backward to exploit their country's resources profitably, the Europeans had to teach them the right way to go about it. What Marlow, however, observes at the Outer Station is the exact opposite of progress: it is "inhabited devastation" (HD 63). At first he cannot make sense of what he sees: "a boiler wallowing in the grass" (HD 63), an "undersized railway-truck" (HD 63) on its back with one wheel off, other "pieces of decaying machinery" (HD 63-64), and "a stack of rusty nails" (HD 64). After a while he notices some activity going on, which he describes in terms similar to the man-of-war shelling the bush: "A horn tooted to the right, and I saw the black people run. A heavy and dull detonation shook the ground, a puff of smoke came out of the cliff, and that was all. No change appeared on the face of the rock" (HD 32). Eventually, a possible explanation dawns on Marlow: "They were building a railway" (HD 64). Given the context, the phrase has already acquired invisible quotation marks. Nothing of the kind is happening and Marlow adds astonished, "The cliff was not in the way or anything; but this objectless blasting was all the work going on" (HD 64). The term 'work', which had a quasi-religious status in imperialist ideology, has here become an expression of contempt. This is not work, order, or progress but simply "a wanton smash-up" (HD 66). Instead of efficiency and profitability there is waste and profligacy: it is, as Marlow says, "men going at it blind" (HD 50). What makes the occurrences at the Outer Station appear even more unsettling is the absence of human agency and intention behind them:

> Everything else in the station was in a muddle, – heads, things, buildings. Strings of dusty niggers with splay feet arrived and departed; a stream of manufactured goods, rubbishy cottons, beads, and brass-wire set into the depths of darkness, and in return came a precious trickle of ivory. (HD 68)

Again we sense the presence of an impersonal controlling mechanism at the back of all this. Although the emphasis on chaos, destructiveness, and futility might call to mind Schopenhauer's conception of the will, it suffices to think about Marlow's audience of businessmen and their place of work to understand where the empire machine derives from and where it is kept in constant motion.

At the Outer Station Marlow also observes the treatment meted out to the colonial subjects. In this context, it is worthwhile recalling how the King of the Belgians, Leopold II, defended his colonization project in the Congo. He claimed that "[o]ur only programme ... is the work of moral and material regeneration, and we must do this among a population whose degeneration in its inherited conditions it is difficult to measure" (quoted in Watts, Notes, *Heart of Darkness* 255). The Lamarckian reasoning behind this statement is that the Africans have acquired degenerative characteristics and that therefore the European regenerative effort has to include the benevolent 'reclaiming' of the natives, that is, raising them to a higher level of evolutionary development. Marlow now sees what the contemporary slogan '*Africa Redivivus*' (cf. Griffith 90) meant in practice. In his harrowing description of the African chain gang Marlow not only emphasizes the natives' suffering due to arbitrary cruelty, slave-work, and starvation but also shows how the colonial system of exploitation has degraded them to the level of beasts of burden: the "[b]lack rags [...] wound round their loins, and the short ends behind wagged to and fro like tails" (HD 64). He also notes the linguistic hypocrisy of the colonialists, who refer to these wretches as "criminals" (HD 64), thus implying that there is some sort of justice involved in their treatment. Similarly ironic is Marlow's reference to the guard as "one of the reclaimed, the product of the new forces at work" (HD 64). So this is 'the level of civilization' to which the Europeans have 'raised' the Africans: they have turned them into members of their native militia. In his attempt to get away from the chain gang Marlow seeks the shade of some trees but finds himself in "the gloomy circle of some Inferno" (HD 66). He has come to what he will later call "the grove of death" (HD 70), where the Africans forced to help in the cause of progress have withdrawn to die. Marlow expresses his horror at what he observes in an extraordinary image:

> The rapids were near, and an uninterrupted, uniform, headlong, rushing noise filled the mournful stillness of the grove, where not a breath stirred, not a leaf moved, with a mysterious sound – *as though the tearing pace of the launched earth had suddenly become audible*. (HD 66; my italics)

What – in addition to expressing Marlow's shock at what he sees – could be the function of this simile, which invokes a cosmic, outer-space perspective? It seems that what Marlow experiences here is a moment of insight which is occasionally granted to Conrad's characters. This epiphany or 'lifting of the veil' does, however, not refer us to Joyce or Woolf but to Schopenhauer. My discussion of the latter's philosophy has shown that the he recognizes special moments in our lives when, through "an external cause or inward disposition," we are, for a short while, snatched "out of the endless stream of willing" (quoted in Safranski 223) and are enabled to gain insight into the universal spectacle of the will. What Marlow understands in this special moment as he, as it were, views the empire machine from the outside is that the ultimate consequence of imperialism is genocide. Although he does not say so explicitly, his description of the scene furnishes sufficient proof for such a reading: "They were dying slowly – it was very clear. They were not enemies, they were not criminals, they were nothing earthly now, – nothing but black shadows of disease and starvation, lying confusedly in the greenish gloom" (HD 66). Marlow is very precise in his delineation of how colonization is responsible for what he sees in "the grove of death." He refers once again to "[t]he work" (HD 66), senselessly but unceasingly going on in the background which has used and then discarded these "moribund shapes" (HD 66) like a machine. In addition, he ironically alludes to Leopold's 'labour tax' (cf. Fothergill 38) and the effects of detribalisation: "Brought from all the recesses of the coast in all the legality of time contracts, lost in uncongenial surroundings, fed on unfamiliar food, they sickened, became inefficient, and were then allowed to crawl away and rest" (HD 66). Far from 'reclaiming' the Africans, the Europeans are, in fact, contributing to their degradation, ruin, and death. Once Marlow has overcome his initial shock, he cannot but react with compassion and offers a dying African "one of my good Swede's ship's biscuits" (HD 67). This act of humanity and pity should be highly evaluated. It sets Marlow worlds apart from the other whites he encounters in Africa, who, due to their racist and sadistic attitudes, would not be capable of reaching out to 'the other'. Because Marlow's act takes place in an instinctive and spontaneous manner, it is reminiscent of Schopenhauer's understanding of compassion, which has, as we have seen, a special place in his philosophy. He regards compassion as a quality that not everyone possesses and that is not at one's disposal all the time. Rather like the rare moments of insight, those of compassion only occur under exceptional circumstances. In such moments the barrier between the ego and the non-ego is broken down and we share the sufferings of a fellow human being in a way in which we normally only feel our own suffering. Something very similar happens to Marlow in this situation. As becomes clear from his observations and comments in the course of his tale, Marlow, in general, possesses what Conrad himself values so highly – a sympathetic and moral imagination that is not patronizing or sentimental. Frequently Marlow also displays a related faculty which Griffith terms the "anthropological urge – to understand and interpret" (62). James Clifford similarly refers to Marlow's narration as "a paradigm of ethnographic subjectivity" (100) and attributes to him "a coherent position of sympathy and hermeneutic engagement" (110). This is evident, for instance, in the way Marlow tries to find a meaning for the "bit of white worsted" (HD 67) tied round the neck of the dying African: "Why? Where did he get it? Was it a badge – an ornament – a charm – a propitiatory act? Was there any idea at all connected with it?" (HD 67). In this way Marlow manages to engage in an, albeit limited and unspoken, dialogue with 'the other' and to transcend "the violence which refuses to listen [and] refuses exchange" that Andrew Gibson (122) regards as constitutive of imperialist ideology and rhetoric.

When Marlow leaves the grove of death and makes "haste towards the station" (HD 67), he encounters his first representative of "the new forces at work" (HD 64), the Company's chief accountant. Marlow's response to the bookkeeper is contradictory, oscillating between amazement, respect, and revulsion. Marlow gives the accountant credit for keeping up appearances "in the great demoralisation of the land" and exclaims, "That's backbone" (HD 68). He also appreciates the way the accountant is "devoted to his books, which [are] in apple-pie order" (HD 68) and even goes so far as to state that he "respected the fellow" (HD 68). Marlow's positive evaluation is, however, undermined by a number of factors. There is, for instance, the accountant's explanation that he manages to sport immaculate linen because he has been "teaching one of the native women about the station," who, at first, "had a distaste for the work" (HD 68). Given the generally appalling treatment of the Africans, we wonder at the accountant's 'teaching methods'. This hint at his possible inhumanity is reinforced by his complete lack of compassion for the dying agent brought into his office, whom he merely regards as a distraction from bookkeeping. For the same reason he has also "come to hate those savages – hate them to the death" (HD 70). Marlow's reference to him as "a hairdresser's dummy" (HD 68) suggests that he has become a 'conscious automaton', whose bureaucratic attitude and efficiency have emptied him of all human values. Michael Levenson, accordingly, sees the bookkeeper as the inevitable product of a certain administrative order that "gives identities, establishes purposes, assigns destinies" (395). It thus encourages the exclusion of any purley personal feeling from the execution of official tasks and produces exactly the kind of inhuman attitude displayed by the accountant. Marlow's ambivalent response to him mirrors his struggle with imperialist ideology in general, sometimes questioning, sometimes embracing it.

5.4   The Central Station

Whereas at the Outer Station the "flabby devil[s] [...] running that show" (HD 72) were, with the exception of the chief accountant, not visible, Marlow gets a closer look at them at the Central Station. Because of the "absurd long staves" (HD 76) the Company agents carry about like fetishes, Marlow refers to them as "a lot of faithless pilgrims" (HD 76). There is, indeed, no doubt that the pilgrims' god is ivory: "The word 'ivory' rang in the air, was whispered, was sighed. You would think they were praying to it" (HD 76). Similar to the silver in *Nostromo*, ivory in *Heart of Darkness* is accorded, in Ross's words, "the status of a fetishized signifier, [...] rounding the ideological field of "reality" as dictated by the profit motive" (71). The epitome of the "imbecile rapacity" which Marlow describes as blowing "through it all, like a whiff from some corpse" (HD 76) is the "invasion, [the] infliction, [the] visitation" of the appropriately named "Eldorado Exploring Expedition" (HD 87). Marlow compares the expedition members' talk to that of "sordid buccaneers" (HD 87) whose desire is "[t]o tear out treasure out of the bowels of the land [...], with no more moral purpose at the back of it than there is in burglars breaking into a safe" (HD 87). As Stephen Ross has put it, they have transferred "libidinal desire onto the object of capitalist desire" by transforming "the product [=ivory] into a fetishized commodity" (72). The lust for ivory and other riches dominates these people to the exclusion of everything else and makes them appear inhuman.

The pilgrims' "show of work" (HD 78) at the Central Station is as much a sham as that at the Outer Station. Inefficient, languid, purposeless waiting is "all the sixteen or twenty pilgrims of them" (HD 77) do; their only desire is "to get appointed to a trading-post where ivory [is] to be had, so that they [can] earn percentages" (HD 78). They beguile their time by "backbiting and intriguing against each other" (HD 78) and enjoy inventing excuses to sadistically torment the natives. Thus, when a grass shed full of trade goods bursts into flames, a culprit is found immediately: "A nigger was being beaten near by. They said he had caused the fire in some way" (HD 76). That the pilgrims are indeed what Valentine Cunningham calls "trigger-happy nigger-killers" (242) is borne out by their behaviour during the attack on the steamer near Kurtz's station. Unthinkingly, they open fire "with their

Winchesters" and "simply squirt[.] lead into that bush" (HD 110). Although Marlow has noticed that "almost all the shots [have] gone too high" (HD 121), one of the pilgrims rejoices: ""Say! We must have made a glorious slaughter of them in the bush. Eh? What do you think? Say?" He positively danced, the bloodthirsty little gingery beggar" (HD 120). When Marlow starts on the journey down-river with Kurtz on board, he can only avoid a massacre by "pull[ing] the string of the whistle" to scare the Africans away as he has already noticed "the pilgrims on deck getting out their rifles with an air of anticipating a jolly lark" (HD 146).

The killing of the natives can go on openly and without much fuss, as it is, at least implicitly, part of the imperialist agenda. There is no doubt, however, that among the whites in Africa murder is in the air as well. A conversation between the manager and his uncle, the leader of the Eldorado Exploring Expedition, makes this clear: ""We will not be free from unfair competition till one of these fellows [= independent traders such as the Harlequin] is hanged for an example,' he said. 'Certainly,' grunted the other; 'get him hanged! Why not? Anything – anything can be done in this country"" (HD 91). This attitude is echoed by the brickmaker, who warns Marlow that "No man – you apprehend me? – no man here bears a charmed life" (HD 84). In contrast to killing an African, the dispatching of a white man demands a lot of scheming and plotting as, after all, appearances have to be observed. That an oblique murder plot lies at 'the heart' of *Heart of Darkness* has first been noted by Cedric Watts in his eminent study of the tale first published in 1977: "If we may describe as a murder plot a scheme to delay a man's relief, in conditions which virtually ensure that without prompt relief the man will succumb to disease and death, then *Heart of Darkness* is a murder story" (*Heart* 83). The victim of this plot is, of course, Kurtz and the murderer the manager, who is encouraged and assisted by his uncle and the brickmaker. Watts has termed the technique Conrad uses to present the murder "*covert or elided plot sequence*" which involves the "conceal[ing] or withhold[ing] [of] narrative elements that a more orthodox novelist would have made evident and prominent" (*Preface* 116). A review of the evidence for the existence of this plot throws light not only on an easily overlooked 'tale-within-the-tale-within-the-tale' but also on the Darwinian theme of *Heart of Darkness*.

When Marlow arrives at the Central Station, he is informed that his "steamer [is] at the bottom of the river" (HD 72). The circumstances of the sinking are rather peculiar and Marlow comments that "the affair was too stupid – when I think of it – to be altogether natural" (HD 72). Marlow's hunch is strengthened by his first interview with the general manager, who knows precisely how long the repairs of the steamer will take. His phrasing even implies that it is *he* who determines the length of time necessary: "Well, let us say three months before we can make a start. Yes. That ought to do the affair" (HD 75). Although at this stage Marlow believes the manager to be "a chattering idiot" (HD 75), he later has to revise his opinion when "it [is] borne in upon [him] startlingly with what extreme nicety he [has] estimated the time requisite for the 'affair'" (HD 75). Marlow's suspicions are further compounded by the dubious character traits of the manager and his assistant, the brickmaker. In his description of the former Marlow emphasizes his ordinariness: he is "commonplace in complexion, in feature, in manners, and in voice"; he is "of middle size and of ordinary build"; his eyes are of "the usual blue"; he is essentially "a common trader"; he is "obeyed, yet he inspire[s] neither love nor fear, nor even respect" (HD 73). He has "no learning, and no intelligence" and merely "keep[s] the routine going – that's all" (HD 74). The manager thus appears to be devoid of any individuality and Marlow speculates that "[p]erhaps there was nothing within him" (HD 74). Even the position he has reached within the Company hierarchy does not seem to be due to his own initiative: "[It] had come to him – why? Perhaps because he was never ill ... He had served three terms of three years out there ... Because triumphant health in the general rout of constitutions is a kind of power in itself" (HD 74). It is in particular this apparent pact with the Darwinian law of the jungle that contributes to the manager's one salient quality: to inspire uneasiness. The brickmaker, too, is a suspicious character. He does "secretarial work for the manager" (HD 83) and is rumoured to be the latter's spy upon the other pilgrims. Although in his exterior – "young, gentlemanly, a bit reserved, with a forked little beard and a hooked nose" (HD 77) – he is reminiscent of the devil, he is only a "*papier-mâché* Mephistopheles" (HD 81; my italics). Indeed, it seems to Marlow that if he tried, he could "poke [his] forefinger through him, and would find nothing inside but a little loose dirt, maybe" (HD 81). This aligns the brickmaker with the manager and the chief accountant, who are also described as 'hollow men'. The conversation with the brickmaker raises Marlow's awareness that he is not only witnessing a murderous "drama of officialdom" (Levenson 395) but that he is also assigned a part in it. The brickmaker assumes that Marlow is acquainted with important people in the Administration and knows about their plans for the Company's stations in Africa. What he is particularly concerned about is the future position of Kurtz:

> To-day he is chief of the best station, next year he will be assistant-manager, two years more and ... but I daresay you know what he will be in two years' time. You are of the new gang

– the gang of virtue. The same people who sent him specially also recommended you. Oh, don't say no. I've my own eyes to trust. (HD 79)

Marlow once again has no control over the identity that is imposed on him. Without having any choice in the matter, he is identified with the Kurtz faction in the manager's and the brickmaker's plot. What is remarkable is that Marlow accepts this ready-made identity by announcing, "When Mr. Kurtz […] is General Manager, you won't have the opportunity [to read the Company's confidential correspondence]" (HD 80). A little later Marlow realizes, however, that by "letting the young fool there believe anything he liked to imagine as to my influence in Europe" he has become "in an instant as much of a pretence as the rest of the bewitched pilgrims" (HD 82). On the other hand his tactics have helped him to perceive what the brickmaker is driving at in his underhand manner: "He, don't you see, had been planning to be assistant-manager by-and-by under the present man, and I could see that the coming of that Kurtz had upset them both not a little" (HD 81). The conversation with the brickmaker has uncovered *one* motive for the attempt to murder Kurtz by delaying his relief. Further motives are furnished by the snatches of dialogue between the manager and his uncle which Marlow overhears while resting on deck of his steamer. Kurtz has, for instance, impressed the higher echelons of the Company with his high ideals and fine rhetoric, which are anathema to the manager. The administrators in Europe have also ignored the manager's advice and fulfilled Kurtz's wish to be posted to the Inner Station "with the idea of showing what he could do" (HD 89). Once there, Kurtz haughtily sent back the assistant the manager appointed to work with him with a contemptuous letter. Furthermore, Kurtz not only sends in "as much ivory as all the others put together" (HD 69) but has also said openly that "he wants to be manager" (HD 91) himself. The uncle expresses sympathy for his nephew's hate of Kurtz and suggests that the "climate may do away with this difficulty for you" (HD 89). There are a number of indications that this might indeed occur. After coming "three hundred miles" down-river Kurtz suddenly decided to turn back to his station, "bare of goods and stores" (HD 90), and his clerk reported that Kurtz "had been very ill – had recovered imperfectly" (HD 90). Finally, there has been no news from the completely isolated Kurtz for "nine months," only "strange rumours" (HD 91). It seems clear that the manager, supported by the brickmaker and his uncle, will not have to do much to finish him off. It will be sufficient to delay the relief of the Inner Station. Otherwise the manager can rely on the Darwinian laws of Natural Selection. As his uncle says, "nobody here, you understand, *here*, can endanger your position. And why?

You stand the climate – you outlast them all" (HD 91). He then refers directly to the jungle as an accomplice:

> 'Ah! my boy, trust to this – I say, trust to this.' I saw him extend his short flipper of an arm for a gesture that took in the forest, the creek, the mud, the river, – seemed to beckon with a dishonouring flourish before the sunlit face of the land a treacherous appeal to the lurking death, to the hidden evil, to the profound darkness of its heart. (HD 92)

The covert murder plot can thus only come off because it is in synchrony with a larger, determinist Darwinian plot in the background. According to Hunter, the manager has "re-interpreted Herbert Spencer's famous catch phrase 'the survival of the fittest' [...] and used it as a law of business" (17). The manager, probably, does not even have to do much 're-interpreting' because, as we have seen in Chapter 2, Spencer actually recommended the Darwinian laws as guidelines not just for business but for a general code of conduct. The manager's inhumanity can therefore be read as an implicit critique of Spencer's and the Social Darwinists' philosophy as it was, for instance, also voiced by T.H. Huxley.

The discussion of the covert murder plot has drawn attention to the evolutionary or Darwinian theme in *Heart of Darkness*, which is most explicit in Marlow's descriptions of African nature. Viewed objectively, nature is, of course, non-human and neutral to man, even though we are its products and subject to its laws. There is, however, a tradition, not least in scientific writing, to anthropomorphise nature. We only have to recall Darwin, who described Natural Selection in *The Origin of Species* as "a power incessantly ready for action" (quoted in Gribbin and White 215) and as "daily and hourly scrutinising, throughout the world, every variation, even the slightest" (quoted in Gribbin and White 216). As we have seen in Chapter 2, Darwin was concerned to emphasize that 'Nature' – significantly usually spelled with a capital 'N' – was in principle benevolent, working for the good of all beings. Towards the end of the nineteenth century, however, Darwin's theory of evolution was interpreted in a much more pessimistic way so that in evolutionary writing Nature was now often portrayed as an alien, even positively hostile force. In analogy to Ruskin's 'Pathetic Fallacy' Cedric Watts refers to this tendency as the "Antipathetic Fallacy" (*Heart* 18), which he locates in Marlow's memorable descriptions of his surroundings. To Marlow the wilderness is, for instance, "something great and invincible, like evil or truth" (HD 76); it exerts both "an appeal" and "a menace" (HD 81); it is characterized by "ominous patience" (HD 92); it is "a thing monstrous and free" (HD 96); it is "pitiless to human weakness" (HD 127); it is like "a mask – heavy, like the closed door of a prison" (HD 129), with an "air of hidden knowledge, of patient expectation, of unapproachable silence" (HD 129). Marlow also combines the antipathetic fallacy with an invocation of evolution's vast time-scales as in the following example:

> The great wall of vegetation, an exuberant and entangled mass of trunks, branches, leaves, boughs, festoons, motionless in the moonlight, was like a rioting invasion of soundless life, a rolling wave of plants, piled up, crested, ready to topple over the creek, to sweep every little man of us out of his little existence. And it moved not. A deadened burst of mighty splashes and snorts reached us from afar, as though an ichthyosaurus had been taking a bath of glitter in the great river. (HD 86)

Marlow feels so oppressed by the massive power he senses hiding in the wilderness that he is actually surprised that the "wall of vegetation" does not move in for the kill. Marlow's suspicion that, in the long run, Nature will prevail and sweep humankind out of existence is implied in his reference to the ichthyosaurus, "which, for all its apparent might, was made totally extinct by the evolutionary process" (Watts, *Heart* 89). From this perspective the white imperialists appear indeed only as a temporary "fantastic invasion" (HD 92). As Watts points out, the references to evolution in the tale also lend precision to "some of the more oratorical comments on the jungle-background [...] which may out of context seem vapid" (*Heart* 90). This concerns, for instance, Marlow's observation during his up-river journey that "this stillness of life did not in the least resemble a peace. It was the stillness of an implacable force brooding over an inscrutable intention. It looked at you with a vengeful aspect" (HD 93). This passage has become notorious because F.R. Leavis in *The Great Tradition* singled it out as a negative example of what he claimed to be Conrad's tendency towards "adjectival insistence upon inexpressible and incomprehensible mystery" (204), whose effect is "not to magnify but rather to muffle" (205). If we consider the Darwinian context, however, and remember that T.H. Huxley, for instance, detected the occurrence of a veritable 'holocaust' in a seemingly peaceful meadow, Conrad's sentences gain in meaning. The "implacable force" recalls the supreme strength of Natural Selection, which, as we have seen, also informs the struggle between Kurtz and the manager. The "intention" is "inscrutable" because, as Huxley has taught us, we cannot know and cannot influence the direction in which evolution moves.

5.5   The journey towards the Inner Station

In the course of Marlow's up-river voyage towards Kurtz another aspect of the evolutionary theme comes into play, namely the way Marlow's perception of Africa and the Africans is torn between Lamarckism – a typical ingredient of imperialist ideology – and an understanding of Darwinism that anticipates present-day positions in evolutionary and anthropological theory. At the Outer Station Marlow emphasized the Africans' humanity by highlighting their suffering at the hands of the colonists. He thus managed to overcome – to some extent at least – the ideologically constructed gulf between himself and 'the other' by sympathetically engaging with the Africans and by asking questions about the riddles African life posed him. This allowed him to recognize the Africans' biological and racial equality and to regard the differences between them and the Europeans as 'merely' culturally conditioned. When he, for instance, wondered whether the African drumming he heard "on some quiet night" (HD 71) might perhaps have "as profound a meaning as the sound of bells in a Christian country" (HD 71), he even suggested that seemingly different manifestations of culture were in fact just variant expressions of the same tribal or societal needs. In a similar feat of cultural relativist thinking he explained the desertion of African villages by asking his audience to imagine the following:

> [I]f a lot of mysterious niggers armed with all kinds of fearful weapons suddenly took to travelling on the road between Deal and Gravesend, catching the yokels right and left to carry heavy loads for them, I fancy every farm and cottage thereabouts would get empty very soon. (HD 70)

By the time Marlow starts on his up-river journey the reader has got so used to Marlow's enlightened "ethnographic subjectivity" that it comes almost as a shock when he suddenly invokes the Lamarckian stereotypes that were used to justify imperialism. He, for instance, clearly refers to developmentalist anthropology when he compares "[g]oing up that river" to "travelling back to the earliest beginnings of the world" (HD 92). A few pages later he imagines himself and his companions to be "wanderers on a prehistoric earth" and the Africans on the shore have become "prehistoric man [...] cursing us, praying to us, welcoming us" (HD 96). This recalls how contemporary anthropology regarded native tribes as 'living fossils' of an earlier evolutionary stage. Another Lamarckian giveaway comes when Marlow explains that the cannibal crew on board did not have "any clear idea of time, as we at the end of countless ages have. They still belonged to the beginnings of time – had no *inherited experience* to teach them, as it were" (HD 103; my italics). This reference to the idea of soft heredity, that is, the inheritance of acquired characteristics, is the clearest evidence in Marlow's narrative that his perception of the Africans is, at times at least, informed by Lamarckism. It is consistent with Marlow's apparent reversion to orthodox imperialist ideology and epistemology that in the pages dealing with the approach to the Inner Station we come across descriptions of Africans which – to the modern reader – are without doubt dehumanising and racist. Thus, Marlow infamously compares his fireman to "a dog in a parody of breeches and a feather hat, walking on his hind-legs" (HD 97) and, during the attack on the steamer, he describes his "fool-helmsman" as "lifting his knees high, stamping his feet, champing his mouth, like a reined-in horse" (HD 110). It is passages such as these which have led Chinua Achebe in his essay, "An Image of Africa: Racism in Conrad's *Heart of Darkness*," to call Conrad – whom he does not distinguish from Marlow – "a thoroughgoing racist" (257).[8] The question is, however, *why* Marlow is all of a sudden so intent on putting as much distance as possible between himself and Africa and the Africans? Maybe he has simply given up trying to understand, question, and empathize and seeks reassurance in a pre-fabricated ideological mind-set. As he, for instance, says at one point,

> [I]t occurred to me that my speech or my silence, indeed any action of mine, would be a mere futility. What did it matter what any one knew or ignored? [...] The essentials of this affair lay deep under the surface, beyond my reach, and beyond my power of meddling. (HD 100)

Watt and Fothergill suggest that, in general, the focus of Marlow's narrative now shifts from a concern with the injustices of colonial practice to a preoccupation with Kurtz and a more philosophical inquiry into the bases of moral conduct and human civilization (cf. Watt, *Conrad* 224 and Fothergill 60). Owen Knowles argues that although the tale "[moves] away from the symptoms of colonial rowdyism," it does not become less topical; in fact, it "devises markedly wider tests in order to probe the credentials of the European mission in Africa" (Introduction xxi). It can indeed be shown that Marlow's sympathetic imagination and urge to question what he sees have not completely disappeared. Indeed, the contradiction between the stereotypes of imperialist ideology he verbally reproduces and his essentially humane actions and observations is intensified. For instance, at the same time as Marlow posits an evolutionary gulf between the advanced Europeans and

---

[8] The essay was first published in 1977 and is based on a lecture Achebe gave two years earlier at the University of Massachusetts.

the "prehistoric" Africans, he also gropes towards a comprehension of the latter by discovering – albeit patronizingly – a "remote kinship with this wild and passionate uproar" and "an appeal [to him] in this fiendish row," which he interprets as the expression of basic human emotions that *all* of humanity share: "Joy, fear, sorrow, devotion, valour, rage" (HD 96). In other words, he perceives "truth stripped of its cloak of time" (HD 97). When Marlow first describes the cannibal crew on board, he notes that "[t]hey were men one could work with, and I am grateful to them" (HD 94). This is a high compliment from someone who places such importance on the work ethic and the duty to a task. The pilgrims, in contrast, are people Marlow certainly cannot work with. Similarly, before the attack on the steamer Marlow talks to the headman of the cannibals "just for good fellowship's sake" (HD 103) but is not interested in speaking with the pilgrims. Although he has painted a disparaging picture of his helmsman, he later asserts that

> I missed my late helmsman awfully [...]. [...] Well, don't you see, he had done something, he had steered; for months I had him at my back – a help – an instrument. It was a kind of partnership. He steered for me – I had to look after him, I worried about his deficiencies, and thus a subtle bond had been created, of which I only became aware when it was suddenly broken. (HD 119)

There is no sense here that Marlow regards the African as his inferior or as a hardly human "prehistoric man." On the contrary, as Wollaeger points out, the helmsman has "carried out one of the most valuable duties a character in Conrad can perform – like Singleton [in *The Nigger of the 'Narcissus'*], he steered" (69). Marlow is also anxious to 'bury' the body as quickly as possible by tipping it overboard in order to save it from the cannibals. Finally, Marlow even states that he is "not prepared to affirm that [Kurtz] was exactly worth the life we lost [i.e. the helmsman] in getting to him" (HD 119). Passages such as these undermine the binary opposition between the savage and the civilized inscribed in the kind of imperialist ideology of which Marlow avails himself sometimes. This subversion is also evident in Marlow's observation of the remarkable restraint exercised by the cannibals, who, although they are starving and outnumber the whites "thirty to five" (HD 104), do not attack them. Marlow starts to look at the Africans

> as you would on any human being, with a curiosity of their impulses, motives, capacities, weaknesses, when brought to the test of an inexorable physical necessity. Restraint! What possible restraint? Was it superstition, disgust, patience, fear – or some kind of primitive honour? No fear can stand up to hunger, no patience can wear it out, disgust simply does not exist where hunger is; and as to superstition, beliefs, and what you may call principles, they are less than chaff in a breeze. (HD 105)

As Griffith has pointed out, the passage refutes the "belief that 'primitive' people [are] utterly unrestrained [which] seems to have been among the most widely distributed stereotypes in writings on non-European cultures" (Griffith 224). It is also significant that the "prehistoric" Africans appear to have restraint, whereas the pilgrims have very little, Kurtz has none, and even Marlow has to fight hard to resist the lure of the wilderness. In this context Allan Hunter has added a caveat. He claims that it is "by no means certain" that the Africans possess restraint as "[a]fter all, fear of the pilgrims' guns may be the cannibals 'restraint'" (118). Marlow, however, makes it sufficiently clear that "[n]o fear can stand up to hunger" (HD 105) and that, furthermore, the cannibals would not have "much capacity to weigh the consequences" (HD 104) of an attack. The cannibals' behaviour appears even more astonishing if we remember that two *European* characters in Conrad's other fiction are rumoured to have resorted to cannibalism when faced with starvation: Old Robinson in *Lord Jim* and the eponymous hero of "Falk." In *Heart of Darkness* there are hints that Kurtz, too, has indulged in anthropophagy *without* any "inexorable physical necessity."

5.6   The character of Kurtz

Kurtz's initial motive to go to Africa seems to have been the same as that of all the other whites Marlow meets in the Congo: to make money. As Marlow says, "He had given me some reason to infer that it was his impatience of comparative poverty that drove him out there" (HD 159). The insatiable greed for ivory Kurtz develops later provides evidence for Marlow's inference. As a typical product of his time and place Kurtz, however, does not acknowledge this motive openly but clothes it in grandiloquent imperialist rhetoric. His eloquence is, of course, Kurtz's most salient characteristic, which is attested to by virtually everyone who comes into contact with him. According to Marlow,

> of all his gifts the one that stood out preeminently, that carried with it a sense of real presence, was his ability to talk, his words – the gift of expression, the bewildering, the illuminating, the most exalted and the most contemptible, the pulsating stream of light, or the deceitful flow from the heart of an impenetrable darkness. (HD 113-114)

Because Marlow is himself fascinated by Kurtz's voice, his evaluation is characteristically ambiguous. One of the most striking comments on Kurtz's rhetorical excellence comes from the journalist friend who visits Marlow in the "sepulchral city" after Kurtz's death. He informs Marlow that "Kurtz's proper sphere ought to have been politics 'on the popular side.' [...] He could get himself to believe anything – anything. He would have been a splendid leader of an extreme party" (HD 154). In this light Kurtz appears to be a propagandist or populist without principles, whose rhetoric is empty but nevertheless dangerous because it has the potential to incite not just himself but also his followers to fanaticism. Kurtz's "gift of expression" is characterized by what Gibson regards as typical of imperialist rhetoric, the "will to dominate through language, through a totalising discourse" (122). Paradoxically, Kurtz talks very little in *Heart of Darkness* and his few direct pronouncements are anything but rhetorically brilliant. We mainly get second-hand impressions of his discursive powers. The brickmaker, for instance, refers to Kurtz as "an emissary of pity, and science, and progress, and devil knows what else" and then starts to "declaim" (HD 79), as if quoting from one of Kurtz's speeches: "We want [...] for the guidance of the cause intrusted to us by Europe, so to speak, higher intelligence, wide sympathies, a singleness of purpose" (HD 79). The most revealing sample of Kurtz's 'ideas' and his manner of expressing them is Marlow's quote from the "opening paragraph" of Kurtz's report for the International Society for the Suppression of Savage Customs:

> He began with the argument that we whites, from the point of development we had arrived at, 'must necessarily appear to them [savages] in the nature of supernatural beings – we approach them with the might as of a deity,' and so on, and so on. 'By the simple exercise of our will we can exert a power for good practically unbounded,' etc. etc. (HD 118)

Kurtz seems to be immensely proud of what he calls "'my pamphlet'" (HD 118) and when he hands it over to Marlow, he asks him to take good care of it as it might further his career in Europe. Although Marlow calls the "peroration [...] magnificent," praises "the unbounded power of eloquence – of words – of burning noble words," and claims that it made him "tingle with enthusiasm" (HD 118), we should bear in mind the journalist colleague's judgement that "Kurtz really couldn't write a bit" (HD 154). The examples quoted above are certainly characterized by what Gibson calls the "overbearing grandiosity" (122) of imperialist rhetoric but they are hardly exceptional or original. They are propagandistic set-pieces that do not differ greatly from the pronouncements of Leopold II, the 'owner' of the Congo, or, indeed, from the expressions used by Marlow's aunt, which the narrator refers to as "rot" and "humbug" (HD 59). Conspicuously, when Kurtz lies dying, Marlow all of a sudden has doubts as to Kurtz's originality and suspects that he might simply be repeating platitudes like an automaton: "I heard him mutter, 'Live rightly, die, die ...' I listened. There was nothing more. Was he rehearsing some speech in his sleep, or was it a fragment of a phrase from some newspaper article?" (HD 148). From this perspective it seems likely that Kurtz has simply absorbed imperialist rhetoric to such a degree that he repeats it like a parrot. He can do this so convincingly because – as his behaviour at the Inner Station shows – he believes in the literal truth of 'his' ideas. Characteristically, the beginning of Kurtz's written report invokes the Lamarckian paradigm: the whites are much further advanced in their biological, mental, and moral development so that they "must necessarily" appear to the savages "in the nature of supernatural beings." Although in the following sentence Kurtz uses a simile – "we approach them with the might *as* of a deity" –, his 'rule' at the Inner Station suggests that he literally conceives of himself as an omnipotent god with unlimited free will. The way Kurtz has succumbed to this illusion is also borne out in his next statement that "[b]y the simple exercise of our will we can exert a power for good practically unbounded." The implication is that only an imperialist situation can lend the will of a white European such supremacy. Kurtz's scrawled postscript "at the foot of the last page" (HD 118) of his report, "'Exterminate all the brutes!'" (HD 118), is not arbitrary or the result of madness: it is the inevitable consequence of the kind of argumentation he employs. A justification of imperialism based on pseudo-scientific theories culled from anthropology, evolution, craniology, and racism cannot come to a different conclusion. Thus, in what Marlow compares to a "luminous and terrifying [...] flash of lightning in a serene sky" (HD 118), Kurtz discloses for a moment the ultimate unspoken consequence of imperialism: genocide. That this revelation should come from someone so imbued with imperialist ideology as Kurtz is certainly no coincidence. As Gibson asserts, without the ideology's "totalising habit of thought and perception [...] the idea of extermination itself is impossible" (121). Characteristically, Kurtz does not just want to exterminate the Congolese or *some* natives but "*all* the brutes." Due to his observations at the Outer and Central Station, Marlow has already become suspicious as to the underlying goals of imperialism in Africa. However, he ascribed what he witnessed to the stupidity, hollowness, and animal-like brutality of the pilgrims and the general manager. He hoped that someone like Kurtz, who appeared to be in opposition to the other whites and who seemed to possess intelligence, moral ideas, and the gift to inspire others, would be different and would redeem imperialism for him. Now he realizes that Kurtz is the epitome of the kind of behaviour and attitude he noted down-river and that, far from being an exception, the extermination of the natives is part and parcel of the imperialist programme.

Ironically, it is Kurtz's conversance with imperialist ideology and his gift of eloquence that have endeared him to the Company bosses in Europe. Historically his 'career' can be explained by the fact that due to mounting international criticism of Belgian activities in the Congo, the officials in Brussels were looking for rhetorically gifted employees with the ability to put up a smoke screen of propaganda as a useful defensive tactic (cf. Smith 193 and Watt, *Conrad* 140). This is probably also the reason why the brickmaker refers to Kurtz as a member of "the new gang – the gang of virtue" (HD 79), in which he also includes Marlow. A further reason for Kurtz's quick rise in the bureaucratic hierarchy is that he proves to be "a first-class agent" (HD 69), which, in the Company's terms, means that he "[s]ends in as much ivory as all the others put together" (HD 69). This is, indeed, something even the manager acknowledges grudgingly (cf. HD 90). Marlow seems to have hoped that Kurtz would have combined his 'economic activities' with some "moral purpose at the back of it" (HD 87). However, as soon as Marlow arrives at the Inner Station, he realizes that the boundless greed for ivory is all that is left of the "original Kurtz" (HD 147). It even appears to Marlow that Kurtz has been transformed into ivory: "And the lofty frontal bone of Mr Kurtz! […] this – ah! - specimen, was impressively bald. The wilderness had patted him on the head, and, behold, it was like a ball – an ivory ball […]." (HD 115). Kurtz is thus merged with the *real* ivory that can be found in such abundance at the station that Marlow thinks that there cannot be "a single tusk left either above or below the ground in the whole country" (HD 115). The Harlequin gives Marlow an idea as to Kurtz's 'business methods'. Although Kurtz has done some exploring too, "mostly his expeditions [have] been for ivory" (HD 128). This uncomfortably reminds us of the "Eldorado Exploring Expedition," whose aim had not been to explore but simply to "tear treasure out of the bowels of the land" (HD 87). When Marlow objects that Kurtz "had no goods to trade with by that time," the Harlequin's evasive reply, "[t]here's a good lot of cartridges left even yet" (HD 128), discloses that Kurtz violently raided the country. What is worse, "he got the tribe to follow him" (HD 128) so that Kurtz had command over his own private army. That Kurtz's appetite for ivory is insatiable is also evident from a personal experience the Harlequin relates: "Well, I had a small lot of ivory the chief of that village near my house gave me. […] Well, he wanted it, and wouldn't hear reason. He declared he would shoot me unless I gave him the ivory and then cleared out of the country […]" (HD 128). The Harlequin, of course, handed over the ivory. This is one more instance of what Gibson has called imperialism's "totalising impulse" (12). Kurtz is not content with a lot of ivory but he wants *all* that there is and have total possession of it. His inability to shake off this obsession is also signalled by the way he makes sure that his last sight on earth is 'his' ivory. Because Marlow and the pilgrims had to pile the ivory on the steamer's deck, Kurtz "could see and enjoy as long as he could see, because the appreciation of this favour had remained with him to the last" (HD 116). Although Kurtz's behaviour is indefensible and has taken him "beyond the bounds of permitted aspirations" (HD 144), it should be noted that his rapacity has been encouraged and abetted by the imperialist-capitalist machine he is part of. After all, for the Company, the best agent is he who sends in most ivory. To some extent Kurtz has therefore also fallen prey to the immoral and inhuman values of a system over which he has no control. Erdinast-Vulcan even claims that "there seems to be no doubt that he [is] fundamentally loyal to his employers" and that he is "an agent who discharges his duties all too well" (*Modern Temper* 101). Indirectly this argumentation gains support from the way the manager judges Kurtz's 'management' of the Inner Station:

> [T]here is no disguising the fact, Mr Kurtz has done more harm than good to the Company. He did not see the time was not ripe for vigorous action. Cautiously, cautiously – that's my principle. [...] The district is closed to us for a time. Deplorable! Upon the whole, the trade will suffer. [...] We must save [the ivory], at all events – but look how precarious the position is – and why? Because the method is unsound. (HD 137)

The manager here embodies the Company's economic viewpoint, which excludes all human or moral considerations. He even seems to be impressed by Kurtz's "method," even though he calls it "unsound." In the manager's view Kurtz's "vigorous action" would certainly be the quickest and most efficient way of obtaining ivory but the time is, unfortunately, not ripe for it yet. What has to be saved, "at all events," is the ivory. Human lives do not count.

Although it could be argued that at the Inner Station Kurtz has tried to realize the promise of complete supremacy and omnipotence held out to the white man by imperialism, Marlow paints the portrait of someone who is anything but free. In a remarkable paragraph he, for instance, first describes Kurtz as wanting to possess everyone and everything in his sourroundings but then reverses his perspective to reveal a man totally possessed by larger forces: "You should have heard him say, 'My ivory.' [...] 'My Intended, my ivory, my station, my river, my –' everything belonged to him. [...] – but that was a trifle. The thing was to know what he belonged to, how many powers of darkness claimed him for their own" (HD 116). The extent of Kurtz's enslavement by the "powers of darkness" can be gleaned from the way he occasionally tries to regain a degree of autonomy but succumbs each and every time to his unrestrained desires. The Harlequin describes the typical course the struggles with his demons take:

> He hated all this, and somehow he couldn't get away. When I had a chance I begged him to try and leave while there was time [...]. And he would say yes, and then he would remain; go off on another ivory hunt; disappear for weeks; forget himself amongst these people [...]. (HD 129)

The Russian also reveals that it was Kurtz who "had ordered the attack to be made on [Marlow's] steamer" because he "hated sometimes the idea of being taken away" (HD 139). When he is finally on the ship, even his severe illness cannot prevent him from falling once again under "the heavy, mute spell of the wilderness" (HD 144) which leads him to crawl on all fours "to the edge of the forest, to the bush, towards the gleam of fires, the throb of drums, the drone of weird incantations" (HD 144). When Kurtz is in thrall to his "forgotten and brutal instincts" (HD 144), he seems to be transformed into "one vast indiscriminate appetite" (Watt, *Conrad* 234). Indeed, it seems to Marlow that Kurtz "wanted to swallow all the air, all the earth, all the men before him" (HD 134). Kurtz thus resembles Freud's conception of the *id*, an irrational and atavistic force with a potential for total destruction. As Marlow describes it, "[t]here was nothing either above or below him [...]. He had kicked himself loose of the earth. Confound the man! he had kicked the very earth to pieces" (HD 144).

Kurtz, however, calls to mind not only Freudian but also Nietzschean concepts, especially the will-to-power and the idea of the super-man. Nietzsche believed the will-to-power to be the most basic human instinct, which informs, to varying degrees, all human actions. He also believed that an increase in power is accompanied by an increase in happiness and freedom. The happiest and therefore freest person is the one who has achieved self-mastery and who has 'becomes who he is' (cf. Hollingdale 162ff). The super-man has then earned the right to be a law-giver, a judge over good and evil, and also an avenger. If we evaluate Kurtz in these terms, it seems obvious that he does *not* achieve self-mastery and therefore cannot be called a super-man. It is, however, also tempting to regard Kurtz as a critique of Nietzsche's thinking. There can be no doubt that Kurtz is striving to increase his power, is aiming at egoistic self-fulfilment at all costs, and sets himself up as a savage god of the jungle whose word is law. However, Kurtz neither finds happiness nor freedom but their opposites. Instead of becoming a *super*-man, he is transformed into a *sub*-human, animal-like creature. By thus turning Nietzsche's concepts on their head, Conrad reveals their premises as dangerous delusions. We could even take this reading of

Kurtz one step further and regard aspects of Kurtz's personality as caricatural references to Nietzsche himself: the philosopher shares with Kurtz a magnificent "gift of expression" (HD 113) and an artistic nature; the ability to fascinate and attract a large following; a penchant for ideas with the potential of misleading others; a shocking descent into madness, accompanied by delusions of divine grandeur; and an end as a pitiable, exhausted shade.

Finally, Kurtz can also be read in the context of Max Nordau's pseudo-scientific theories of degeneration, which consisted of a muddled mixture of anthropology, psychology, criminology, and evolutionary theories and enjoyed great popularity during the *fin-de-siècle* period.[9] Degeneration refers to the reversion to an earlier phase of evolution understood in a Lamarckian sense. Nordau imagined degeneration to occur according to the commonly held belief that ontogeny recapitulates phylogeny, which means that the development of the individual mirrors that of the species (cf. Griffith 220-221). A degenerate would therefore, first of all, shed the refined qualities and higher moral sensibilities that characterize European civilization, would then descend to the level of 'savages' and 'primitives', and, finally, resemble our progenitors, the apes. The application of this theory to Kurtz is obvious: whereas in his notorious pamphlet he still appeals "to every altruistic sentiment" (HD 118), his note "scrawled evidently much later" (HD 118) shows that he has lost his moral sense. Kurtz then sets himself up as a tribal leader by 'going native' and possibly even resorts to cannibalism, behaviour stereotypically ascribed to 'savages'. Thus he reaches a "state of unrestricted desire" (Griffith 153), which is, according to Nordau, a basic characteristic of the degenerate. Finally, Kurtz does not even walk upright any longer but crawls on all fours towards members of his tribe dancing round a fire in the guise of animals. Cedric Watts (cf. *Heart* 132ff) claims that Kurtz even conforms to a special type in Nordau's taxonomy, the 'higher degenerate', which Nordau defines as follows:

[J]ust as he occasionally exhibits gigantic bodily stature ....., has some mental gift exceptionally developed at the cost, it is true, of the remaining faculties, which are wholly or partially atrophied..... I do not share Lombroso's opinion that highly-gifted degenerates are an active force in the progress of mankind. They corrupt and delude [...]. They [...] are leading men along the paths they themselves have found to new goals; but these goals are abysses or waste places. They are guides to swamps like will-o'-the wisps, or to ruin like the ratcatcher of Hammelin. (quoted in Watts, *Heart* 133)

---

[9]   I will return to Nordau's theories in my discussion of *The Secret Agent*.

Kurtz, who is twice referred to as a "universal genius" (HD 83 and 154), certainly has an exceptionally developed gift, the "gift of expression" (HD 113), whereas his other faculties might indeed be "atrophied." He also possesses "the power to charm or frighten rudimentary souls [= the natives] into an aggravated witch-dance in his honour" and to "fill the small souls of the pilgrims with bitter misgivings" (HD 119). In addition, he also fascinates the Intended, the Harlequin, and Marlow himself. Kurtz even displays the characteristic of the "gigantic bodily stature": to Marlow he looks "at least seven feet long" (HD 134). Nordau detected highly-gifted degenerates in particular among artists and Kurtz, too, is variously referred to as a poet, a musician, and a painter.

How are we then to evaluate Kurtz? Is he indeed "a *special* being" (HD 79; my italics), whose break-up in the jungle is deplorable but should be regarded as an aberration, something that would not happen to everyone? Or does Kurtz's fate raise more general questions about the state of European civilization? The answers Marlow provides are contradictory. On the one hand he claims that "there was something wanting in [Kurtz] – some small matter which, when the pressing need arose, could not be found under his magnificent eloquence" (HD 131). The implication is that other people who do not have this deficiency would behave differently under the circumstances and would not succumb to the lure of the wilderness. However, a few lines later Marlow asserts that "[Kurtz] was hollow at the core" (HD 131). This trait identifies him with the other 'hollow men' Marlow has encountered down-river. According to this reasoning, Kurtz is not all that exceptional but shares characteristics with the pilgrims, who are average white Europeans turned imperialists. But Marlow goes even further and declares that "[a]ll Europe contributed to the making of Kurtz" (HD 117). This allows the inference that Kurtz should be regarded as an embodiment of that particular culture so that, consequently, his fortune *does* reflect back on the conditions of European society. Such a reading gains support from the two occasions in his narration during which Marlow harangues and mocks his audience for their complacency and false sense of security. The first passage is ostensibly a defence of Marlow's near break-down and momentary loss of self-restraint as a reaction to the death of his helmsman during the attack on the steamer (cf. HD 114-115). The second, occurring just one and a half pages later and worded in a very similar manner, is an attempt to make his listeners comprehend Kurtz's behaviour:

> You can't understand. How could you? – with solid pavement under your feet, surrounded by kind neighbours ready to cheer you or to fall on you, stepping delicately between the butcher and the policeman, in the holy terror of scandal and gallows and lunatic asylums –

how can you imagine what particular region of the first ages a man's untrammelled feet may take him into by the way of solitude – utter solitude without a policeman – by the way of silence – utter silence, where no warning voice of a kind neighbour can be heard whispering of public opinion? These little things make all the great difference. (HD 116)

In this passage Marlow wants his audience to see that their restraint would have crumbled just as Kurtz's if they had been exposed to similar circumstances. To appreciate the full subversive power of the paragraph, however, we should remember that restraint was regarded at the time as a basic form of morality that many thinkers – especially those of a Lamarckian persuasion – believed to have become innate in Western societies (cf. Griffith 226). Marlow, however, undermines this assumption by suggesting that in European societies restraint has not become an inherited instinct but is externally imposed. He implicitly distinguishes between what Louis Althusser has termed 'repressive' and 'ideological' structures (cf. Barry 164). Examples of the first, which originate in state institutions and operate by direct force, are the penal system (the "policeman," the "gallows") and the mental health system (the "lunatic asylum"). They curb our aggressive and irrational impulses and regulate our social and mental behaviour. The primary example of the second, the ideological structures, which work in a more indirect but hardly less constraining manner, is "public opinion" enforced by "kind neighbours ready to cheer you or to fall on you." Marlow's mention of "the butcher" has a particularly ominous ring to it, especially as it follows so close upon his disquisition on the restraint of the "cannibal crew." According to Adams, Marlow implies that in Europe you "do not need to worry about the morality or advisability of eating the inhabitants of neighbouring villages if there is, in your own, a butcher able at all times to satisfy your demand for fresh meat" (66). In his earlier address to his friends, Marlow has also referred to their "excellent appetites" (HD 114), which reminds us both of the cannibals' hunger and Kurtz's voracity. What Marlow appears to drive at is, once again, cultural relativism: *all* human beings possess cannibalistic instincts but within European civilization they have been sublimated and redirected because their expression has – due to the existence of butchers – become unnecessary and has been outlawed. Marlow's suggestion that European civilization might be nothing more than a web of external constraints that constitute what has been deemed to be an innate moral sense had been voiced in a similar manner by a number of Victorian and Late-Victorian thinkers. In "Signs of the Times" Thomas Carlyle, for instance, argued that "the 'superior morality,' of which we hear so much, [...] is properly rather an 'inferior criminality,' produced not by greater love of Virtue, but by greater perfection of Police; and of that far subtler and stronger Police, called Public Opinion" (81). Carlyle's proposed panacea to what he perceived to be the moral emptiness of his contemporaries was spiritual renewal, coupled with a commendation of the work ethic. In his "Evolution and Ethics" Huxley, too, doubts that the moral sense has become ingrained. He, therefore, commends the imposing of external constraints, such as "[l]aws and moral precepts," because they are "directed to the end of curbing the cosmic process" ("Evolution" 328), which Huxely identifies with the brutal and unethical laws of evolution. In *Heart of Darkness* Marlow's position as regards the innateness of the moral sense veers from the ambiguous to the sceptical. On the one hand he argues that some people *do* possess a moral instinct whereas others do not. Twice, in contexts that imply that he is also talking about himself, Marlow refers to "innate strength" (HD 116) and one's "own true stuff" (HD 97) which may serve as protection against the loss of restraint. Others, like Kurtz, who lack this instinct, may succumb to the "powers of darkness" (HD 116). Marlow's own actions and viewpoints throughout his narrative are certainly informed by a pragmatic humanitarian ethos which seems to be largely instinctual with him. On the other hand Marlow undermines this position by emphasising the way our behaviour and values are simply expressions of a set of control mechanisms forced on us by our culture, which we lose as soon as we leave it behind. From this point of view it an be argued that Kurtz loses all restraint because he completely surrenders his cultural identity, whereas Marlow actively ensures that his own remains inviolate by clinging to the confines of his steamer, which, for him, functions as a vestige of European civilization. Marlow combines this strategy with a "deliberate belief" (HD 97), which he does not define explicitly but which seems close to Huxley's recommendations about how the "cosmic process" should be curbed in favour of the "ethical process."

The debate on whether morality is instinctual or not has repercussions for the related concept of moral responsibility and its prerequisite, free will. If morality is just another word for restraint, which is, furthermore, imposed from the outside, then genuine moral responsibility and the possibility of free choice might be equally illusory. Although this scepticism is present in Huxley's and Marlow's argumentation, their response to these doubts is not one of resignation. To ensure that human beings do not lose their humanity, a "deliberate belief" in moral concepts and therefore also in limited human freedom is necessary, despite the awareness of the possible illusory nature of this belief. With regard to *Heart of Darkness*, Jacques Berthoud has referred to this position as "the concept of positive illusion" which allows Marlow to "survive tragic knowledge without incurring self-deception – that is to say, affirm the values of the active life without blurring his sense of its underlying contradictions" (*Conrad* 63). As Kurtz's development demonstrates, freedom certainly cannot be found in the liberation of the instincts or extreme individualism. Paradoxically, the constraints of European civilization, which may limit personal freedom, may also safeguard a minimum of morality and individual autonomy.

5.7   The 'death-bed cry' and Marlow's relationship with Kurtz

Any interpretation of Kurtz's death-bed cry cannot be separated from Marlow's contradictory view of it. To understand the latter it is needful to look in more detail at the remarkable relationship between the two protagonists, for instance at the way Marlow experiences Kurtz as part of the deterministic forces that exert an astonishing degree of control over his African adventure. Ian Watt has pointed out that it is typical of Conrad's character portrayals that he

> sees relationships between individuals not as essentially personal, but as parts of a larger structure in which [...] chance, occasion, occupational activities, and general attitudes toward the physical and moral world, have enormous determining power, and allow very little autonomy to the wishes of the individual concerned. (*Conrad* 241)

In *Heart of Darkness* the "larger structure" of which both Kurtz and Marlow are part is the empire machine, which also produces the bureaucratic conflict between Kurtz and the manager. We have already seen how Marlow – without having any choice in the matter – is identified by the pilgrims with the Kurtz faction in this quarrel. Marlow accepts this ready-made role in the manager's "sordid farce" (HD 61) with "a sort of eager fatalism" (HD 127)[10] even though he is aware that he thus becomes "as much of a pretence as the rest of the bewitched pilgrims" (HD 82). It is from this moment onwards that Marlow starts to view the projected journey towards the Inner Station to relieve an ailing agent – which has so far been simply part of his job – as a very personal search for someone whom he, too, increasingly regards as a "special being" (HD 79). Due to Marlow's deeply upsetting experiences down-river his desire for explanation and meaning has become overwhelming. This is partly the reason why he turns Kurtz into an

---

[10]   These are the words Marlow uses to describe the Harlequin's devotion to Kurtz but they are surely applicable to Marlow's relationship with Kurtz as well.

imaginary, larger-than-life figure from which he expects ultimate clarification. As Daphna Erdinast-Vulcan puts it, "Kurtz becomes the embodiment of [an] originary presence to which Marlow addresses his faith. [...] The journey towards Kurtz is perceived as a promise of homecoming, a recovery of a lost truth, a return to an authentic point of origin" ("Ends of Man" 25). If we bear this in mind, it becomes easier to understand Marlow's "startling extravagance of emotion" (HD 114) when, after the attack on the steamer, he presumes Kurtz to be dead:

> I thought, By Jove! it's all over. We are too late; he has vanished – the gift [of expression] has vanished, by means of some spear, arrow, or club. I will never hear that chap speak after all, – [...]. I couldn't have felt more of lonely desolation somehow, had I been robbed of a belief or missed my destiny in life.... (HD 114)

Once Marlow has arrived at the Inner Station, he soon realizes that Kurtz does not correspond at all to his idealized conception of him and will not provide the illumination he seeks. What Marlow discovers at 'the heart' of Kurtz is not meaning but mere emptiness: "[H]e was hollow at the core" (HD 131). Far from being different from the pilgrims, Kurtz is, in Erdinast-Vulcan's words, the epitome of their "blind omnivorous greed" and represents the "culmination of the hollowness which is their essence" (*Modern Temper* 100). We might assume that at this point Marlow's fascination with Kurtz would evaporate and give way to disgust and revulsion. That this does not happen is one of the major paradoxes of the tale, especially because there can be no doubt that Marlow condemns Kurtz's deeds. He says clearly that Kurtz was "no idol of mine" (HD 132), at one point doubts whether Kurtz was "exactly worth the life we lost [=the helmsman] in getting to him" (HD 119), and also regards the Harlequin's unthinking devotion to Kurtz "as the most dangerous thing in every way [the young man] had come upon so far" (HD 127). How can we then account for Marlow's continuing fascination with Kurtz? According to Cedric Watts, Kurtz, "[l]ike Janus, [...] presents two contrasting faces to Marlow [...]. One face has a vacuous expression: he's a hollow man. The other face has a ferociously intense expression: he's a remarkably full man" (*Deceptive Text* 21). It is this second face which differentiates Kurtz from the other whites in Africa and which mesmerizes Marlow: "In the extremity of his ambitions, of his corruption and of his depraved appetites, Kurtz in ontological fullness offers a challenging *contrast* to the long line of hollow men. This Kurtz commands awe rather than dismissive contempt [...]" (Watts, *Deceptive Text* 22). Therefore, when confronted once again with the amoral hypocrisy of the manager, who refers to Kurtz's activities as "unsound method," Marlow turns "mentally to Kurtz for relief – positively for relief" (HD 138) and exclaims that "it was something to have at least a choice of nightmares" (HD 138).

The latter statement implies that Marlow freely decided to choose Kurtz as his preferred bad dream. However, as has been noted earlier, it was the pilgrims and the Company Administration in Europe that made that choice for him quite a long time ago down the river. Later in his tale Marlow will himself voice doubts whether he is in control of his fascination with Kurtz. He, for instance, announces enigmatically that "it *was ordered* I should never betray [Kurtz] – it *was written* I should be loyal to the nightmare of my choice" (HD 141; my italics). In direct contradiction to what he has said earlier, he asks himself how and why he has come to accept "this unforeseen partnership, this choice of nightmares *forced upon me* in [this] tenebrous land" (HD 147; my italics). When he runs after Kurtz, who is crawling towards his tribe, he remembers the "knitting old woman with the cat" from the Company offices in Europe and imagines her "to be sitting at the other end of such an affair" (HD 142). Thus Marlow seems to regard his dealings with Kurtz as part of destiny or larger deterministic forces that he cannot influence. Marlow's struggle with Kurtz to get him back to the steamer tightens the bond between them even further. As Marlow says, "at this very moment [...] the foundations of our intimacy were being laid – to endure – to endure – even to the end – even beyond" (HD 143). Kurtz on his part – not least due to the "special recommendations" (HD 135) from Europe – regards Marlow as his natural ally. He not only gives him his infamous pamphlet but also "a packet of papers and a photograph" (HD 148) as if to exhort Marlow to take on the role of keeper of his memory. This is, of course, exactly what Marlow will do, thus serving Kurtz's will even after his death. The symbiosis between the two protagonists is so pronounced that a number of commentators have interpreted Kurtz as Marlow's 'Double' or, indeed, as a facet of his unconscious (cf. Watts, *Deceptive Text* 82ff and Guerard).

That Marlow is determined to wring some consoling meaning out of his encounter with the "hollow sham" (HD 147) that Kurtz has become is evident from his evaluation of his death-bed cry. Peter Brooks has drawn attention to the way Marlow's narration is here informed by the traditional belief that

> the meaning of a life cannot be known until the moment of death: it is at death that a life first assumes transmissible form – becomes a completed and significant statement – so that it is death that provides the authority or 'sanction' of narrative. The deathbed scene of the nineteenth-century novel eminently represents the moment of summing-up of a life's meaning and a transmission of accumulated wisdom to succeeding generations. (74)

This is certainly the kind of significance Marlow wishes to give to Kurtz's cry and the reason why he elaborately 'stages' the pronouncement of Kurtz's last words. Thus he first of all notes that a "change [...] came over his features" (HD 149) which is "as though a veil had been rent" (HD 149). He then sees on his face, as if in rapid succession, the expression of extreme emotions: "of sombre pride, of ruthless power, of craven terror – of an intense and hopeless despair" (HD 149). Next he "evokes the tradition of the 'panoramic vision of the dying'" (Brooks 76) by wondering whether Kurtz "live[d] his life again in every detail of desire, temptation, and surrender during that supreme moment of complete knowledge" (HD 149). Finally, the theatrical climax is reached when Kurtz

> cried in a whisper at some image, at some vision – he cried out twice, a cry that was no more than a breath –
> 'The horror! The horror!' (HD 149)

Later on Marlow will remain adamant that Kurtz "had summed up – [...] had judged" (HD 151) and that "perhaps all the wisdom, and all truth, and all sincerity" (HD 151) had been compressed into that utterance at the moment between life and death. The problem here is that Kurtz's final words, taken on their own, are not all that meaningful and that therefore the claims Marlow makes for them seem excessive. According to Brooks,

> 'The horror! The horror!' is more accurately characterised when Marlow calls it a 'cry'. It comes about as close as articulated speech can come to the primal cry, to a blurted emotional reaction of uncertain reference and context. [...] More than a masterful, summary, victorious articulation, 'The horror!' appears as minimal language, language on the verge of reversion to savagery, on the verge of a fall from language. (Brooks 77)

Still, Marlow is intent on endowing Kurtz's cry with ethical significance, which is why he ends his commentary on it on a consoling and moral note: "It was an affirmation, a moral victory paid for by innumerable defeats, by abominable terrors, by abominable satisfactions. But it was a victory! That is why I have remained loyal to Kurtz to the last, and even beyond [...]" (HD 151). This interpretation implies that, due to the conventions of the traditional death-bed scene, Kurtz has repented, has recognized that his deeds are the result of his own free choice, and has accepted responsibility for them. His final words thus refer to his own actions and constitute an insight into the evil he has done. This is the reading of Kurtz's cry that Marlow most insists upon, probably because it conforms to the notions that make up his "deliberate belief" discussed earlier. Although Marlow's moral interpretation has the potential to provide a comforting closure not only to Kurtz's but also to his own story, he undermines it by hinting at other possible meanings of Kurtz's exclamation that offer no hope for any sort of redemption. Cedric Watts (cf.

Heart 117) has described three such alternative readings. Firstly, Kurtz regards as horrible but also as desirable the temptations to which he has succumbed: his whisper is characterized by a "strange commingling of desire and hate" (HD 151) and is therefore no moral victory at all. Secondly, Kurtz deems horrible the nature of all humankind: "No eloquence could have been so withering to one's belief in mankind as his final burst of sincerity" (HD 145). Thirdly, Kurtz is horrified by the whole universe, the whole scheme of things: "[T]hat wide and immense stare embracing, condemning, loathing all the universe" (HD 156). As Watts points out, this third reading suggests that rather than a self-condemnation Kurtz's cry is a self-justification: "[F]or in so horrifying a universe, any code of conduct, however destructive and violent, may be justified, so long as it enables a man to stamp his individuality on the senseless environment" (*Deceptive Text* 23). Although, therefore, Marlow's ostensibly comforting interpretation of Kurtz's final words is not entirely convincing, he nevertheless seems to manage to still – at least temporarily – not just his own need for ultimate meaning but, presumably, also that of his listeners, who, as we have seen, certainly do not want their complacency disturbed.

When Marlow is back in the "sepulchral city" near the end of his tale, he finds that far from relenting, Kurtz has tightened his grip on him. He also realizes that even a version of Kurtz's story that ends with his death-bed repentance would not be conducive to his posthumous reputation, especially given the light it would throw on the imperialist project in Africa. On his return he is therefore, as Watt puts it, "immediately engaged in the suppression of the truth about Kurtz's final degradation" (*Conrad* 242). Thus he tears off the infamous "postscriptum" (HD 153) to Kurtz's pamphlet before presenting it to the journalist colleague. Famously, he also lies to the Intended about Kurtz's last words. Due to the emphasis Marlow puts on the latter, the lie to the Intended is usually regarded as particularly noteworthy. However, Marlow's decision to censor Kurtz's report before passing it on to a representative of the press is much more problematic because of its political significance. Through this act Marlow goes beyond being a mere accomplice to imperialism, or, as he ironically puts it, "a part of the great cause of these high and just proceedings" (HD 65). He actively contributes to the proliferation of imperialist propaganda and suppresses evidence as to the genocidal dimensions of colonization in Africa. Marlow mentions the torn off postscriptum only in passing, as if this were not worth commenting on. The implication of his deed, however, dawns on him later, when he places such inordinate emphasis on his lie to the Intended. He realizes that, once again, he is concealing the truth about Kurtz in order to uphold a consoling fiction.

During the scene with the Intended many of the themes discussed earlier interpenetrate. For instance, Marlow presents his decision to visit her as the result of forces over which he has no control: "I had no clear perception of what it was I really wanted. Perhaps it was an impulse of unconscious loyalty, or the fulfilment of one of these ironic necessities that lurk in the facts of human existence. I don't know. I can't tell. But I went" (HD 155). As Marlow crosses the doorstep, Kurtz's haunting presence becomes so palpable and intense that it/he "seem[s] to enter the house with [him]" (HD 155). While Marlow waits in front of "a mahogany door on the first floor," it seems to him that Kurtz "stare[s] at [him] out of the glassy panel" (HD 156). What Marlow really sees is, of course, his own face but the suggestion is that, like a double, he has taken on Kurtz's features. During the visit the sense of Kurtz's presence continues, which is evoked not merely through Marlow's memories that almost overwhelm him but also through the Intended's gestures that ironically reproduce those of Kurtz's African mistress. The 'conversation' between the Intended and Marlow hardly deserves that name because she is "more inclined to talk than to listen. She controls the direction of the conversation. She requires agreement on particular points. She puts words into her interlocutor's mouth [...]" (Adams 97). The Intended takes it for granted, for instance, that Marlow admires Kurtz and even goes so far as to finish sentences for him:

'It was impossible not to –'
'Love him,' she finished eagerly, silencing me into an appalled dumbness. (HD 158)

Although it is Marlow who starts talking about Kurtz's last words – which is not surprising as they have been on his mind all the time – the Intended once again does not leave him any choice but to tell her what *she* wants to hear. As Anthony Fothergill has pointed out, Marlow's lie – "[t]he last word he pronounced was – your name" (HD 161) – is therefore "the melodramatic, romantically conventional closure to the official love story of Kurtz that the Intended [...] has constructed for Marlow to utter" (106).

Marlow reacts to his lie as if he has done something unforgivable and catastrophic: '[i]t seemed to me that the house would collapse before I could escape, that the heavens would fall upon my head' (HD 162). What has, *in fact*, happened is that, firstly, the Intended left Marlow little choice in the matter and that, secondly, he merely obeyed the rules of decency: you do not normally tell a grieving person that his or her beloved partner turned into an irresponsible monster before his or her death. Marlow seems to realize that he has overreacted when he registers with surprise that "nothing happened" because the "heavens do not fall for such a trifle" (HD 162). His initial reaction, however, becomes understandable, if we see his lie not just as upholding the Intended's "great and saving illusion" (HD 159) but also that of European civilization in general. This view is also taken by Anthony Fothergill, who sees the words "your name," which are, after all, addressed to someone whom we only know as the *Intended*, as

> a metonym for social and sexual relations which embody order, coherence and civilized reproduction of the same. Marlow passes on to the Intended the image of marital continuity. [...] [H]er ideal of the two of them [thus] remains intact and with it the social, moral and sexual values this ideal endorses – and which Kurtz's actual experience [...] has done everything to undermine and deconstruct. (106)

If we connect Marlow's lie – seen in this light – to the political implication of his suppression of Kurtz's scrawled note, he indeed has something to feel guilty about. Thus it can be argued that a primary motivation for Marlow to tell his tale in the first place springs from a need to testify, to tell, if not *the true* story, then at least *a truer* story about the practice of imperialism and one of its protagonists. Similarly, Erdinast-Vulcan views *Heart of Darkness* as "the belated testimony of a witness haunted by his own failure to testify" ("Millenial Footnotes" 56). Certainly, Marlow's claim that he "laid the ghost of [Kurtz's] gifts at last with a lie" (HD 115), is blatantly contradicted by his narrative as a whole. It rather confirms Marlow's later assertion that he will *not* be able to lay Kurtz's memory and all it represents "for an everlasting rest in the dustbin of progress" (HD 119) because "you see, *I can't choose*. He won't be forgotten" (HD 119; my italics).

5.8   Determinism and Indeterminism

As we have seen, Marlow has to cope with a great number of impersonal forces that throw his possibility of free agency into doubt: imperialism and ideology; capitalism and bureaucracy; evolution and an inimical African nature; his own psychological needs and drives, such as his fascination with Kurtz and his compulsion to narrate his story. We could therefore assume that the implicit position regarding the freedom-of-the-will-problem in *Heart of Darkness* is hard determinism. However, as we have seen in earlier chapters, 'classical' hard determinism, due to its postulation of universal causation, holds out the hope that ultimate truth is discoverable and accessible to the human mind. *Heart of Darkness* offers little ground for such optimism. Revealingly, Marlow defines the human condition as a "mysterious arrangement of merciless logic for a futile purpose" (HD 150). Although the reference to "merciless logic" invokes the hard determinist paradigm – the absolute, necessitating rule of cause and effect – the words *"mysterious* arrangement" and *"futile* purpose" suggest scepticism as to our ability to uncover *the* truth and to exercise control over our lives. Marlow's definition thus describes the first of the three positions regarding free will and determinism that we come across in Conrad's works: hard determinism combined with scepticism as regards our ability to discover a singular truth about ourselves and the world. Marlow's scepticism, however, sometimes also leads him towards solipsism or radical indeterminism. This position manifests itself most notably in Marlow's insistence on the unreal, dream-like nature of his experience. Already during Marlow's journey along the African coast he feels himself to be "within the toil of a mournful and senseless delusion" (HD 61) and compares his voyage to a "weary pilgrimage amongst hints for nightmares" (HD 62). The activities he observes at the Central Station are "as unreal as everything else" (HD 78) and the steamer on the River Congo "toil[s] along slowly on the edge of a black and incomprehensible frenzy" (HD 96). Marlow's most sustained expression of a solipsistic viewpoint is the passage in which he addresses his listeners and wonders if they can make sense of his narration:

> It seems to me I am trying to tell you a dream – making a vain attempt, because no relation of a dream can convey the dream-sensation [...].
> "... No, it is impossible; it is impossible to convey the life-sensation of any given epoch of one's existence - that which makes its truth, its meaning – its subtle and penetrating essence. It is impossible. We live, as we dream – alone...." (HD 82)

The passage conveys Marlow's feelings of powerlessness and helplessness both with regard to the nature of his experience and his ability to communicate it in a comprehensible narrative form. He couples the solipsistic perspective with the linguistic scepticism typical of Modernism. It seems that the reality confronting Marlow in Africa has baffled his conceptualising abilities to such a degree that he has begun to feel that the words at his disposal no longer fit their referents and have become devoid of genuine communicative meaning. As Owen Knowles puts it, Marlow has come to view language as insufficient "to express anything more than a frustrated desire for meaning" (xxviii). Arguably, the quoted paragraph is the most extreme expression of loss of control we come across in *Heart of Darkness*.

Indeterminism, however, does not just manifest itself in the tale's themes but also in its formal aspects, such as its use of the "'oblique narrative' convention" (Watts, *Heart* 22) of the frame tale. Indeed, in *Heart of*

Darkness we are not just dealing with *one* tale within another tale but with various frames and framed tales (cf. Brooks 82-84 and Knight 16ff). Thus it can be argued that Kurtz's and the Harlequin's tales are additionally embedded in Marlow's own. Brooks claims that if *Heart of Darkness* were a traditional frame narrative, such as Mary Shelley's *Frankenstein*, we would have a structure in which

> the first narrator presents Marlow as the second narrator, who presents Kurtz as the third narrator; then Kurtz would tell his tale to its end and fall silent; Marlow would then finish his own tale, framing Kurtz's; and the first narrator would reappear to close the outer frame. (83)

Such a "pattern of nested boxes, bracketed core structures, nuts within shells" (Brooks 83) obviously does not exist in Conrad's tale. Kurtz's story – just as the Harlequin's – remains incomplete and is merely "suggested to [Marlow] in desolate exclamations, completed by shrugs, in interrupted phrases, in hints ending in deep sighs" (HD 129). Although Marlow is driven by the desire to give his experience a determinate meaning and to provide closure to his story, the form his narrative takes suggests that this is impossible. Marlow seems to recognize this himself when he admits that "the essentials of this affair lay deep under the surface, beyond my reach, and beyond my power of meddling" (HD 100). When Marlow ceases to talk and the primary narrator takes over, he does not provide a closing comment or summing-up either. Instead he seems to avoid an explicit reaction to Marlow's narrative. According to Brooks, the last sentence of the tale[11] is merely 'a generalisation of the darkness at the heart of Marlow's (and Kurtz's) stories, rather than any defining illumination' (83). Therefore the fact that the frames of tales within tales do not close properly but remain open to varying extents reinforces the indeterminism and opacity of the whole narrative. As Hillis Miller puts it, "*Heart of Darkness* is posited on the impossibility of achieving its goal of revelation [;...] it is a revelation of the impossibility of revelation" ("Revisited" 212).

Another formal aspect of the tale that contributes to this effect is the use of 'delayed decoding'. This technique, which was first defined by Ian Watt, emphasizes Marlow's epistemological perplexities in Africa. It represents the combination of "the forward temporal progression of the mind, as it receives messages from the outside world, with the much slower reflexive process of making out their meaning" (Watt, *Conrad* 175). The protagonist *and* the

---

[11] "The offing was barred by a black bank of clouds, and the tranquil waterway [...] seemed to lead into the heart of an immense darkness" (HD 162).

reader are thus made to experience a gap between sense impression and decoding and "the delay in bridging the gap enacts the disjunction between the event and the observer's trailing understanding of it" (Watt, *Conrad* 176-177). By presenting, as Watts explains, "the *effect* [...] while withholding or delaying an understanding of its *cause*" (*Deceptive Text* 43-44) an element of indeterminism is inserted into the process of making sense of reality, which is conventionally imagined to take place in an ordered, rational, cause-and-effect manner. Although eventual decipherment may be provided, the sense of a 'defamiliarized' reality will remain. A prominent example in *Heart of Darkness* is the attack on the steamer near Kurtz's station. Marlow is at first bewildered by a sequence of sense impressions which he registers only as "a gratuitous change in the normal order of things" (Watt, *Conrad* 177). He sees his "poleman give up the business suddenly, and stretch himself flat on the deck, without even taking the trouble to haul his pole in" (HD 109); at the same time "the fireman [...] sat down abruptly before his furnace and ducked his head" (HD 109). As yet, Marlow (and with him the first-time reader) has no idea what is going on and is simply "amazed" (HD 109). Then he notices "[s]ticks, little sticks [...] flying about – thick: they were whizzing before my nose, dropping below me, striking behind me" (HD 109). Still, Marlow does not understand. Only after having circumvented a snag he finally hits upon the explanation: "Arrows, by Jove! We were being shot at!" (HD 110). Although in this case the reader probably grasps more quickly than Marlow what is actually happening, this is not true for all examples of the technique. A first-time reader of *Heart of Darkness* will, for instance, believe with Marlow that the notes in the book he finds in the Harlequin's hut are "in cipher" (HD 99) or that the "round carved balls" (HD 121) on the posts surrounding Kurtz's station are merely ornaments. This reader will then also share Marlow's surprise when he has to revise his initial interpretation and find out that the notes are in Russian and the 'ornaments' are skulls. According to Watts, the concept of delayed decoding cannot just be applied to shorter "descriptive passages" in Conrad's work but also "to longer narrative sequences and ultimately to the narrative strategies of whole works" (*Deceptive Text* 45). Thus the covert murder plot, which only careful re-readings can unveil, can be understood as another example of the technique.

Another element that destabilizes and decentres the narrative is the shifting distance between the narrating and the experiencing selves of the two main narrators, Marlow and the narrator of the frame tale. As John Lyon has pointed out, there is a time-gap between

the experiences of Marlow as protagonist, journeying up the Congo, and the experiences of Marlow as narrator, unfolding his narration on board the *Nellie*, although, in the pages of the novel, these two series of events *run concurrently*. And a second, though perhaps less important gap in time may exist between the anonymous *hearer* on board the *Nellie* as he *listens* to Marlow, and the experiences which he, having become the anonymous *narrator*, now offers to us, *his* audience, although these two series of events also *run concurrently*. (*Heart of Darkness* xxiv-xxv)

Sometimes Marlow makes a clear distinction between discourse and story time but often these time levels are blurred, for instance when Marlow's narrative threatens to break down. An example is the passage occurring before the start of Marlow's narrative proper in which he appears to justify imperialism:

> What redeems it is the idea only. [...] – something you can set up, and bow down before, and offer a sacrifice to...."
> He broke off. (HD 51)

What happens here is that Marlow's mind is thrown forward in terms of his narration and backwards in terms of his experience of Kurtz (cf. Lyon, *Heart of Darkness* xxx-xxxi). His juggling with at least three time levels leads Marlow to choose words which, he realizes, undermine the pro-imperialist sentiments he wanted to express and lead him to stop in his narration altogether. Another example is Marlow's recounting of the psychological crisis he experiences in the wake of the helmsman's death (cf. Lyon, *Heart of Darkness* xxxiii-xxxv). The description of his dismay at the thought of never being able to hear Kurtz speak brings his narrative once again to the point of collapse:

> Of course I was wrong. The privilege [of listening to Kurtz] was waiting for me. [...] And I heard – him – it – this voice – other voices – all of them were so little more than voices – and the memory of that time itself lingers around me, impalpable, like a dying vibration of one immense jabber, silly, atrocious, sordid, savage, or simply mean, without any kind of sense. Voices, voices – even the girl herself – now –"
> He was silent for a long time.
> 'I laid the ghost of his gifts at last with a lie,' he began suddenly. 'Girl! What? Did I mention a girl? Oh, she is out of it – completely. (HD 115)

To a first time reader of *Heart of Darkness* this passage probably indeed appears to be "one immense jabber" without coherence or sense, the representation of a mind on the brink of disintegration. Only on a second reading will the reader be in a position to decode the passage and follow Marlow's train of thought. His proleptic reference to the granted privilege of listening to Kurtz also brings the trauma of that experience to the surface, which expresses itself in Marlow's incoherent memories of that time. The horrors of the encounter with Kurtz that Marlow recalls push his mind further into the narrative future to the meeting with the Intended and his lie. The destabilization of Marlow's tale is so severe that after the passage quoted above he feels the need to insert another long proleptic digression until he finally manages to pick up the thread of his story. Although it is sometimes impossible to distinguish Marlow's narrating self from his experiencing self, it is nevertheless clear that such a difference exists. With regard to the primary narrator this is less obvious. Although, as Diana Knight points out, the latter "does not take up the possibility of telling us what he thinks about Marlow's tale with the benefit of hindsight" (18), critics such as Jakob Lothe claim that the former's narrative *does* show signs of a learning process which enacts the temporal indeterminism between the narrating and experiencing self. As Lothe puts it, "although the personal narrator at first appears to be strikingly simple compared to Marlow, this simplicity (both in attitude and insight) is more noticeable at the very beginning of his narrative than it is later on" (24-25). The frame narrator's naivety seems evident in his praise of British imperialism, which Marlow famously undercuts by pointing out that "this also [...] has been one of the dark places of the earth" (HD 48). Immediately after Marlow's laconic statement, the primary narrator's profound understanding and apt description of Marlow's inconlsuive method of presenting his tale contradict his seeming simplicity:

> [T]o [Marlow] the meaning of an episode was not inside like a kernel but outside, enveloping the tale which brought it out only as a glow brings out a haze, in the likeness of one of these misty halos that sometimes are made visible by the spectral illumination of moonshine. (HD 48)

The narrator's warning that we cannot hope to find a clearly defined and stable meaning at the centre of Marlow's story but that it will have to be actively sought for at the margins, suggests that indeterminism and deferral are fundamental organising principles of the tale. The primary narrator's closing remarks can also be taken as evidence that a learning process has taken place. Although his last sentence may not constitute an explicit comment on Marlow's story, it might be read as an implicit reaction to it and therefore as an enactment of the shifting distance between his narrating and his experiencing self. Whereas in his introduction he has praised the Thames as a bringer of light, as helping to bear the "spark from the sacred fire" (HD 17), his emphasis now falls on the encompassing darkness. This, according to Cedric Watts, can be taken to reflect what has become his "sombre and chastened mood" (*Heart* 127).

As we have seen, elements of indeterminism in *Heart of Darkness* are not just embodied on a thematic but also on a narratological-structural level and have to be set against the deterministic aspects that also make up the tale. As regards free will and determinism, we have seen that the tale sometimes takes a hard determinist perspective mixed with scepticism and, occasionally, a solipsistic one. The combination of determinism and indeterminism also brings to mind the position of near determinism, which has been discussed with reference to T.H. Huxley's theory of evolution. It postulates an overall deterministic system but also recognizes indeterministic elements. The consequences Huxley draws from this view for the concepts of morality and conduct are also reflected in *Heart of Darkness*. Although Marlow frequently feels that he is controlled by impersonal forces and at other times senses that his grasp on reality is slipping away, he nevertheless doggedly sticks to his possibly illusionary "deliberate belief" in practical ethical values which inform his actions. Although he is to an extent compromised by his participation in the imperialist exploitation of Africa and by his initial suppression of the truth about his experiences, his feelings of guilt and his desire to narrate his story show that he accepts responsibility for what he has seen and done. Although he sometimes despairs at the inadequacy of language and the impossibility "to convey the life-sensation of any given epoch of one's existence" (HD 82), it is nevertheless in his dogged persistence in narrative transmission that morality and a measure of freedom become manifest.

6. *Nostromo* and the Mechanics of History

The process of history becomes *Nostromo*'s dominant theme through Conrad's narrative strategies concerning time, place, and characters. Despite its title the focus of *Nostromo* is not on a particular figure but on a whole country, the fictional South American state Costaguana. Although the central action of the novel – the events leading up to the foundation of the Occidental Republic – spans just a few days in 1890 (cf. Watts, *Nostromo* 61-66), there are countless references to the past as far back as the Spanish Conquest in the sixteenth and seventeenth centuries and to about ten years to the future of the secession of Sulaco from Costaguana. Conrad's use of such a large time-scale enables him to give the reader multiple perspectives of the main events. He can zoom in on the characters involved in the War of Separation but he can show at the same time that this upheaval is just one of many similar ones that have occurred in the past and will occur again in the future. Not only the treatment of time and place thus draws attention to the process of history but also the social panorama that is presented. In the course of the narrative we come across representatives of numerous classes and ethnic groups that constitute the society of the country. This enormous canvas facilitates the identification of the characters with a certain social class and/or ethnic group and allows for the action of the novel to be analysed in abstract political and historical terms. *Nostromo*'s concern with the historical process inevitably raises questions related to the freedom-of-the-will-problem. Which forces 'produce' history? Is history progressive or is its movement cyclical or even circular? What is the relationship between the individual and history? Do human beings have any possibility of influencing the historical process or are they completely determined by it? Are human beings in a position to uncover 'the truth' about history or are all our attempts to do so coloured by ideological preferences that are again the result of subjective motives? In the following questions such as these will be examined by looking at the main events of the novel from the perspective of three concepts of history: the Whig or bourgeois/capitalist view, the Marxist view, and a Darwinian view based on T.H. Huxley's theory of evolution. By analysing which of the three perspectives corresponds best to the representation of history in *Nostromo* conclusions can be drawn regarding the implicit attitude towards the freedom-of-the-will-problem.

6.1   The Whig or bourgeois/capitalist perspective

The history of Costaguana is one of constant political turmoil: since the War of Independence to throw off Spanish colonial rule, periods of civil war have alternated with ruthless dictatorships, revolutions, and constantly changing governments. The politicians appear to be exclusively motivated by greed, rapacity, and the lust for power. The institutions of the state are devoid of meaning and simply serve as instruments for money-grabbing and the arbitrary wielding of authority. Because of the endemic political instability and its geographical position the Sulaco Province, which provides the main setting of the novel, has remained relatively untouched by industrialisation. Trading by sea is made difficult by the absence of wind from the Golfo Placido, trading by land by the enormous mountain range, the Cordillera, which cuts off the province from the rest of Costaguana. The "solemn hush of the deep Golfo Placido" (N 3) is first broken by the arrival of steamships and the setting up of the Oceanic Steam Navigation Company (O.S.N.). The economy, however, remains based on plantations and cattle breeding, together with the export of indigo, indiarubber, cotton, and ox-hides. Sulaco's biggest asset is the San Tomé silver mine, which has, however, not been exploited successfully for decades due to the ubiquitous political chaos and corruption. The concession of the mine has been thrust upon the wealthy merchant Gould, who has no knowledge of mining but is forced to pay royalties on the estimated output and fines for negligence. When Gould dies, his son Charles, who is in Europe for his education, decides to come to Sulaco with his wife Emilia, intending to make the mine a success. Charles is convinced that the introduction of material interests to the Occidental Province and the ensuing industrialisation will exert a stabilizing influence on the whole country, bringing not *just* material progress. Gould's credo echoes the theories of eighteenth and nineteenth century economists and utilitarians:

> What is wanted here is law, good faith, order, security. Any one can declaim about these things, but I pin my faith to material interests. Only let the material interests once get a firm footing, and they are bound to impose the conditions on which alone they can continue to exist. That's how your money-making is justified here in the face of lawlessness and disorder. It is justified because the security which it demands must be shared with an oppressed people. A better justice will come afterwards. That's your ray of hope. (N 84)

Gould's determination to make the working of the mine not just a financial but also a moral success is reinforced when he travels the province with his wife to look for labourers and is confronted everywhere with a feeling of resignation and hopelessness, the result of decades of political chaos. Costaguana appears to the Goulds as "a great land of plain and mountain and people, suffering and mute, waiting for the future in a pathetic immobility of patience" (N 88). In the households of the Blancos, the aristocratic families of Spanish descent, the Goulds hear

> stories of political outrage; friends, relatives, ruined, imprisoned, killed in the battles of senseless civil wars, barbarously executed in ferocious proscriptions, as though the government of the country had been a struggle of lust between bands of absurd devils let loose upon the land with sabres and uniforms and grandiloquent phrases. And on all the lips [they] found a weary desire for peace, the dread of officialdom with its nightmarish parody of administration without law, without security, and without justice. (N 88)

Charles is only able to set his plans into motion because he forms a number of strategic alliances. On a private level the most important one is with his wife, who passionately believes in her husband's claim that materialism is just a means to a higher end, namely to bring about a better future for Costaguana. Emilia not only travels the country with Charles but also oversees the setting up of the mining villages and establishes the Casa Gould as a central meeting place open to representatives of all sections of Sulaco society. Even more so than her husband Emilia believes in the symbolic power of the silver and endows the first ingot from the mine "with a justificative conception, as though it were not a mere fact, but something far-reaching and impalpable, like the true expression of an emotion or the emergence of a principle" (N 107). Within the Sulaco Province Charles's most influential political ally is Don José Avellanos, a patriotic, liberal aristocrat, and the "Nestor-inspirer" (N 144) of the Blanco party. Avellanos has had a long, distinguished career as ambassador to various European nations and has suffered atrociously under one of Costaguana's most bloodthirsty dictators, Guzman Bento. Although he is by now "too old to descend personally into the centre of the arena at Sta. Marta" (N 140), the capital of Costaguana, Avellanos is still powerful and knows how to pull strings in the higher political spheres. Don José regards the alliance with Gould as his last chance to realize his desire to bring to the country "peace, prosperity, and [...] "an honourable place in the comity of civilized nations"" (N 140). Charles's chief financial backer is the North American tycoon Holroyd. The latter refers to Costaguana as "the bottomless pit of 10 per cent. loans and other fool investments" (N 76-77) but lets himself be swayed by Gould's determination and competence.

In a very short time the mine becomes a huge success. Gould seems to be proved right not only in his belief that the silver will spread security and stability across the province but also in his confidence in being able to channel and mould material interests according to his plans. The number of miners, who mainly belong to the most exploited section of Costaguana society, the Indians, quickly rises to "over six hundred" (N, 100): "Whole families had been moving from the first towards the spot in the Higuerota range, whence the rumour of work and safety had spread over the pastoral Campo, forcing its way also [...] into the nooks and crannies of the distant blue walls of the Sierras" (N 101). The area of the mine soon becomes, as Don José calls it, an "Imperium in imperio" (N 111), consisting of three mining villages, a hospital, a presbytery, a miners' chapel, a store house, and other administrative buildings. The miners become a noticeable new segment of Sulaco society and their presence alters

> the outward character of the crowds on feast days [...] by the number of white ponchos with a green stripe affected as holiday wear by the San Tomé miners. They had also adopted white hats with green cord and braid [...]. A peaceable Cholo wearing these colours [...] was somehow very seldom beaten to within an inch of his life on a charge of disrespect to the town police; neither ran he much risk of being suddenly lassoed on the road by a recruiting party of lanceros – a method of voluntary enlistment looked upon as almost legal in the Republic. (N 97)

The mine has thus greatly improved the situation of the poorest of the poor in Sualco and it seems justified that the mine's colours are white and green – green being, of course, the colour of hope. Every three months the "increasing stream of treasure" (N 115) is brought down to the harbour from the San Tomé mountain and is shipped to North America. For both the Goulds "each passing of the [silver] escort under the balconies of the Casa Gould [is] like another victory gained in the conquest of peace for Sulaco" (N 115). Soon the mine turns into an

> institution, a rallying point for everything in the province that needed order and stability to live. Security seemed to flow upon this land from the mountain-gorge. The authorities of Sulaco had learned that the San Tomé mine could make it worth their while to leave things and people alone. This was the nearest approach to the rule of common-sense and justice Charles Gould felt it possible to secure at first. (N 110)

Revealingly, Charles acquires the nickname "King of Sulaco" (N 93). Despite his success, Gould still feels hampered and humiliated by "the mire of corruption that was so universal as to almost lose its significance" (N 85). This is why, together with Don José Avellanos and after "confidential communications" with "the head of the silver and steel interests far away in California" (N 143), he decides to finance another revolution to bring about the (supposedly) five-year dictatorship of Don Vincente Ribiera, "a man of culture and of unblemished character, invested with a mandate of reform by the best elements of the State" (N 117). Ribiera is "a doctor of philosophy from the Cordova University" (N 144) and the "first civilian Chief of the

State Costaguana had ever known" (N 119). His five-year mandate encourages foreign investment and the material interests in Sulaco gather substance more and more rapidly: there is "a loan to the State, and a project for systematic colonization of the Occidental Province, involved in one vast scheme with the construction of the National Central Railway" (N 117). Sir John, an influential financier and chairman of the London railway board, travels in person to Costaguana to ensure that the government keeps to the conditions of the loan and that the construction of the railway goes forward as planned. The turning-of-the-first-sod celebration in the Sulaco harbour, at which the complete new ruling elite of Costaguana is present, is Charles Gould's greatest triumph. It seems that his faith in material interests to establish "law, good faith, order, security" (N 84) and to give a progressive direction to the country's history is vindicated.

However, about six months after the inaugural celebrations the Sulaco capitalists suffer an almost fatal setback. In the capital Santa Marta a revolution led by General Montero, the former Blanco military chief, and his brother breaks out which threatens to engulf the whole country. The Monterists are completely insincere but effective demagogues who claim to be for the people and against the aristocrats and foreign capitalists that are flooding the country. Although the Occidental Province is at first hardly touched by the revolutionary upheavals, it is "in the very forefront of the defence with men and money" (N 146). The situation changes dramatically when news reaches Sulaco that the capital is in the hands of Montero and that Ribiera is fleeing across the mountains. With pressure mounting on all sides and a Monterist invasion imminent, the Sulaco intellectual and journalist Martin Decoud comes up with the only possible way out for the Blancos: the secession of the Occidental Province from Costaguana. Decoud's plan is not only inspired by Sulaco's isolated geographical position but also by the various forces present in the province which, in alliance, might be able to defeat the Monterist invasion: the Blanco aristocrats, the capitalists, and their overseas backers; the miners, the railway engineers, and imported workers; the dockers and employees of the Oceanic Steam Company; General Barrios and his army; Hernandez, the bandit, and his well-organised mounted gang whose support the Blancos have bought. This time Charles Gould is forced to commit himself openly to the Sulaco revolution and clinches the alliance with promises of financial rewards. He feels debased by the sordid compromises he is obliged to make but realizes that he would do anything – even blow up the mine – to save his enterprise. Eventually, the Blanco forces manage to defeat Montero and the Costaguana-Sulaco War is ended by "an international naval demonstration" led by the "United States cruiser,

Powhatten, [which] was the first to salute the Occidental flag" (N 487). The novel does not describe the Blanco victory but shows its effects about six years later when Captain Mitchell takes a group of businessmen on a guided tour of the new Sulaco. We thus witness all the changes that the development of material interests has brought to the province. There are now "cable cars running along the streets of the Constitution, and carriage roads far into the country [...] where the foreign merchants and the Ricos generally have their modern villas, and a vast railway goods yard by the harbour" (N 95). There is a new Custom House, a Sulaco National Bank, and new clubs and bars for "mining engineers and businessmen" (N 474). The mine has greatly expanded as well and its "territory, containing gold, silver, copper, lead, cobalt, extends for miles along the foot-hills of the Cordillera" (N 504). Although at the end of the novel there are hints at new unrest and revolutionary agitation, the young Republic appears prosperous and stable.

If this summary of the main events of *Nostromo* were the gist of the representation of the historical process in the novel, one could indeed conclude that, at the end of the narrative, Gould's belief in material interests is vindicated. Through the introduction of capitalism as the driving force of events, he has managed to break – at least in Sulaco – the vicious circle of revolution and counter-revolution and has created the possibility of a linear, progressive, and goal-oriented development. *Nostromo* would thus be in line with nineteenth-century Whig historiography and would bear out the theories of Adam Smith, Herbert Spencer, Lord Macaulay, H.T. Buckle and others. The implied attitude towards the freedom-of-the-will-problem would be a compatibilist one: although materialist forces circumscribe our lives, we have enough freedom to understand how they work and to use and mould them to our advantage. Some critics have indeed read *Nostromo* in such a manner. Robert Penn Warren, for instance, analyses the denouement of *Nostromo* as follows: "There has been a civil war, but the forces of 'progress' – that is the San Tomé mine and the capitalistic order – have won. And we must admit that the society at the end of the book is preferable to that of the beginning" (584). This rings especially true if one takes as "the beginning" Guzman Bento's savage tyranny or the various civil wars and as "the end" the period of regeneration, stability, and rule of law in the years following the War of Separation. Certain sections of Sulaco's society, such as the Indians, have without doubt also profited from material progress. The mine has not only given them employment but has become for them a source of "well-being, security, and justice" (N 397). Furthermore, the capitalist Sualco is certainly preferable to an arbitrary Monterist dictatorship.

However, such a view of the central developments neglects aspects of the novel which should also influence the evaluation of the representation of the historical process: the pervasive scepticism as to whether material interests really bring progress; the disillusioned views of some of the protagonists of the events they are involved in; the characters' general inability to control the materialist forces they come into contact with; the nature of the society portrayed; or the function of the novel's formal complexities. What should also make us suspicious of a teleological reading of Costaguana's history is the actual presence of two historians in the novel whose Whig view of history is clearly revealed to be inadequate. One of them, the aristocrat and former diplomat, Don José Avellanos, believes in constitutionalism, national unity, and political probity. Before the War of Separation he was just putting the finishing touches to his history of Costaguana called *Fifty Years of Misrule*. In it Avellanos tries to give meaning to his country's bloody and chaotic history by fitting it into a liberal and progressive conceptual framework. Its aim is to show that Costaguana is moving towards prosperity and civilization in a meaningful and linear fashion. The first highpoint of this development is supposed to be the Ribiera-Administration, which both Avellanos and Gould have been instrumental in bringing about. The degree to which Avellanos has to distort historical occurrences to suit his agenda can be gauged from his attempt to find a meaningful place even for one of Costaguana's most bloodthirsty dictators, Guzman Bento, under whom Don José himself suffered terribly (cf. N 142). That Avellanos's perspective on his country's history is just wishful thinking and an ideologically biased interpretation becomes obvious when Ribiera is toppled by the Monterists, which, in turn, leads to the secession of Sulaco. The old aristocrat is completely broken by these events and dies soon afterwards. It is not clear whether he actually condones Decoud's idea of an independent Occidental Republic, which would mean the abandonment of one of his most cherished political principles, national unity. On a metaphorical level Avellanos's view of history is cruelly mocked by the way the first copies of his book, fresh from the Blanco press, are treated by the Monterist rebels. As Decoud exclaims,

[H]asn't he seen the sheets of 'Fifty Years of Misrule' [...] littering the Plaza, floating in the gutters, fired out as wads for trabucos loaded with handfuls of type, blown in the wind, trampled in the mud? I have seen pages floating upon the very waters of the harbour. (N 235)

The second character in the novel who fulfils the role of a historian is the pompous but likeable Captain Mitchell, appropriately nicknamed "Fussy Joe" (N 10). Twice in the novel he takes a group of distinguished foreign visitors on a tour of Sulaco, joyfully relating all the 'historic' occasions he witnessed during the past years. Whereas Don José consciously moulds Costaguana's history to fit his beliefs and purposes, Captain Mitchell unthinkingly repeats Blanco propaganda. He is, as Hillis Miller puts it, the unwitting "spokesperson for an exemplary "official history," with its naïve conception of "historical events" as following one another in a comprehensible linear and causal succession" (""Material Interests"" 161). This becomes particularly noticeable during Mitchell's second appearance as a tour guide towards the close of the novel when he not only points out all the signs of economic prosperity but also draws attention to the new national monuments and rituals that are meant to give solidity and permanence to the Blancos' version of past events. Mitchell's tale of heroic martyrs and glorious victories is ironically undercut not only by the narrator's contemptuous view of Fussy Joe but also by the novel's form: its unchronological placement immediately after the relation of the chaos of the War of Separation and immediately before that of Decoud's suicide makes the account resemble a complacent fiction. By thus revealing Mitchell's and Avellanos's 'histories' as ideologically motivated constructs, *Nostromo* can be said to mock the inadequateness of bourgeois/capitalist historiography in general. For these reasons we should reject the Whig view of history and its compatibilist position with regard to free will and determinism as a suitable interpretative framework. Because the characters in the novel appear so exclusively determined by one particular force – materialism, in the shape of the ubiquitous silver – many critics have turned to Marxism as a key to reading the novel.

6.2   The Marxist view of history

According to Cedric Watts (cf. *Nostromo* 69) it is in particular three elements in the novel that bring Marxism to mind. Firstly, the recurrent emphasis on economics as a key to history and the suggestion that the quest for material gain provides the base beneath the ideological superstructure of society. Secondly, the implication that the success of the protagonists' schemes depends on their compatibility with global economic forces. Thirdly, the stress the novel puts on the ways in which a state's political apparatus can be manipulated in the interests of the wealthy. To these elements should be added the novel's presentation of its characters as representatives of types and classes rather than as fully-fledged individuals and the frequent suggestion that they are mere puppets of larger, impersonal forces.

A summary of *Nostromo* from a Marxist perspective might start out by highlighting that Costaguana, as a typical South American country, has been subject to European economic exploitation since the Spanish Conquest in the fifteenth century. The novel not only frequently draws attention to this long history of foreign interference but establishes many parallels between the *conquistadores* of old and the new influx of European capitalists in the late nineteenth century. As Jacques Berthoud points out, one of the principal reminders of Spanish colonial rule is the city of Sulaco itself, whose ground plan "reduplicates the structure of virtually all the fifty-odd cities founded by Spain between 1498 and 1550" ("Sulaco" 145). These cities were designed "to operate as engines for extracting wealth, particularly silver and gold" (Berthoud, "Sulaco" 148). The attraction of Sulaco lies in the San Tomé silver mine, whose history the reader is acquainted with in the course of the novel:

> Worked in the early days mostly by means of lashes on the backs of slaves, its yield had been paid for in its own weight of human bones. Whole tribes of Indians had perished in the exploitation; and then the mine was abandoned, since with this primitive method it had ceased to make a profitable return, no matter how many corpses were thrown into its maw. (N 52)

In general, the Spanish-American colonies functioned as mere instruments of colonial mercantilism and were thus not able to establish their own markets and their independence. Their economies remained confined to the export of raw materials in exchange for manufactured goods and their social structures were controlled by an overseas bureaucratic elite and quasi-feudal landlords owning enormous estates. During Mrs Gould's travels around the Occidental Province she realizes that the early colonisation of the country was exclusively based on materialist greed and contempt for human life: "The heavy stonework of bridges and churches left by the conquerors proclaimed the disregard of human labour, the tribute-labour of vanished nations" (N 89). However, the rapacity, inhumanity, and ruthless exercise of power remained the salient characteristics of the tumultuous history of Costaguana even after the Spanish colonial yoke had been thrown off. According to Berthoud, one of the reasons for this development was that after the War of Independence the South American countries remained conditioned by their colonial identities (cf. "Sulaco" 149-150). This applies not only to the immature political scene and the arbitrary conception of government displayed by the countries' leaders but also to the influx of foreign investors, entrepreneurs, and adventurers, which increased after the disappearance of mercantilism.

When Charles and Emilia Gould come to Sulaco, the constant sequence of revolutions, civil wars, and dictatorships has long been accepted as "something inherent in the nature of things," even "by people of intelligence, refinement, and character" (N 109). Charles Gould, however, is – at least at the beginning of his venture – determined to effect a complete change by developing the economic resources of the country on an unprecedented scale. Charles thereby knows himself to be in tune with emerging global capitalism in the wake of imperialism and with the technological progress of the nineteenth century. He knows that, even if his own project fails, "the great silver and iron interests shall survive, and some day shall get hold of Costaguana along with the rest of the world" (N 82). A similar position is taken up by Charles's backer, the North American tycoon Holroyd, who sees himself as an agent of that divine destiny or inevitable development which will lead the United States to a position in which she can exercise global control in all areas through sheer economic clout:

> Of course, some day we shall step in. We are bound to. But there's no hurry. Time itself has got to wait on the greatest country in the whole of God's Universe. We shall be giving the word for everything: industry, trade, law, journalism, art, politics, and religion, from Cape Horn clear over to Smith's Sound, and beyond, too, if anything worth taking hold of turns up at the North Pole. And then we shall have the leisure to take in hand the outlying islands and continents of the earth. We shall run the world's business whether the world likes it or not. The world can't help it – and neither can we, I guess. (N 77)

Although the last sentence shows that Holroyd is dimly aware that even he is not in complete control of historical-economic forces, this does not bother him. He is buoyed by the complacent compatibilist attitude towards free will and determinism typical of the adherents of the Victorian ideology of progress. The narrator takes a scathing view of Holroyd and his smug, uncritical attitude towards his undertakings and comments that – in a manner similar to Kurtz – it was "all Europe" that contributed to the making of Holroyd:

> [H]is massive profile was the profile of a Caesar's head on an old Roman coin. But his parentage was German and Scotch and English, with remote strains of Danish and French blood, giving him the temperament of a Puritan and an insatiable imagination of conquest. (N 76)

Metaphorically speaking, Holroyd thus not only looks back to the age of 'classic' European colonialism – military conquest followed by trade – but also forward to the new 'American-century', for which a form of global economic imperialism would become characteristic. Although Holroyd remains in the background throughout *Nostromo* we are frequently made aware that without him the working of the mine, the setting up of the Ribiera dictatorship, and the establishment of the Occidental Republic would not have been possible.

As Holroyd is after all a minor character the question whether it is he who controls large-scale economic processes or whether it is they that control him is not examined in detail. The case is different with Charles Gould: his development can be read as a case study of the precarious relationship between an individual will and a vast impersonal force, capitalism. When he first arrives in Sulaco, Charles is convinced that his project will be all the more successful *because* it is in tune with worldwide economic trends. He regards the wealth of the mine "as a means, not as an end" (N 75) and believes that he is only making use of what he sees. Although Charles's initial success seems to vindicate his idealism, a number of factors soon throw doubts on his probity. To go about his business unmolested, Charles, for instance, has to resort to large-scale bribery and intrigue in the corrupt Costaguana style he so abhors: "The Gould Concession had to fight for life with such weapons as could be found at once in the mire of corruption that was so universal as to almost lose its significance. He was prepared to stoop for his weapons" (N 85). Thus the San Tomé mine, for instance, has "its own unofficial pay list, whose items and amounts [are] fixed in consultation by Charles Gould and Señor Avellanos" (N 116). Charles feels debased by these methods and, for a moment at least, suspects that "the silver mine, which had killed his father, had decoyed him further than he meant to go" (N 85). Nevertheless he decides to try and rid himself from his subjection to the country's corruption by financing a Blanco revolution. This not only appeases his outraged sense of right but is also sound business policy: the working of the mine will become more profitable and the floodgates of foreign investment will be opened. Indeed, in due course, a loan to the State is floated, the construction of the National Central Railway is begun, and telegraph lines are laid. *Nostromo* leaves no doubt that the new dictator, Don Vincente Ribiera, is merely a puppet on a string: he is, as Sir John puts it, the Blancos' "own creature" (N 38). Behind Ribiera is the politician Avellanos, behind Avellanos the capitalist Gould, and behind Gould the tycoon Holroyd. It is characteristic of this chain of dependencies that the Ribierist party can only take "practical shape under the eye of the administrator of the San Tomé mine" after Holroyd has given his assent and a credit has been opened "by the Third Southern Bank (located next door but one to the Holroyd Building)" (N 143). That the Ribiera-dictatorship has been set up by Blanco capitalists with the backing of foreign investors and with the primary aim of maximising profits remains implicit in the book version of *Nostromo* but is made explicit in the serial version, which appeared in *T.P.'s Weekly*:

> The Señor Administrador of the Gould concession was pleased with the wording of the Five-year Mandate, which suspended the fundamental laws of the estate [sic], but at the same time aimed at keeping private ambitions from interfering in the work of economic reconstruction. Peace at home and credit abroad! Nothing could be more sane. This was not politics; it was the common-sense watchword of material interests which, once established, would safeguard the honest working of these political institutions which, sound in themselves, had been the shield of plundering demagogues. (quoted in Watts, *Nostromo* 53)

The "fundamental laws" of Costaguana are suspended so that the capitalists can develop their ventures without interference. The passage also highlights Gould's increasing hypocrisy: although he originally wanted to inaugurate an era of justice, peace, and progress he has intrigued to establish yet another dictatorship. Charles's belief that material interests will somehow by themselves safeguard the probity of political institutions is shocking in its naïveté.

It is from the installation of the new dictator and the ensuing "systematic colonization of the Occidental Province" (N 117) onwards that the much-vaunted material progress takes on a life of its own and becomes threatening and sinister. The new telegraph poles, for instance, are said to bear a wire which is "like a slender, vibrating feeler of that progress waiting outside for a moment of peace to enter and twine itself about the weary heart of the land" (N 166). In another passage a "locomotive" takes on a nightmarish life of its own as it rolls quickly out of sight "under a white trail of steam that seem[s] to vanish in the breathless, hysterically prolonged scream of warlike triumph" (N 171-172). The notion of capitalism as a panacea for Costaguana's problems is further undermined by the suggestion that the exploits of entrepreneurs such as Charles Gould are essentially the same as those of the *conquistadores* a few centuries earlier. One of the old gateways into Sulaco, for example, bears "a grey, heavily scrolled, armorial shield of stone above the apex of the arch with the arms of Spain nearly smoothed out as if in readiness for some new device typical of the impending progress" (N 173). Although the names and symbols may change the economic exploitation that they are meant to disguise, remains essentially the same. This idea is also present in the nickname Charles Gould acquires, "King of Sulaco" (N 93). He not only has absolute control over the mine, which covers a huge area and is referred to by Don José Avellanos as an "*Imperium in imperio*" (N 111), but his reign also spreads across the Province and, after the Ribierist coup, across the whole country. It is not surprising, therefore, that at one point Gould is

compared to Charles IV of Spain, the last of the Spanish emperors of South
America:

> His way would lie along the old Spanish road – the Camino Real [= Royal Road] of popular
> speech – the only remaining vestige of a fact and name left by that royalty [...] whose very
> shadow had departed from the land; for the big equestrian statue of Charles IV at the
> entrance of the Alameda [...] was only known [...] as the Horse of Stone. The other Carlos
> [...] looked as incongruous, but much more at home than the kingly cavalier reining in his
> steed on the pedestal [...]. (N 48-49)

Later in the novel, when Gould puts himself at the head of what he calls "a
provincial revolution" (N 379) in order to save the mine and all it stands for,
he realizes that he is, in fact, no different from the foreign exploiters and
adventurers of old:

> After all, with his English parentage and English upbringing, he perceived that he was an
> adventurer in Costaguana, the descendant of adventurers enlisted in a foreign legion, of men
> who had sought fortune in a revolutionary war, who had planned revolutions, who had
> believed in revolutions. For all the uprightness of his character, he had something of an
> adventurer's easy morality [...]. (N 365)

That the development of material interests progresses not quite as smoothly
and unproblematically as the Blancos have hoped is driven home to them
only half a year after the Ribierist triumph. General Montero and his brother
Pedrito, motivated by boundless vanity and rapacity, instigate another
revolution in the capital. The slogans the Monterists employ are reminiscent
of Marxist rhetoric: they oppose the "sinister land-grabbing designs of
European powers" and condemn "the "miserable Ribiera," who [has] plotted
to deliver his country, bound hand and foot, for a prey to foreign speculators"
(N 146). Although *Nostromo* leaves no doubt that the Monterists are
insincere and cynical demagogues, the novel also shows that there is a grain
of truth in their propaganda. For instance, when the narrator describes the
"systematic colonization" (N 117) of the Province, he ironically tells us that
"the ignorant were beginning to murmur that the Ribierist reforms meant
simply the taking away of the land from the people. Some of it was to be
given to foreigners who made the railway; the greater part was to go to the
padres" (N 195). This statement is borne out by the activities of the fanatical
Catholic priest, Father Corbelán, whose "idea of political honour, justice, and
honesty [...] consists in the restitution of the confiscated Church property"
(N 188-189). Another instance is the ruthless behaviour of the ostensibly
civilized and sophisticated Sir John, the British financier and head of the
London railway board. To acquire land for the railway he resorts to bribery
and would not even shy away from violent means: "The Government was

bound to carry out its part of the contract with the board of the new railway company, even if it had to use force for the purpose" (N 37). The consequences of the new distribution of property for the populace become clear on the occasion of a colourful traditional festival held on the Campo near the harbour. Charles Gould, who witnesses the celebrations, comments nonchalantly, "All this piece of land belongs now to the Railway Company. There will be no more popular feasts held here" (N 123).

The period between the Monterist coup in Santa Marta, the invasion of Sulaco, the Blanco counter-revolution, and the establishment of the independent Occidental Republic appears tumultuous and chaotic. Marxist critics have attempted to make sense of these events by analysing them in terms of conflicts and allegiances between the various classes that make up Sulaco society. Gareth Jenkins (cf. 161), for instance, distinguishes between six different classes: (1) the indigenous Indians, of whom many work for the San Tomé mine and who will become the new proletariat; (2) the poor farmers and peasants who work on the Campo and are so oppressed by changing governments that banditry such as Hernandez's arises; (3) the impoverished and brutalized workforce that forms the 'mob' and 'rabble' responsible for the riot in Sulaco and that later follows Pedrito Montero when he makes his entrance into the town;[12] (4) what Jenkins calls the "aristocracy of labour" (161), consisting of both the native *cargadores* handpicked by Nostromo and the imported European workers, mainly Italians, employed by the O.S.N. and the National Central Railway; (5) small shop-keepers, merchants, and traders, comprising both the Blanco Anzani, the general store owner on the main plaza of Sulaco, and the Monterist Gamacho, the ex-pedlar, who becomes a kind of disreputable tribune of the people; (6) the conservative landowners, aristocrats, and members of the bourgeoisie, which include capitalists such as Gould, high-ranking Churchmen such as Corbelán, politicians such as Don José Avellanos, and intellectuals such as Martin Decoud. In addition to these six classes, Jenkins (cf. 161) adds three other groups that play decisive roles in the shaping of events: the army, the government bureaucracy, and non-Costaguaneros such as the English engineers who have no direct financial stake in the country but serve imperialist-capitalist concerns.

The Blanco victory comes about by a coalition between these classes, motivated either by direct financial dependence or by common economic interests. It is characteristic of the nature of this alliance that, due to class

---

[12]   Fleishman refers to that group as "Lazarones" or "Lumpenproletariat" (*Conrad's Politics* 166).

antagonisms, it breaks apart fairly soon after the establishment of the Republic of Sulaco. Conspicuous is also the acceptance of Hernandez, the robber, into the Blanco fold. The narrator clearly relishes the irony that the turning of "a bandit into a general [was the] memorable last official act of the Ribierist party, whose watchwords were honesty, peace, and progress" (N 352-353). Although it is Father Corbelán who pleads the case for "that most pious robber" (N 352), it is left to Charles Gould, practically the only person with genuine power left in the Province, to clinch the deal by promising financial support. The negotiations with Hernandez's emissary reveal the idealism with which Gould has surrounded his capitalist venture as an illusion:

> "Has not the master of the mine any message to send to Hernandez, the master of the Campo?"
> The truth of the comparison struck Charles Gould heavily. In his determined purpose he held the mine, and the indomitable bandit held the Campo by the same precarious tenure. They were equals before the lawlessness of the land. It was impossible to disentangle one's activity from its debasing contacts. (N 360)

It is this encounter that makes Charles Gould realize that his project has, in its moral essence, failed. He has not been able to channel material interests for any other than economic ends and not even they are under his control. As regards his implicit stance towards free will and determinism, Charles has to recognize that his hitherto complacent compatibilist attitude corresponding to the ideology of progress is not adequate to account for his present experience of complete lack of control. Although Charles is dimly aware of his failure, he also knows that he cannot stop now. The materialist forces he has unleashed have him under their control and his thoughts and acts start to resemble those of a monomaniac or, indeed, a terrorist (cf. Fleishman, *Conard's Politics* 181). After all, Gould is prepared to "blow up the whole San Tomé mountain sky high out of the territory of the Republic" (N 365) rather than let it fall into the hands of the Monterists. He imagines himself to be writing "in letters of fire" (N 379) to Holroyd, declaring that he has been "forced to take up openly the plan of a provincial revolution as the only way of placing the enormous material interests involved in the prosperity and peace of Sulaco in a position of permanent safety" (N 379). Although it is not clear whether such a letter is sent, Holroyd's support manifests itself in an "international naval demonstration" led by the "United States cruiser, *Powhatten*" (N 487), which brings the Sulaco-Costaguana war to a conclusion. That Britain and the United States support an independent Sulaco is historically plausible. As Berthoud explains, by the end of the nineteenth century foreign finance [...] was in control of the economies of the [South American] continent. With the London market in the lead, it owned all the shipping lines and submarine cables, nearly all the railways, many of the harbours, etc.; and a large number of corporations – especially from the United States in northern South America – were engaged in mining metals. ("Sulaco" 153)

Cedric Watts (cf. *Nostromo* 24) also points out that the detail of the United States as "the first great power to recognize the Occidental Republic" (N 485) is an astute reference to the emergence of economic imperialism of the North American kind at the end of the nineteenth century. Watts draws attention to the parallels between the secession of Sulaco from Costaguana and of Panama from Colombia. The latter was also made possible by the arrival of a warship from the United States eager to control the Panama Canal. *Nostromo* leaves no doubt that America supports the manufacturing of a new state to get a better deal for investors such as Holroyd and to ensure that the new country will be stable and tractable in dealing with American business.

When Captain Mitchell, the purveyor of Sulaco's 'official history', takes his guests on a tour of the capital about six years after the defeat of the Monterists, he praises the economic prosperity and stability of the young Republic. The narrator, however, undermines Mitchell's account by juxtaposing it to examples of how the vaunted material progress has degraded or even destroyed the lives of most of the protagonists. Emilia Gould, for instance, memorably describes the effect her husband's exploitation of the mine has had on their private lives:

[S]he would never have [Charles] to herself. [...] [S]he saw clearly the San Tomé mine possessing, consuming, burning up the life of the last of the Costaguana Goulds; mastering the energetic spirit of the son as it had mastered the lamentable weakness of the father. [...] An immense desolation, the dread of her own continued life, descended upon the first lady of Sulaco. With a prophetic vision she saw herself surviving alone the degradation of her young ideal of life, of love, of work – all alone in the Treasure House of the World. (N 521-522)

However, not just on a private but also on a public level Mrs Gould comes to view her husband's endeavours as a failure, in particular his initial idealistic plan to use the wealth of the mine as the material means to an immaterial and moral end: "She saw the San Tomé mountain hanging over the Campo, over the whole land, feared, hated, wealthy; more soulless than any tyrant, more pitiless and autocratic than the worst Government; ready to crush innumerable lives in the expansion of its greatness" (N 521). In its bleakness this passage is reminiscent of Conrad's comparison of the universe to an inhuman knitting machine that determines our lives by iron necessity. Similarly, for Emilia, the San Tomé mine has taken on a destructive existence of its own, grinding along inexorably without reference to human lives or values. Dr. Monygham supports her view by claiming that there can be "no peace and no rest in the development of material interests. They have their law, and their justice. But it is founded on expediency, and is inhuman" (N 511). Mrs Gould's and Dr. Monygham's analysis is corroborated by the many hints at the end of the novel that the stability of the Occidental Republic will only be temporary. We first hear about new unrest and new revolutionary agitation from Captain Mitchell:

> The Democratic party in opposition rests mostly [...] on these socialistic Italians [...] with their secret societies, camorras, and such-like. There are lots of Italians settled here on the railway lands, dismissed navvies, mechanics, and so on, all along the trunk line. There are whole villages of Italians on the Campo. And the natives, too, are being drawn into these ways... (N 479)

The Italians have originally been 'imported' to build the railway. Now that this project is largely completed, they have been made redundant and feel underprivileged. They have become class-conscious and organize themselves politically to fight their former employers. A significant development is Mitchell's hint at an alliance between the natives and the Europeans, between whom there has been no contact before. Furthermore, there is labour trouble at the mine. Dr. Monygham reveals as much in a conversation with Mrs Gould when he asks rhetorically, "Do you think that now the mine would march upon the town to save their Señor Administrador?" (N 511). The last glimpse we have of Charles Gould in the novel is when he starts for the mountains as "[t]here is some trouble with the workmen to be feared" (N 555). By turning the Indians into miners Charles has created a new proletariat that has now become conscious of its status and demands its rights. A third dangerous element of instability is the precarious relationship between the Occidental Republic and Costaguana. As Monygham explains the (now) Cardinal-Archbishop Corbelán and Antonia Avellanos, who passionately believe in national unity, "are conspiring with the refugees from Sta. Marta" (N 510) for the invasion of Costaguana and seek support from "the secret societies amongst immigrants and natives" (N 511).

As Cedric Watts summarizes, Marxist critics have read the dénouement of *Nostromo* as a demonstration of the way in which

> capitalism, emerging from feudalism, re-shapes in its own interests the political institutions of a country, thrives and prospers for a while, but eventually, through the tendency to monopoly and the creation of a vast and discontented work-force, reaches the phase of internal contradictions which ensures its own downfall. (*Nostromo* 71)

The capitalist order of the Occidental Republic at the end of the novel is thus regarded as an intermediary phase. According to Marxists, the next revolution, which can already be sensed in the closing pages of the novel, will be a proletarian one and will bring better justice for the Costaguaneros. Avrom Fleishman thus reads *Nostromo* as "a record of the transition from a precapitalist to capitalist – and, prospectively, to post-capitalist – society" (*Conrad's Politics* 171). He points out the irony that Gould, by turning the Indians into miners and by forming an alliance with Hernandez and his peasant band, "must become a party to the future proletarian revolution in the very process of securing the capitalist-backed separatist revolution" (*Conrad's Politics*, 167). Irving Howe goes even further than Fleishman and claims that *Nostromo* "verifies [...] Leon Trotsky's theory of the 'permanent revolution'" (101): the bourgeois separatist revolution is a necessary one but it breeds new, capitalist evils which generate a proletarian revolution leading to the final stage of progress, the socialist utopia. Although the events in *Nostromo* may appear chaotic, Marxist critics detect in them signs of an inevitable, goal-oriented process rigidly determined by economic determinism, which, they believe, also drives history. Although progress in a bourgeois/capitalist sense is denied, there is hope for it in a Marxist sense if the events depicted lead to a proletarian revolution that manages to establish a socialist state. The question, however, is whether the novel actually provides any grounds for the hope that a socialist revolution would lead to more justice and stability and whether any characters are depicted that could actually serve as leaders or inspirers of a socialist movement.

Conspicuously, towards the end of the novel, a genuine Marxist puts in an appearance. However, like Donkin, the trade union agitator in *The Nigger of the 'Narcissus'*, he is a despicable creature. When he presides at one of the socialist meetings that take place in honour of Nostromo in Sulaco he is described as "an indigent, sickly, somewhat hunchbacked little photographer, with a white face and a magnanimous soul dyed crimson by a bloodthirsty hate of all capitalists, oppressors of the two hemispheres" (N 528). When Nostromo lies dying, the Marxist is the only one with him. As is typical of Conrad's characterisations of villainous or detestable minor characters, the Marxist is compared to an animal. He perches upon a stool, "shock-headed, wildly hairy, like a hunchbacked monkey" (N 562). The Marxist is thus reminiscent of the vulture, "this patient watcher for the signs of death and corruption" (N 413), that observes "with an air of voracious anxiety" (N 413) the slumbering Nostromo just back from the silver exploit in the Golfo Placido. Revealingly, the main reason for the Marxist's presence at Nostromo's death-bed is not pity or compassion but the request to bequeath his wealth to the socialist cause. He argues that "[t]he rich must be fought with their own weapons" (N 562). Although, at first glance, this appeal may appear reasonable, we are reminded of Charles Gould, who had also regarded the wealth of the mine as a weapon in his fight for a "better justice" but who had to learn that it is "dangerous to the wielder, too" and is "always ready to turn awkwardly in the hand" (N 365). In general, the novel is full of characters whose judgment is corrupted by the silver or the prospect of possessing it. Therefore there is little hope that the Marxist would be less "short-sighted in good and evil" ("Author's Note" ix) than the others. This is also indicated by his enquiry whether Monygham is "really a dangerous enemy of the people" (N 563). The grim irony implicit in this question is that the doctor, who has suffered once already under Guzman Bento, might suffer again in the future at the hands of someone proclaiming the liberation of the oppressed. Although the Marxist's beliefs may be ideologically sounder than the empty, hypocritical rhetoric of the Monterists, it is likely that even if a proletarian revolution took place in Sulaco, the story of bloodshed and exploitation would continue.

A character Marxist critics often regard as a promising representative of the emerging new proletariat and the new socialist communities in Sulaco is Nostromo. Irving Howe, for instance, claims that Nostromo's "history anticipates those fissures of consciousness that will soon work their way through the masses, his estrangement [from the capitalists] represents the dawning realization of distinct class interests and sharpening class antagonisms" (108). Fleishman goes even further and regards Nostromo's development throughout the novel as representative of

> an entire class, the proletariat – its enlistment and exploitation in the industrialisation of the country, its entry into the separatist revolution (fighting for class interests not directly its own), its growth of self-consciousness and discovery of an independent political role, its temptation by the materialistic drives of capitalism, and its purgation by traditional idealists in its own camp. (*Conrad's Politics* 163-164)

A closer look at Nostromo's career reveals, however, that the actual evidence for these readings is slight. When we first come across the eponymous hero, he works for Captain Mitchell as foreman of the dockers. He is so successful and reliable that Mitchell develops "[a] mania for 'lending you my Capataz de Cargadores'" which, in turn, brings "Nostromo into personal contact [...] with every European in Sulaco, as a sort of universal factotum – a prodigy of efficiency in his own sphere of life" (N 44). Nostromo does not display any political interests or class consciousness and does not seem to mind being *nostre uomo*, our man, to the ruling elite as long as this enhances his reputation, which seems to be the only thing he cares about. Throughout the novel almost all of Nostromo's important actions are in the interests of the capitalists: he rescues the fleeing ex-dictator Ribiera, he suppresses the riot of the mob, he delivers the message to Hernandez which turns him into a supporter of the Blanco cause, he removes the silver from Sulaco to save it from seizure, and he rides to Cayta to summon General Barrios's troops to defeat the Monterists and bring about the secession. These are reasons why Decoud refers to Nostromo as the "active usher-in of the material implements for our progress" (N 191). It is only towards the end of the novel that Nostromo distances himself from the Blancos. The turning point comes when – after he has left Decoud and the load of silver on the Great Isabel – Nostromo wakes up in a Sulaco which is in the hands of the Monterists. He realizes that in this new political situation the only thing he ever cared about, his reputation, is irretrievably lost. He also understands how intimately his fate is intertwined with that of the Blancos and that from now on he will be regarded as "a marked Ribierist for any sort of vengeance Gamacho, for instance, would choose to take, now the Montero party had, after all, mastered the town" (N 417). For the first time he grasps that he has been used by the Blancos all along as a "perfect handy man" (N 320), a cogwheel in the capitalist machinery but has not been treated as an individual in his own right. The Blancos have taken it for granted that he would risk his life for a load of silver whose loss is of no great consequence to its owners. Nostromo feels betrayed and that his "fidelity [has] been taken advantage of" (N 417). All of a sudden he remembers old Viola's teachings: "Kings, ministers, aristocrats, the rich in general, kept the people in poverty and subjection; they kept them as they kept dogs, to fight and hunt for their service" (N 415). It is primarily this insight into his class status as an exploited worker and his patronage of socialist meetings later on why Marxist critics see Nostromo as an embodiment of the working class and its development. The novel, however, seems to emphasise not so much Nostromo's allegiance to a certain class or political ideology but his subjection to the silver which he decides to keep for himself. Whereas before his theft Nostromo regarded the silver more as an accoutrement of his great reputation, he now becomes enslaved by its material nature:

> His audacity, greater than that of other men, had welded that vein of silver into his life. And the feeling of fearful and ardent subjection, the feeling of his slavery – so irremediable and profound that often, in his thoughts, he compared himself to the legendary Gringos, neither dead nor alive, bound down to their conquest of unlawful wealth on Azuera - weighted heavily on the independent Captain Fidanza [...]. (N 526-527)

It is highly ironic that Nostromo, who is now the owner of a schooner and trades along the coast, calls himself Captain *Fidanza*. After all, as the narrator emphasizes, he can no longer be trusted because of his obsession with the silver: "[T]he genuineness of all his qualities was destroyed. He felt it himself, and often cursed the silver of San Tomé. His courage, his magnificence, his leisure, his work, everything was as before, only everything was a sham. But the treasure was real" (N 523-524). This, of course, also applies to his patronage of the socialist meetings, where he listens "with his mind far away" and walks off "unapproachable, silent, like a man full of cares" (N 528). Although Nostromo has managed to rid himself of his dependence on the Blancos by becoming self-employed, his position is invalidated by its being inextricably tied up with the stolen silver. He pretends to support 'the people' by making socialist gestures but, in fact, he no longer engages actively with anybody else at all. His only reality is the treasure. The moment he develops class consciousness he is corrupted by the silver that belongs to an opposing class. Funk-Rieselbach even goes so far as to claim that "Nostromo has become a capitalist instead of a revolutionary" (32). Jenkins also asserts that

> [m]ost of us would have difficulty in recognising Nostromo as a proletarian. Although he is a *cargador* (docker), we rarely see him at work, and his work-situation does not carry over into any other sphere of his life. *Cargador* he may be at the beginning of the novel, at the end he is a ship-owner – hardly a very proletarian occupation for all his participation in socialist politics. (166)

In contrast to Nostromo, his mentor, Giorgio Viola, has always regarded himself as emphatically of and for 'the people'. His nickname, Garibaldino, reveals that he is a fervent follower of the Italian republican and patriot Garibaldo, for whom he fought in Italy and South America. Viola's "simple devotion to a vast humanitarian idea" has instilled in him an "austere contempt for all personal advantage" (N 31). He despises money as a matter of principle. Although this sets Giorgio apart from the other characters in the novel that fall under the spell of the silver, it would be an exaggeration to call his anti-materialism Marxist. According to Peter Christmas,

> Viola's republicanism and anti-clericalism can be aptly described as simply the heroic phase of 19th century liberalism rather than the prelude to socialism. [...] Viola is the expression of a pre-1848 Left whose principal aspiration was national independence and the end of rule by despotic decree: a far cry, that is to say, from the preoccupation with public ownership and proletarian control of the post-1848 Left. (Christmas 623)

The narrator frequently stresses how out of touch Giorgio is with the new power structures that are determined exclusively by material interests. He, for instance, laments that "[t]oo many kings and emperors flourished yet in the world which God had meant for the people" (N 31) but does not see that he himself lives under one, Charles Gould, the King of Sulaco. Neither is he aware that his home and source of livelihood, the *Albergo d'Italia Una*, is left standing only because Mrs Gould has begged its preservation of Sir John, who wanted to tear it down for the building of the harbour branch of the railway. Giorgio is also inconsistent in so far as he claims with Garibaldi to be for the "poor, suffering, and oppressed in this world" (N 31) but applies this stance only to the European workers in Sulaco. For the natives or the mob he has nothing but contempt, which becomes clear in his comments on the riot after the Ribierist defeat:

> These were not a people striving for justice, but thieves. Even to defend his life against them was a sort of degradation for a man who had been one of Garibaldi's immortal thousand in the conquest of Sicily. He had an immense scorn for this outbreak of scoundrels and leperos, who did not know the meaning of the word "liberty." (N 20-21)

It seems therefore that the two major representatives of the working class in the novel, Nostromo and Giorgio, do not fit easily into a reading of the novel in Marxist terms. It is also pertinent that the most outspoken criticism of the existing power structures and of the fatal dynamism unleashed by the development of material interests cannot be found among the workers but the bourgeois Blancos. Whereas Martin Decoud, for instance, uses a standpoint of extreme scepticism to reveal the Blanco talk of progress and patriotism as mere propaganda hiding egoistic motives, Emilia Gould and Dr Monygham criticize the belief in material interests from a moral or humanitarian position. We can conclude that in general Marxism is a more adequate model to account for the representation of history and the freedom-of-the-will-problem in *Nostromo* than the bourgeois/capitalist one. This is mainly due to the negative view Marxism takes of capitalism, which corresponds to *Nostromo*'s scepticism regarding "material interests." The Marxist emphasis on economic determinism and the consequent incompatibilist attitude towards free will and determinism also tallies with the experience shared by many characters in the novel that once they have come into contact with the silver they seem to lose a measure of control over their lives. On the other hand the novel does not endorse Marxist teleology, the belief that class struggle will inevitably bring about a socialist utopia. This is partly due to the pessimistic view the novel takes of human nature: we are all "short-sighted in good and evil" ("Author's Note" ix) and are therefore bound to be corrupted due to our basic greed and egoism. Even though economic determinism is a most significant force in the novel it is not the only one that drives history and determines the characters' actions.

6.3   The individual and the historical moment

Charles Gould is the character that most conspicuously contributes to set into motion the central events of the novel. His decision to take up the exploitation of the mine is determined by the history and tradition of his family, which has been "established in Costaguana for three generations" (N 46). His grandfather "had fought in the cause of independence under Bolivar" (N 46-47) and one of his uncles had been "the elected President of that very province of Sulaco [...], and afterwards had been [...] shot by the order of the barbarous Unionist general, Guzman Bento" (N 47). With "a relative martyred in the cause of aristocracy," the Blancos consider Charles "as one of themselves" (N 47). This also means that he naturally occupies a position at the very top of the ethnic and social hierarchy of the Occidental Province. Although "no one could be more of a Costaguanero than Don Carlos Gould" (N 47), his heritage is not only South American but also English. In fact, the latter is so pronounced in his aspect that in "the talk of common people he was just the Inglez – the Englishman of Sulaco" (N 47). The strength of these cultural and familial determinants is formidable: "[T]here was something [...] indelible in all these ancestral Goulds – liberators, explorers, coffee planters, merchants, revolutionists – of Costaguana [...]" (N 48). The use of the word "indelible" implies that to take up these various roles is something genetically ingrained in the Gould family. Pre-programmed in this way Charles also continues the tradition that the Goulds "always [go] to England for their education and their wives" (N 46). His decision, after many years in Europe, to return to Sulaco to work the San Tomé silver mine is the direct result of his father's fate. For Gould Senior "the perpetual concession of the San Tomé mine" (N 53), which a corrupt government had thrust upon him, had taken on the "eternal character of a curse" (N 57) and had ruined him financially and physically. He had therefore implored Charles in his letters "never to return to Costaguana, never to claim any part of his inheritance there, because it was tainted by the infamous Concession" (N 57). On Charles, of course, this injunction had the opposite effect. He studied mining and by "the time he was twenty had, in his turn, fallen under the spell of the San Tomé mine" (N 59). Paradoxically, it is because of his father's failure to cope with the concession that Charles feels personally and morally linked to the mine: "The mine had been the cause of an absurd moral disaster; its working must be made a serious and moral success. He owed it to the dead man's memory" (N 66). Charles's actions therefore not only happen to be in tune with larger economic trends but can also be traced to his individual psychological predicament: he wants to rehabilitate his father and at the same time atone for defying the latter's wish to stay away from Costaguana. Similarly, his faith in material interests to bring not only economic but also moral progress to Costaguana is not just the expression of a contemporary belief but also the consequence of his family background and individual disposition. Martin Decoud adds another reason for Gould's idealistic rhetoric, his cultural heritage. As an Englishman, Decoud argues, Charles "cannot act or exist without idealizing every simple feeling, desire, or achievement. He could not believe his own motives if he did not make them first a part of some fairy tale" (N 215). This analysis seems to be corroborated by the narrator, who, later in the novel, claims that there is a contrast between the ingrained character traits of the English and those of the Costaguana natives: "There is always something childish in the rapacity of the passionate clear-minded, Southern races, wanting in the misty idealism of the Northerners, who at the smallest encouragement dream of nothing less than the conquest of the earth" (N 333). As regards Gould *Nostromo* emphasizes that he is *both* an Englishman *and* a Costaguanero so that we can assume that he shares the traits of both cultures. Indeed, in the course of the novel Charles's idealism is revealed as an illusion which masks base desires. When the exigencies of material interests force him to participate actively in another revolution – his second since his arrival in Sulaco – it appears that his heritage has finally caught up with him. He not only acts like the foreign exploiters of old but his monomania regarding the mine seems increasingly similar to the greed and rapacity exhibited by Sotillo, the Montero brothers, and other native leaders. The sceptical Decoud has hinted all along that the difference between the apparently 'civilized' Blancos and the seemingly 'primitive' Monterists exists merely on the surface. What unites them is their basic egoism that informs all their talk and actions. According to Decoud, the lofty convictions of people like Gould, Holroyd, or Corbelán are, in fact, just "particular views of [their] personal advantage either practical or emotional" (N 189). Although Decoud is being deliberately provocative, Gould's development in the novel largely bears out his analysis. Although Charles might originally have been actuated by a combination of various motives, at the end of the novel there is only one left, his egoism. Even the practically minded engineer-in-chief notices this: "[W]e all here know [Gould's] motive, and he has only one – the safety of the San Tomé mine with the preservation of the Gould Concession in the spirit of his compact with Holroyd" (N 317).

The San Francisco billionaire's character prompts a similar analysis. There is, for instance, a comparable stress on the importance of his cultural heritage. He is of "German and Scotch and English [extraction], with remote strains of Danish and French blood, giving him the temperament of a Puritan and an insatiable imagination of conquest" (N 76). Holroyd also idealizes his motives, which is so pronounced that Decoud calls him an "utter sentimentalist" (N 240). Holroyd, after all, claims that his monetary schemes will not only introduce "justice, industry, peace, to the benighted continents but also [...] a purer form of Christianity" (N 240). Thus he believes to be fulfilling both his country's destiny and God's will. Revealingly, however, the novel clearly shows that Holroyd's immediate motives for backing Gould are personal and rooted in his psychological make-up: he is looking for diversion, for a new hobby (cf. N 81). He gives his personal attention to the San Tomé enterprise because he finds in it "the imaginative satisfaction which other minds would get from drama, from art, or from a risky and fascinating sport" (N 378). The working of the silver mine, which will affect hundreds of lives and the fate of a whole country, is, therefore, from Holroyd's perspective merely "a great man's caprice" (N 80). He derives immense satisfaction from the thought that in Sulaco

> [h]e was not running a great enterprise [...]; no mere railway board or individual corporation. He was running a man! A success would have pleased him very much [...]; but [...] it was incumbent upon him to cast it off utterly at the first sign of failure. A man may be thrown off. (N 81)

Holroyd's talk of godliness and patriotic duties is thus revealed as hypocritical rhetoric, as a cover for his immense egoism. *Nostromo* thus emphasises that, as in the case of Gould, Holroyd's participation in the events that shape Costaguana's history is not only a result of global economic forces but also of a mixture of cultural, psychological, and biological determinants.

A third example of how individual characteristics and historical developments are intertwined is Pedrito Montero, who, together with his brother, the General, is responsible for toppling Ribiera and invading Sulaco. The exact nature of Pedrito and his brother's family background is unclear but it appears that the two are of mixed ethnic origin and have early encountered European culture. We are told that they are "both bald, with bunches of crisp hair above their ears, arguing the presence of some negro blood" (N 386). There are rumours that they

> had been brought up by the munificence of a famous European traveller, in whose service their father had lost his life. Another story was that their father had been nothing but a charcoal burner in the woods, and their mother a baptised Indian woman from the far interior. (N 39)

The fact that they hail from the poorest section of Costaguana society but have had extensive contacts with European adventurers may have partly predestined them for the careers they later embark on. Like the other native leaders that appear in *Nostromo*, Pedrito is subject to uncontrollable rapacity. Whereas Holroyd and Gould clothe their greed in altruistic or religious rhetoric, Pedrito is in a sense more straightforward in that his confessed goal is to wield as much power as possible and "to acquire a serious fortune for himself" (N 388). However, the reasons why he seeks to realize his selfish dreams through turning himself into a politician of sorts and starting a revolution are rather curious. As the narrator comments, "[h]is actions were usually determined by motives so improbable in themselves as to escape the penetration of a rational person" (N 387). Pedrito used to work for the Costaguana Legation in Paris as a "lackey or inferior scribe" and spent his free time "devouring the lighter sort of historical works in the French language" (N 387), for instance those about the Second Empire. This gave him the idea of "an existence for himself where, like the Duc de Morny, he would associate the command of every pleasure with the conduct of political affairs and enjoy power supremely in every way" (N 387). No historian intent on unravelling the causes of the Montero brothers' coup would be able to guess that. Nevertheless, as the narrator analyses,

> this was one of the immediate causes of the Monterist Revolution. This will appear less incredible by the reflection that the fundamental causes were the same as ever, rooted in the political immaturity of the people, in the indolence of the upper classes and the mental darkness of the lower. (N 387)

In this passage the narrator explicitly draws attention to the interaction between the personal and the impersonal, the particular and the general that bring about a historical event. The Monterist revolution is the result of Pedrito's unbridled egoism, expressed in his dream of living like the Duc de Morny, combined with the socio-economic factors that determine Costaguana at that particular moment in history. In his delineation of Pedrito the narrator stresses his animal characteristics, thus touching upon the Darwinian theme of atavism in *Nostromo*. Pedrito is said to display "an ape-like faculty for imitating all the outward signs of refinement and distinction, and [...] a parrot-like talent for languages" (N 386). His unrestrained greed informs his decision to invade the wealthy Occidental Province and to brave the dangerous ride across the mountains. It is indicative of what the narrator calls "the political immaturity of the people" (N 387) that it is exactly the free reign Pedrito gives to his basic instincts which impresses his followers. Although there is no doubt that Pedrito is a villain, *Nostromo* suggests that Gould's monomania and Holroyd's "insatiable imagination of conquest" (N 76) are not far removed from Pedrito's rapacity. Furthermore, Holroyd's reason for backing Gould – he is looking for a new hobby – is hardly less whimsical than Pedrito's for supporting his brother's coup.

It seems clear that it is not just economic determinism that must be taken into account in an analysis of the nature of the relationship between the individual and history. A particularly conspicuous force is egoism, which is rooted in humankind's biological and psychological make-up and can, on the surface level of our actions and talk, appear in many, seemingly unrelated guises. When egoism is combined with materialism – as in the case of Gould, Holroyd, and Montero – it may be blown out of all proportions and reduce human beings to the level of animals. This draws our attention to the presence of evolutionary determinism in *Nostromo* and prompts a Darwinian reading of the representation of history and the freedom-of-the-will-problem.

6.4   The Darwinian view of history

Costaguana's society frequently appears to be informed by Social Darwinism as formulated by Herbert Spencer: the maxims of evolution – the struggle for survival and the survival of the fittest – appear to be taken as guidelines for human action. Such an analysis is emphasized by the stress the novel puts on Costaguana's brutal history of colonialism, economic exploitation, and revolutions. Furthermore, the various groups that make up this society are shown to be so disparate culturally, ethnically, and economically that social cohesion or interconnectedness informed by common traditions or by an overarching national purpose is hardly possible. In this context Hillis Miller has indeed spoken about Sulaco's "noncommunity" (""Material Interests"" 164). Except in an economic and exploitative sense there is no link between these disparate groups. If we regard the novel's title as a metaphor for the way the Costaguaneros deal with each other, it appears that everyone is *nostre uomo* to everyone else. The characters use each other for their selfish purposes which are usually materialist in kind. Thus Gould is 'our man' to Holroyd, Ribiera is 'our man' to Gould and Avellanos, the chief-engineer is 'our man' to Sir John, and Nostromo is 'our man' to Captain Mitchell. All of them are 'our man' to their selfishness in general and material interests in the guise of the silver in particular. The latter corrupts Costaguana society and taints all of the relationships represented in the novel. It cuts people off from each other and leaves them intensely loney. In this way *Nostromo* establishes a clear link between egoism, materialism, and human isolation. A case in point is the scene where the King of Sulaco, Charles Gould, holds court in the reception room of the Casa Gould where politicians, government officials, aristocrats, businessmen, and traders from Europe and North America have gathered. At first glance this seems to be a meeting of friends to discuss the future of Sulaco. A closer look reveals, however, that they have all come out of expediency. They are either, like the politicians and government officials, on the mine's unofficial pay list, or, like the businessmen and traders, hope to clinch lucrative deals by an association with Charles Gould. As Brook Miller has pointed out "[b]oth Gould and the silver are appropriated as symbols of a progressive, capitalist vision of history" (20), which results in Gould being "a fetish object as well as a fetishizing subject" (21). When Gould's courtiers leave, it is difficult to imagine a more isolated and lonely figure than their host: "And now the Europeans were dropping off from the group around Charles Gould till the Administrador of the Great Silver Mine could be seen in his whole lank length, from head to foot, left stranded by the ebbing tide of his guests on the great square of carpet [...]" (N 199). The hollowness of the ties between Gould and his admirers is also revealed when, after Montero's temporary victory, they are immediately prepared to leave their mentor in the lurch and contemplate how best to ingratiate themselves with the new powers. Charles's obsession with the silver has also led to an estrangement in his marriage. To his wife it seems that her husband "dwell[s] alone within a circumvallation of precious metal, leaving her outside with her school, her hospital, the sick mothers, and the feeble old men" (N 222). At the end of the novel she envisions herself "surviving alone the degradation of her young ideal of life, of love, of work – all alone in the Treasure House of the World" (N 522). Due to his secret treasure, Nostromo, too, cuts himself off from the people closest to him. He betrays Teresa by choosing to save the silver instead of fetching a priest to her deathbed; Giorgio by appearing to adopt his political principles but violating the most important of them, the contempt for material gain; Giselle by making passionate love to her while only caring about the silver; Linda by marrying her perfunctorily while carrying on an affair with her sister under Linda's very eyes. At the end of his life Nostromo appears to be completely isolated, his only reality being the silver. The novel thus appears to argue that because material interests reinforce the instincts of greed and egoism, they will inevitably inspire actions that divide people from each other rather than unify them. This is not only borne out on a private but also on a public level. The various sections of Costaguana society sometimes form temporary allegiances when this is to everyone's advantage. However, as soon as the goal is attained, theses allegiances break apart because the various parties pursue once again their individual interests. The primary example of this process is the way the Republic of Sulaco is established and how, soon afterwards, new tensions and strife develop. In the following the focus will be once again on the creation of the new state but not on the, as it were, 'macrolevel' of events but on the 'microlevel', on the actions of Decoud, Nostromo, Hirsch, and Monygham, who intentionally and unintentionally become the originators of the Occidental Republic.

The idea of an independent Sulaco is first hatched by the Blanco Martin Decoud, whose roles in the novel include those of intellectual, journalist, propagandist, arms dealer, and lover of Antonia Avellanos. Although Decoud was born in Costaguana, he grew up in Paris where he "studied law" (N 151), "dabbled in literature" (N 151) and "condescended to write articles on European affairs for the *Semenario*, the principal newspaper in Sta. Marta" (N 151-152). The narrator takes a scathing view of Decoud. He calls him an "idle boulevardier" (N 152) and a "nondescript dilettante" (N 153) and regards his "Frenchified – but most un-French – cosmopolitanism [as] mere barren indifferentism posing as intellectual superiority" (N 152). Nevertheless, throughout the novel, Decoud's "habit of universal raillery" (N 153) provides a corrective to the Blancos' hypocritical rhetoric. Thus he, for instance, reveals Charles Gould's, Father Corbelán's, and Nostromo's talk and action to be driven by their respective obsessions with the mine, the restitution of confiscated Church property, and personal reputation. Decoud extends his scepticism to himself and his own motives: "I am not a sentimentalist, I cannot endow my personal desires with a shining robe of silk and jewels. Life is not for me a moral romance derived from the tradition of a fairy tale. [...] I am not afraid of my motives" (N 218). Thus, when he first voices his idea of an independent Sulaco to Mrs Gould, he claims to be actuated exclusively by his desire not to be separated from Antonia:

> She won't leave Sulaco for my sake, therefore Sulaco must leave the rest of the Republic to its fate. Nothing could be clearer than that. [...] I cannot part with Antonia, therefore the one and indivisible Republic of Costaguana must be made to part with its western province. Fortunately it happens to be also a sound policy. (N 215)

As Decoud has said earlier, he has no "patriotic illusions" (N 189). He is not inspired by a sense of responsibility for his country, his friends, and countrymen but only by "the supreme illusion of a lover" (N 189). That he refers to being in love as an illusion is in accord with his Darwinian or Nietzschean perspective on human affairs. For Darwin love is just an evolutionary ploy to veil reproductive urges, for Nietzsche it is a particularly pernicious expression of the will-to-power. However, despite Decoud's protestations, these biological instincts in the guise of his illusions as a lover do not have much hold on him. As soon as he has left Sulaco for his night journey on the Golfo Placido "[e]ven his passionate devotion to Antonia into which he had worked himself up out of the depths of his scepticism had lost all appearance of reality" (N 267). The reader suspects that Decoud's love has lacked substance all along and that the role of the 'burning lover' is just one of his many impersonations. Nevertheless, it is pertinent that the reasons Decoud gives for his participation in the attempt to save the load of silver on the lighter – his love for Antonia and his fear for his life[13] – have nothing to do with patriotic high-mindedness or selfless sacrifice to a communal cause but can be analysed as forms of selfishness.

Decoud is joined in the lighter by Nostromo, who is also not inspired by a belief in national independence or the meaningfulness of political action but by desire for personal prestige, which Decoud analyses as "that finest form of egoism which can take on the aspect of every virtue" (N 300). The Blancos feed Nostromo's vanity by telling him that he is the only person fit to save the silver of the mine and he responds by resolving "to make this the most desperate affair I was ever engaged on in my whole life" (N 256). Although one should assume that, thrown together on the lighter, Nostromo and Decoud would be united in their common cause to ship the silver across the Golfo Placido, their essential isolation from each other is thrown into even sharper relief:

> [T]hey seemed to have become completely estranged, as if they had discovered [...] that the loss of the lighter would not mean the same thing to them both. This common danger brought their differences in aim, in view, in character, and in position, into absolute prominence in the private vision of each. There was no bond of conviction, of common idea; they were merely two adventurers pursuing each his own adventure, involved in the same imminence of deadly peril. Therefore they had nothing to say to each other. (N 295)

This estrangement is exacerbated by the interference of chance: the discovery of Hirsch on the boat is followed by the near fatal collision with Sotillo's steamer during which Hirsch clings to the ship's anchor and is whisked off into the night. These unlikely events gain significance later on when it transpires that they notably contribute to the Blanco victory.

Although Nostromo and Decoud become involved in the political upheavals for reasons that have – at first glance at least – nothing to do with the great cause of secession, they nevertheless act with confidence and intention. Señor Hirsch, on the other hand, is a helpless victim of the dynamics of events, whose outcome he, however, unwittingly influences. As

---

[13]   He is aware that, as the foremost Blanco propagandist, he will be first against the wall if Sulaco should fall into the hands of the Monterists (cf. N 215-216).

Mark Wollaeger remarks, "Hirsch [...] is both a crucial cog in the novel's narrative machinery and a victim of it" (134-135). We first meet Hirsch, a Jewish hide-merchant from Esmeralda, in the Casa Gould, to which he has travelled in the hope of striking a business deal with Charles. After his unsuccessful petition he does not leave Sulaco immediately and is surprised by the riot that breaks out after Montero's victory. From then on Hirsch can no longer think rationally as he is completely controlled by his survival instincts manifesting themselves in boundless terror. As the narrator says, "Hirsch was one of those men whom fear lashes like a whip" (N 273). In his panic to find a way out of the town he acts like a cornered animal: "He crouched, crept, crawled, made dashes, guided by a sort of animal instinct, keeping away from every light and from every sound of voices" (N 272). Finally he reaches the harbour and throws himself into the very lighter that will be used to transport the silver. When he is discovered, Decoud realizes that "Hirsch could not be spoken to, reasoned with, or persuaded into a rational line of conduct" (N 274) and Nostromo fittingly remarks that "[h]is being here is a miracle of fear" (N 274). The way Hirsch falls into Sotillo's hands just a short time later is hardly less wonderful. Although Hirsch immediately 'confesses' all he knows about the silver to Sotillo, the colonel does not believe him: "[T]he idea that he had destroyed the principal object of his expedition was too intolerable to be accepted" (N 294). Dr Monygham later supports Sotillo in his conviction that the silver can still be found and that, consequently, Hirsch is lying. Monygham pursues this strategy in order to prevent Sotillo from invading the town and uniting with the approaching Montero. Hirsch therefore becomes a pawn in the risky power game played by Monygham. Although the doctor is successful, thus making the Blanco victory possible, Hirsch is brutally tortured and murdered by Sotillo. Ironically, the merchant thus becomes one of the 'martyrs' of the War of Secession and a founding father of the new Republic. However, his contribution can only be appreciated by the attentive reader who realizes that, as Wollaeger puts it, the "development of the narrative [...] *requires* the dissemination of Hirsch's misinformation [about the silver]" (133).

Similar to Decoud, Dr Monygham is a clear-sighted, sceptical commentator on the unfolding events. He, too, has no illusions about humankind in general and people's motives in particular. He is, furthermore, a most incisive critic of the capitalists' claim that moral aims can be achieved with the help of material interests. Unlike Decoud's scepticism, however, Monygham's is not an empty pose but based on bitter experience and firm moral standards. In the time of the dictator Guzman Bento Monygham was imprisoned and forced to inform on his friends by gruesome torture. This betrayal destroyed his self-respect and left him with contempt for his failure to live up to the severe ideal of conduct he had set himself: "Dr. Monygham's view of what it behoved him to do was severe; it was an ideal view, in so much that it was the imaginative exaggeration of a correct feeling. It was also, in its force, influence, and persistency, the view of an eminently loyal nature" (N 375-376). Consequently, Monygham also created for himself "an ideal conception of his disgrace" (N 375) which informs his scepticism: he is "disillusioned as to mankind in general, because of the particular instance in which his own manhood had failed" (N 433). After his release from prison Monygham lived like an outcast, disregarded and disliked by the other Europeans who regarded him as "something between a clever vagabond and a disreputable doctor" (N 372). This changed with the arrival of the Goulds, to whom it was apparent that "for all his savage independence he could be tamed by kindness" (N 311). Monygham is especially moved by Mrs Gould's "humanizing influence" (N 45), believes her "worthy of every devotion," and settles the "great fund of loyalty in [his] nature [...] on [her] head" (N 376). His growing love for Emilia is the only reason why he becomes involved in the Sulaco revolution. The mine "presented itself to his fifty-years' old eyes in the shape of a little woman in a soft dress with a long train" (N 431) and he becomes convinced that "his devotion was the only thing that stood between an admirable woman and a frightful disaster" (N 431). Furthermore, he concludes that due to his personal history and the contempt he has for his own actions, he is the only person fit "to play [a] game of betrayal with Sotillo, and keep him off the town" (N 410). At first glance, the reader cannot but admire Monygham's self-sacrifice. In contrast to almost all of the other characters' motives Monygham's appear to be unselfish and informed by moral principles. Neither is there any doubt, as in the case of Decoud, about the sincerity of his love for Emilia. Nevertheless, as Darwin, Nietzsche, and others have warned us, *true* altruism does not exist in a materialist universe. It is always infused to some extent by egoism or the will-to-power. That Monygham's actions cannot be called unreservedly 'good' becomes clear in his attempt to hold Sotillo at bay, a task that he undertakes "in a fanatical spirit" (N 439). Because of his exclusive concern with the safety of Mrs Gould, all of his scruples vanish and his "thinking, acting, individuality [becomes] extremely dangerous to himself and to others" (N 431). When he encounters Nostromo in the deserted Custom House, whom everybody believes to be drowned along with Decoud and the silver, he does not "think of him humanely, as of a fellow-creature just escaped from the jaws of death. The Capataz for him [is] the only possible messenger to Cayta. The very man" (N 431-432). Blinded by his obsession, Monygham almost ruins his plans as at that moment Nostromo, who labours under his sense of betrayal by the Blancos, desires nothing *but* interest in himself as an individual human being as this "would have restored to him his personality – the only thing lost in that desperate affair" (N 434). Revealingly, the ensuing long conversation between the two men takes place under the dead eyes of the murdered Hirsch, hanging from a beam, "disregarded, forgotten, like a terrible example of neglect" (N 435). When Nostromo suggests to the doctor that if he "had not confirmed Sotillo in his madness, he would have been in no haste to give the estrapade to that miserable Hirsch" (N 438), Monygham is only momentarily startled. As the fanaticism of "his devotion [...] had left his heart steeled against remorse and pity" (N 438), he is able to shrug off any feelings of guilt and sees the fate of Hirsch "as part of the general atrocity of things" (N 439). After a while the doctor manages to hit the right note with Nostromo by telling him that he is indispensable to the Blancos and the only man fit to ride to Cayta and bring back Barrios's army to defeat the Monterists. Nostromo responds to the familiar flattery of his vanity and, after receiving Giorgio's sanction, starts on his mission.

At this point the narrative breaks off, leaving a time gap of several years. We can only infer the success of Monygham's and Nostromo's undertakings from Mitchell's complacent and ideologically biased relation of the Blanco victory. By leaving out decisive events such as the miners' march on the town or Barrios's defeat of Montero, the narrative emphasis falls on the microlevel of events described above. The implication is that it is *they* that determine the outcome of the revolution. However, neither Decoud, nor Nostromo, nor Monygham, nor Hirsch, are motivated by the desire to genuinely contribute to the secession. The latter is, at best, a secondary consideration or, is indeed, not on their minds at all. Each of the four characters is actuated by idiosyncratic reasons: Decoud because of his precarious love for Antonia and his survival instinct, Monygham because of his devotion to Emilia Gould, Nostromo because of his vanity, and Hirsch because of his inordinate fear. Although – and this is remarkable in the context of the novel – none of the characters is, at this particular moment, driven by material interests, their motives are nevertheless variants of egoism. Because each character thus acts for himself, wrapped in his own world, isolated from the others, it seems a matter of arbitrary chance that the result of their actions is some kind of unintentional cooperation which ultimately leads to the realisation of the 'master plan', the secession. From this perspective the establishment of the Occidental Republic appears to be the result of a complex chain of accidents. If we take this as an example of the way history is made in *Nostromo*, it appears to be a combination of deterministic forces – materialist and biological in nature – and random chance. Such a view would broadly conform to late nineteenth-century models of evolution as advanced by T.H. Huxley and to the position with regard to the freedom-of-the-will-problem that Ted Honderich has termed near-determinism.

Both thematic and formal aspects of the novel support an analysis in these terms. There is, for instance, the frequent withdrawal of the narrator from the characters and the central events to give the reader a distant, panoramic view that can be identified with a non-human, Darwinian perspective. Thus the timeless, serene, and enigmatic beauty of Sulaco's natural features, such as the Campo, the Golfo Placido, the Isabels, the Cordillera mountain range, or Mount Higuerota, is juxtaposed to the human atrocities committed in its midst, making them appear meaningless and futile. A famous example is the depiction of the riot preceding the Monterist invasion: "[T]he movements of the animated scene were like the passages of a violent game played upon the plain by dwarfs mounted and on foot, yelling with tiny throats, under the mountain that seemed a colossal embodiment of silence" (N 27). Another instance occurs in the scene where Decoud rows out into the Golfo Placido to commit suicide. His desperation and hopelessness are seemingly mocked by an uncaring nature: "Taking up oars slowly, he pulled away from the cliff of the Great Isabel, that stood behind him warm with sunshine, as if with the heat of life bathed in a rich light from head to foot as if in a radiance of hope and joy" (N 500). Passages such as these emphasize the paradoxes of the human condition in a Darwinian universe, such as the idea that even though nature is inhuman and not concerned with the individual, we are nevertheless its products and subject to its laws. *Nostromo* indeed shows that the characters are to a large extent controlled by their biological instincts, programmed by evolution, which contribute to the cruelty and suffering depicted. Because the view of evolution in the novel is Darwinian rather than Lamarckian, there is no hope that the human condition might change in the foreseeable future or that human beings might be able to contribute significantly to such a change. This is the dark undercurrent of Costaguana's chaotic history and a further reason why, at the end of the novel, the reader is left with little hope that the Blanco victory will inaugurate a genuinely better future for the country. That human nature is fundamentally flawed due to forces beyond our control is also stressed by certain key-statements in the text, uttered partly by the characters and partly by the narrator, which cannot only be read as comments on the developments in the narrative but also on the human condition in general. There is, for instance, Decoud's analysis of Costaguana's history as a carnivalesque repetition of the unchanging same (cf. N 152 and 186), his belief that people's ideals are nothing but sublimations of their egoistic desires (cf. N 189), and his claim that "every conviction, as soon as it [becomes] effective, turn[s] into that form of dementia the gods send upon those they wish to destroy" (N 200). There is also Mrs Gould's view that "[t]here [is] something inherent in the necessities of successful action which carrie[s] with it the moral degradation of the idea" (N 521). This is amplified by the narrator's deterministic assertion that "[i]n our activity alone do we find the sustaining illusion of an independent existence as against the whole scheme of things of which we form a helpless part" (N 497).

The narrator's use of the cosmic or Darwinian viewpoint and the deterministic statements about the human condition should be contrasted to the subjective, solipsistic perspective, which is also employed in the novel. Solipsism, which can be considered either as the reverse coin of determinism or as the logical consequence of indeterminism, is most prominent in the passages dealing with Decoud's night journey in the Golfo Placido and his suicide near the Great Isabel. The moment the lighter is launched into the Gulf Decoud's perception of the surrounding world is radically altered:

> [T]he enormous stillness, without light or sound, seemed to affect Decoud's senses like a powerful drug. He didn't even know at times whether he were asleep or awake. Like a man lost in slumber, he heard nothing, he saw nothing. Even his hand held before his face did not exist for his eyes. The change from the agitation, the passions and the dangers, from the sights and sounds of the shore, was so complete that it would have resembled death had it not been for the survival of his thoughts. (N 262)

For Decoud external reality has been transformed into a mirage-like flux, has lost its material solidity, its cause-and-effect sequences and can no longer be grasped intellectually. Only his isolated consciousness remains, suspended in space and time: "All his active sensations and feelings from as far back as he could remember seemed to him the maddest of dreams" (N, 235). This solipsistic experience is reinforced when Nostromo leaves him alone on the Great Isabel. The narrator clearly relishes the irony that Decoud cannot cope with isolation on the island even though he has always prided himself on his intellectual aloofness and enjoyed pouring scorn on the pretensions of society and his friends' illusions. Although Decoud has always styled himself as an intellectual outsider, commenting sardonically from the sidelines, he now has to recognize that he can only play this role *within* society; outside it his constructed identity loses all substance. Indeed, after having had to spend three days on the Great Isabel Decoud "caught himself entertaining a doubt of his own individuality. It had merged into the world of cloud and water, of natural forces and forms of nature. [...] Decoud lost all belief in the reality of his action past and to come" (N 497). On the fifth day the "people of Sulaco" (N 497) appear to him like "jibbering and obscene spectres" and he starts to behold "the universe as a succession of incomprehensible images" (N 498). Due to the disappearance of his habitual reality and to his want of faith in himself and others, Decoud sees no other way out than to shoot himself. The "glittering surface" of the Gulf remains "untroubled by the fall of his body" and he disappears "without trace, swallowed up in the immense indifference of things" (N 501). The solipsistic episode is thus concluded with a return to the deterministic, evolutionary perspective: nature does not care about an individual life.

A Darwinian or, rather, Huxleyan reading of *Nostromo* makes the belief in progress, in economic development, or in the beneficial effects of political action seem illlusionary. The question remains whether we can at least fall back upon morality. Can a moral principle, as Dr. Monygham suggests, serve as a guideline for human conduct and give us hope for a better future? There is no doubt that the world portrayed in *Nostromo* is non-theological but scientific-materialist in nature. There is no hint at the possible existence of a transcendental entity that could give our lives meaning or provide unquestionable ethical standards. Although religious characters feature in the novel, their religion seems to be a mere fig leaf to cover their selfishness. Father Corbelán, for instance, is only interested in the restoration of church property; Holroyd, the Evangelical billionaire, looks upon God as a business partner who gets a share of his profits in the endowment of churches; and Father Beron of Guzman Bento's era derived sadistic pleasure from torturing innocent prisoners such as Monygham. It is therefore needful to read the concept of morality in *Nostromo* in a materialist and Darwinian context.

If we look at some of the minor characters, it seems possible – at first glance at least – to distinguish between what would conventionally be called good and evil, moral and immoral, humane and inhumane figures. Don Pépé, Padre Romàn, and Barrios conform to the Sancho-Panza-like character types in Conrad's fiction. They are rather simple-minded and slightly comic but at the same time function as sustainers of communal, ethical values due to their integrity and their sense of duty, honour, and responsibility. Don Pépé, for example, a retired senior major of humble origins who is in charge of the mining population, is characterized by "a sort of sane, humorous shrewdness, and a vein of genuine humanity so often found in simple old soldiers of proved courage who have seen much desperate service" (N 99). Padre Romàn, who cares for the spiritual welfare of the miners, is also said to have a humane temperament and is, in strong contrast to almost all the other characters in the novel, "incapable of fanaticism to an almost reprehensible degree" (N 399). Barrios, who commands the Blanco army, is untypical of a Costaguana military leader in that he is referred to as "a man of perfect honesty" (N 162) and is liked for his "humane temper, which was like a strange and precious flower unexpectedly blooming on the hotbed of corrupt revolutions" (N 163). However, in *Nostromo*'s complex Darwinian world of multiple, constantly shifting perspectives undiluted good and unquestionable ethical principles no longer exist. The reader is, for instance, made aware that Don Pépé runs the mining community like a military camp and is, together with Padre Romàn, a compliant cogwheel in the exploitative, capitalist machinery set up by Gould and others. This also holds true for Barrios, who, furthermore, contributes actively to the plight of the indigenous population by his recruiting methods: his army consists of Indios "only caught the other day" (N 167). Nevertheless, these three characters are preferable to the likes of Sotillo, the Montero brothers, or Gamacho, who are mere villains. They are devoid of any moral principles, corrupt to the core, and only interested in laying their hands on as much 'plunder' or 'booty' as possible. The narrator, for instance, describes Sotillo's "want of a moral sense" as being "of a profound and innocent character. It bordered upon stupidity, moral stupidity. Nothing that served his ends could appear to him really reprehensible" (N 350). Although, as readers, we might want to condemn *Nostromo*'s scoundrels unequivocally, we have to recognize that the behaviour of the Blanco capitalists frequently only appears to be more civilized. The intricate system of analogies that informs the novel suggests that in the case of the Blancos we are often dealing with the same kind of rapacity that motivates the Monterist leaders. Thus an action or plan that ostensibly serves an ethical end, such as the establishment of an independent Sulaco to promote "law, good faith, order, security" (N 84) is revealed to be a mere trick to secure the capitalists' economic advantage. As we have seen, a case in point is Charles Gould, whose linking of moral and material progress is disclosed as a complacent, self-serving illusion. Similarly, Nostromo's honourable and charitable actions are shown to be the product not of a moral principle but of his desire to be well-spoken of. Later on, his obsession with the silver leads him to betray each member of the Viola family. Nostromo's father-in-law, Giorgio, extends his humanitarian principles derived from Garibaldi exclusively towards the European workers and has only scorn for the Costaguana natives whom he refers to as "thieves" (N 20) and "scoundrels and leperos" (N 21). Neither does he see that he has become completely dependent on the good will of the Blanco capitalists, who, according to his principles, he should oppose. As we have seen earlier, even Dr Monygham's behaviour, which he deliberately bases on a rigorous, ethical code of conduct, may appear selfish and callous. To a certain extent this also holds true for the other protagonist in the novel who actively strives for ethical standards, Emilia Gould. When she first arrives in Sulaco, Emilia is convinced that her husband loves her and that the profitable working of the mine will be the material means to a higher moral end. When Charles declares that he pins "his faith to material interests" in order to bring about a better future for Costaguana, Emilia "glance[s] up at him with admiration. He was competent; he had given a vast shape to the vagueness of her unselfish ambitions" (N 84). The "vast shape" is the industrialisation of a whole country; her "unselfish ambitions" are to do as much good as possible. With amazing energy she embarks on her new role: she travels the country with her husband in search of labourers; she oversees the setting up of the mining villages together with hospitals, schools, and a church; and she establishes the Casa Gould as a central meeting place for everybody of note in Sulaco. When the first silver ingot is turned out from the mine, Emilia, who, according to the narrator, is wanting in "even the most legitimate touch of materialism" (N 75), endows it "with a justificative conception, as though it were not a mere fact, but something far-reaching and impalpable, like the true expression of an emotion or the emergence of a principle" (N 107). Fairly soon, however, Mrs Gould has to recognize that the material interests unleashed by the mine adhere to principles that have nothing to do with ethics but are, in Monygham's words, "founded on expediency, and [...] inhuman" (N 511). Emilia first voices such doubts when the Ribiera government is overthrown. On trying to discuss the future of the mine and their own compromised position with her husband, she is shocked to see that "all sign of sympathy or any other feeling [has] disappeared" (N 207). Charles's announcement in a matter-of-fact tone that he would go "[a]ny distance, any length" (N 208) in order to preserve the mine, causes her to shudder. Her profound disillusionment is memorably expressed later on when she contemplates the San Tomé mine in the following terms:

> It was a long time now since she had begun to fear it. It had been an idea. She had watched it with misgivings turning into a fetish, and now the fetish had grown into a monstrous and crushing weight. It was as if the inspiration of their early years had left her heart to turn into a wall of silver-bricks, erected by the silent work of evil spirits, between her and her husband. He seemed to dwell alone within a circumvallation of precious metal, leaving her outside with her school, her hospital, the sick mothers and the feeble old men, mere insignificant vestiges of the initial inspiration. (N 221-222)

Emilia thus draws a clear parallel between the failure to bring lasting peace and stability to Costaguana through the development of material interests and the sterility of her marriage. It is revealing that Emilia feels that her husband has "left her outside" along with her charitable projects. She has thought that the latter would be at the centre of Charles's undertakings but now she understands that they have been mere accoutrements, by-products of his profit-making. She starts to question Charles's grandiloquent phrases of bringing a new justice to Sulaco and suspects them of being part of a hollow rhetoric of benevolence to which her projects are supposed to give credibility. Rebecca Carpenter puts this even more relentlessly:

> The narrative allows us to see how Emilia's charitable actions provide a perfect cover for Charles Gould's imperial exploits; her outward acts of charity enable his profit-taking by putting a positive face on his actions, while at the same time his exploitative industry enables Emilia's charitable works. (86)

If we thus take a postcolonial view not only of Charles's but also of Emilia's actions, then the latter's philanthropy, too, becomes suspect. After all, she is actively involved in her husband's colonization of Sulaco and it is questionable whether her charitable acts, which Carpenter describes as being "colored by paternalism and sanctimony" (86), are always in the interests of the colonized. In a psychoanalytic analysis Joyce Carol Oates argues that Emilia's "care for the community is a kind of sublimation of her unfulfilled marriage" (594). From this perspective, too, it is doubtful whether Emilia's motives are truly moral and above criticism.

Should we therefore conclude that one of *Nostromo*'s 'lessons' is that apparent altruism is egoism in disguise? This is certainly what Martin Decoud suggests when he defines a conviction as a "particular view of our personal advantage either practical or emotional" (N 189). Ironically, however, it is also Decoud's fate that demonstrates that such corrosive scepticism tending towards nihilism cannot be an adequate response to life. In his analysis of *Heart of Darkness* Jacques Berthoud has spoken of the "concept of positive illusion" (*Conrad* 63) that Marlow believes in. *Nostromo* seems to endorse this concept as well. Although from some perspectives morality may appear as a complacent or even self-serving illusion, it is nevertheless a life- and freedom-enhancing one because it is essential to what makes us human. Without this illusion, we would indeed be reduced to the level of mere animals and would be completely controlled by external and internal forces. *Nostromo* certainly takes a generally positive view of characters such as Emilia Gould and Dr Monygham who adhere to moral principles without being blind to the fact that in a materialist world 'pure' morality no longer exists. Thus the novel does not emphasize Mrs Gould's hypocrisy but her suffering due to her "transformation from a young bride, future mother, and social philanthropist to an older, childless woman, no longer beloved by her husband, and no longer confident in her ability to improve the condition of the natives" (Carpenter 85). We should also note that in the very passage at the end of the narrative in which Emilia voices her dread of the tyranny of the San Tomé mine and her despair at her loneliness and failed love, she also reaffirms her moral commitment, half-conscious that it might be an illusion: "It had come into her mind that for life to be large and full, it must contain the care of the past and of the future in every passing moment of the present. Our daily work must be done to the glory of the dead, and for the good of those who come after" (N 520-521). The circumstances in which these thoughts occur to Emilia can serve as an apt summary of the status of morality in *Nostromo*. Even though Emilia is aware that her aim of bringing moral regeneration to Costaguana has dismally failed both on a private and public level, she nevertheless knows that this failure does not devalue moral principles as such. In order to remain human she has no other choice but to reaffirm them.

Many of the conclusions reached in the course of the preceding analysis are reflected in the formal complexities of the novel. They, for instance, emphasise epistemological questions, the sense that all human endeavour is futile, and, most importantly, the idea that history is not and cannot be represented as a cause-and-effect, linear, progressive process. Among the formal techniques the novel employs Cedric Watts (cf. *Nostromo* 75-80) has identified perspectival mobility as being of particular importance. Temporal mobility, for instance, is especially pronounced in Part First, "The Silver of the Mine," where actions and events from different time levels are thrust at the reader, who is not as yet in a position to order them chronologically or to assess their significance. Captain Mitchell, for example, recalls the escape of the President-Dictator Ribiera from the capital as a past occurrence, but a few pages later we witness the inaugural celebrations of the Ribierist regime. It is only towards the end of Part Second, "The Isabels," that we learn the details about how and why Ribiera had to flee. Thus an analepsis within Part First proves to be a prolepsis of Part Second. The mobility of perspective in *Nostromo* is not only temporal but also visual. Sometimes the viewpoint is high above the ground, taking a bird's-eye-view of the Costaguaneros' activities amidst the breathtaking beauty of the landscape; sometimes it is in the thick of the crowd; sometimes it is largely congruent with that of a character; sometimes it seems to correspond to that of an inhuman, Darwinian nature. One effect of this flexible movement between an extremely remote and an intimately close view of humankind is to underline the paradox between the significance of the individual as a thinking, suffering being that deserves our compassion and its utter insignificance with regard to the impersonal forces of history and evolution. Narratorial mobility is employed in the novel by the way in which information about the unfolding events is provided by a great number of informants. We are, for instance, acquainted with the views of Captain Mitchell, Mr Gould, Mrs Gould, Dr Monygham, or Nostromo, which strongly contrast with each other and therefore make us aware of how biased the characters' observations are. Although we can, on the whole, rely on the guidance of an authorial narrator, he is a mere voice in the background that never steps forward to comment on or clarify the actions and events. It is pertinent that at the opening of Chapter 8 in Part First the narrator identifies himself as a 'mere' character, an anonymous visitor to Costaguana, "whom business or curiosity took to Sulaco in these years before the advent of the railway" (N 95). This revelation might be taken as a hint that his perspective, too, is biased and far from omniscient. Ambiguity is also created through the way the narrative shifts between an authorial and a figural narrative situation so that it is often difficult to distinguish between a character's thoughts and opinions and those of the narrator. Analogical mobility, finally, refers to "the postulation of analogies between different characters or entities" (Watts, *Nostromo* 79). This means that when we consider one character in our analysis, we suddenly find that an unexpected analogy shifts our consideration to another character so that we are obliged to establish a comparative judgement. Due to *Nostromo*'s attempt to portray the society and history of a whole country, this perspectival device is particularly prominent. For instance, when contemplating Gould's obsession with the San Tomé mine, we also have to think about Nostromo's obsession with its product, the silver, and contrast both to Monygham's "inexhaustible treasure" and "unlawful wealth" (N 504) that is his love for Emilia Gould. Analogical mobility also contributes to the novel's strain of atavism and the sense that nothing ever changes in the history of the country. Thus the Blancos' apparently civilized values and manners appear to be just a veneer, hiding the same basic desires that motivate the likes of Montero and Sotillo. Charles Gould, who is referred to as the King of Sulaco, is compared to Charles IV, the last of the Spanish emperors of South America, suggesting that the former is just another imperialist exploiter (cf. N 48-49). Similarly, Nostromo's enslavement to the silver is compared to the way the *gringo*-ghosts in the folk legend related in Chapter 1 are condemned to hover forever over the treasure they have discovered on Azuera (cf. N 4-5).

As in *Heart of Darkness* delayed decoding also plays an important role in *Nostromo*. Minor examples include Decoud's perception of the collision with Sotillo's steamer in the Golfo Placido; Nostromo's discovery of the murdered

Hirsch in the Custom House; Monygham's inference from Nostromo's reappearance that the lighter's cargo of silver is lost; or Viola's assumption that the nocturnal visitor on the island is Ramirez and not Nostromo. In all of these instances the first-time reader shares the characters' initial misunderstanding of or bewilderment by the unfolding events. On a larger scale delayed decoding is used with regard to the representation of the historical process in the novel. It is in particular the frequent time-shifts referred to above that inhibit our decoding of developments. In "The Silver of the Mine," for instance, Captain Mitchell tells his visitors about how he saved the toppled Ribiera, who fled to Sulaco on a mule (cf. N 11ff). At this stage we are led to believe that this event is past history, outstripped by the unfolding narrative. Subsequently, however, the narrative slowly spirals further back in time so that six chapters after Ribiera's downfall we are told of the inauguration of his regime (cf. N 116ff). Then the narrative gradually moves forward in time so that we hear about Ribiera's flight in detail as an event that occurred "yesterday" in Decoud's letter to his sister (cf. N 224ff). It is therefore only once we are half way through the book that we are able to piece together the linear sequence of the central events. As first-time readers we are bewildered by the time-shifts, which delay our decoding of what is going on and force us to share the characters' own short-sightedness. Indeed, in Part First, where various time-levels coalesce, we behold the fictional universe like Decoud on the Great Isabel: "as a succession of incomprehensible images" (N 498). Although the reader will eventually overcome the resistance to comprehensibility, the initial bewilderment will have "invoked the possibility that the world, truly perceived, may be recalcitrant to man's decoding endeavours" (Watts, *Nostromo* 83). The time-shifts also reinforce the sense that history does not evolve in an ordered, progressive manner but is repetitive, without goal, or random. The cyclical relation of Ribiera's fate is again a good example: we witness his downfall, then his inauguration, and finally again his downfall. The implication is that nothing is ever achieved. Although names and ideologies may change the pattern of revolution and counter-revolution, of exploitation and suffering will continue.

As we have seen, the novel's modernist narrative strategies largely support a Darwinian reading of its representation of the historical process. History can thus be grasped as a random, basically directionless process which often seems to be a repetition of the unchanging same. A historical event appears to be the product of a combination of various determinants, including chance, so that we cannot hope to discover the definitive truth about it. The position with regard to free will and determinism that emerges from a Darwinian reading can best be described as near-determinism, which, in some scenes of the novel, is transformed into solipsism or radical indeterminism. Although the characters appear to have little or no free will, those figures appear freer and more human who exhibit a moral sense. If there is any hope in *Nostromo*, it certainly does not lie in political action or economic enterprise but in a moral, immaterial principle that we have to adhere to despites its paradoxical and illusionary nature.

7. *The Secret Agent* and the Urban Jungle

7.1   The representation of London

In his "Author's Note" to *The Secret Agent* Conrad claims that part of his inspiration to write the novel was

> the vision of an enormous town [...], of a monstrous town more populous than some continents and in its man-made might as if indifferent to heaven's frowns and smiles, a cruel devourer of the world's light. There was room enough there to place any story, depth enough there for any passion, variety enough there for any setting, darkness enough to bury five million of lives. (6)

This paragraph anticipates the kind of London portrayed in *The Secret Agent*, a place much more than mere setting. In his "Note" the author stresses the town's immensity, its teeming population, and its infinite variety. He introduces the contradiction between the city's "*man*-made might" and its inhuman monstrosity, suggesting that even though human beings have built London, it has slipped from their control. The town's characteristic Conrad most insists upon, however, is its darkness; indeed, it *devours* "the world's light." That the city's salient quality should be darkness does, however, not just remind us, by way of contrast, of the comparative brightness of *Nostromo* or of the tales of the sea but also of the setting of the frame tale of *Heart of Darkness*. From his location in the Thames estuary, the primary narrator repeatedly notes the "brooding" and "mournful gloom" (HD 45) over "the place of the monstrous town" (HD 48) some miles off and Marlow famously remarks that "this [i.e. London] also [...] has been one of the dark places of the earth" (HD 48). When, in *The Secret Agent,* we move directly into "the very centre of the Empire on which the sun never sets" (SA 162), we find that it is *still* a place of darkness. At its heart we find the Verlocs' household in Soho, which is "hidden in the shades of [a] sordid street seldom touched by the sun" (SA 34). This is the perfect environment for Verloc and his professions: he is "a seller of shady wares" (SA 11), i.e. pornography, and derives additional income from being a secret agent, an occupation also associated with night. Even in the few scenes set during daytime the "peculiarly London sun" (SA 15) is fighting a losing battle against the urban darkness. The sun is never bright but – at the most – "bloodshot" (SA 15) or "rusty" (SA 26). When it does manage to "struggl[e] clear of the London mist," it only produces "a lukewarm brightness" (SA 26). Although the novel's main action is set during "early spring," the sky is "grimy" and the day "gloomy" (SA 65), "choked in raw fog to begin with, and [then] drowned in cold rain" (SA 80). Michael Whitworth has therefore claimed that there is a "general sense of the sun's decay" (44) in *The Secret Agent*, which invokes the contemporary idea of entropy and reinforces the novel's theme of degeneration. It is poignant to note that the primary narrator in *Heart of Darkness* also credits London with the capacity to put out the sun. He fears that it will be "stricken to death by the touch of that gloom brooding over a crowd of men" (HD 46).

Darkness, therefore, provides a link between such seemingly disparate novels as *Heart of Darkness* and *The Secret Agent*. By suggesting that the 'heart of darkness' might be located in London and not in the so-called 'Dark Continent' both narratives subvert binary oppositions, such as civilization/savagery, morality/immorality, decency/indecency, or progress/degeneration. As Rebecca Stott has pointed out (cf. 202), the idea to "superimpose" Africa and all it stood for in the European imagination on London was not unique in *fin-de-siècle* writing. In his *In Darkest England and the Way Out* William Booth, for instance, claimed that if "the stony streets of London" could speak, they would "tell of tragedies as awful, of ruin as complete, of ravishments as horrible, as if we were in Central Africa; only the ghastly devastation is covered, corpse-like, with the artificialities and hypocrisies of modern civilisation" (quoted in Gill 26). The notion that London's 'nether world' mirrors the "colonial Otherworld" (Stott 202) was facilitated by the way the discourses of evolution, anthropology, and race, which had been used to justify imperialist expansion, were combined with criminology and theories of degeneration to identify so-called 'evolutionary throwbacks' among the city's underclass. Indeed, as I will show later on, *The Secret Agent* is peopled with a great number of characters that could be labelled degenerates so that the city, in Harrington's words, emerges as "an evolutionary laboratory in which "the fittest" survive" (63).

The urban environment in *The Secret Agent* is often given organic or anthropomorphic qualities so that it fulfils a similar thematic function to nature in *Heart of Darkness* and *Nostromo*. For instance, in the streets of Soho, the Assistant Commissioner, whose career has indeed "begun in a tropical colony" (SA 79), feels as if "ambushed all alone in a jungle many thousands of miles away from departmental desks and official inkstands" (SA

116). Earlier his "descent into the street" from his office has been compared to that into

> a slimy aquarium from which the water had been run off. A murky, gloomy dampness enveloped him. The walls of the houses were wet, the mud of the roadway glistened with an effect of phosphorescence, and when he emerged into the Strand out of a narrow street by the side of Charing Cross Station the genius of the locality assimilated him. (SA 114)

In this passage London appears to be a vast living and breathing organism with the ability to swallow up an individual and give him a new identity. The mysteriousness of the urban environment is amplified by what Cedric Watts calls "a form of negative mystification or "antipathetic fallacy"" so that the city appears "wilfully oppressive or [is] given a totalising, apparently unqualified, negativity" ("Monstrous Town" 18). Indeed, the darkness London generates often seems to be alive, tangible, and inimical to human beings, such as when the Assistant Commissioner advances into "an immensity of greasy slime and damp plaster interspersed with lamps, and enveloped, oppressed, penetrated, choked, and suffocated by the blackness of a wet London night, which is composed of soot and drops of water" (SA 116). Even more insidious is Winnie's encounter with the urban darkness, which seems to encroach upon her slowly and, eventually, claims her for its own. As Stott has noted, already before her murder, "as a consequence of dressing herself in black, her contours begin to dissolve" (207). After her deed she takes on qualities of the surrounding darkness: "A tinge of wildness in her aspect was derived from the black veil hanging like a rag against her cheek, and from the fixity of her black gaze where the light of the room was absorbed and lost without the trace of a single gleam" (SA 195). Just as London is the "cruel devourer of the world's light" ("Author's Note" 6), Winnie's eyes have developed the power to absorb the light of the room. Later on, her "black form [is] merged in the night, like a figure half chiselled out of a block of black stone" (SA 209-210). Before she meets her watery death in the Channel, Winnie metaphorically drowns in London's darkness: "She was alone in London: and the whole town of marvels and mud, with its maze of streets and its mass of lights, was sunk in a hopeless night, rested at the bottom of a black abyss from which no unaided woman could hope to scramble out" (SA 203).

As we have seen, one important aspect of London in *The Secret Agent* is its organic totality and its ability to enshroud its inhabitants in sinister darkness. However, the extremes of alienation and isolation the characters experience are also due to another, directly contrasting aspect of the city, its *in*organicism. As Hugh Epstein notes, "it is the inhuman *material* quality of

London that impresses itself upon the reader's memory" ("Pier-glass" 189; my italics). The city, of course, is basically made up of inorganic, non-human matter, which, in its monolithic urban immensity, may be experienced as a hostile force. When Verloc, for instance, leans his "forehead against the cold window pane [of his bedroom]" one night, he experiences the "enormity of cold, black, wet, muddy, inhospitable accumulation of bricks, slates, and stones" with a "force approaching to positive bodily anguish" (SA 48). According to Hillis Miller, this impression of hostility is due to "a stubborn recalcitrance in matter, a passive resistance to man's shapings or valuings" (*Poets* 49). It is "outside time, since time cannot change it, and it transcends all attempts to understand or control it. Matter is static and perdurable, and therefore alien to man, creature of time and change" (Hillis Miller, *Poets* 49). A particularly good example of Hillis Miller's analysis is the description of the private road along which Verloc walks to the Embassy: "In its breadth, emptiness, and extent it had the majesty of inorganic nature, of matter that never dies. [...] The polished knockers of the doors gleamed as far as the eye could reach, the clean windows shone with a dark opaque lustre. And all was still" (SA 17). The reference to "a doctor's brougham arrested in august solitude close to the curbstone" (SA 17) establishes a contrast between human mortality and the apparent indestructibility of the surroundings, which is further emphasized by the sudden "eruption of vitality" (Fleishman, "Symbolic World" 207) in the guise of "a butcher boy, driving [round the corner] with the noble recklessness of a charioteer at Olympic Games" (SA 17). However, just at the moment when an opposition between the organic and the inorganic, the mortal and the immortal has been established, it is thrown into doubt again. As Verloc continues walking, he observes what amounts to a strange symbiosis between the human and the non-human. First of all, a "guilty looking cat issu[es] from under the stones" (SA 17), as if the latter had given birth to the animal and then "a thick police constable, looking a stranger to every emotion, as if he too were part of inorganic nature, surg[es] apparently out of a lamp post" (SA 17). If this were not surprising enough, the street, which has so far seemed unassailable in its orderliness and stolidity, suddenly becomes unreadable and mysterious:

> Mr Verloc pursued his way along a narrow street [...] which, for some inscrutable reason, had No.1 Chesham Square written on it in black letters. Chesham Square was at least sixty yards away [...]. At last [...] he reached the Square, and made diagonally for the number 10. This belonged to an imposing carriage gate in a high, clean wall between two houses, of which one rationally enough bore the number 9 and the other was numbered 37; but [...] this last belonged to Porthill Street [...]. (SA 17)

The comic narratorial comment that there are "strayed houses" in London which have to be compelled by an Act of Parliament to "return where they belong" (SA 17) implies that inorganic matter might have a life of its own after all. Far from being fixed, London's topography may suddenly shift and prove recalcitrant to our decoding endeavours. The city can thus not only be regarded as a static totality but also, as Frank Kermode has put it, as "a whole made up of a million randomnesses" (137).

The characters' frequent journeys – by cab and by foot – through London give occasion to explore not only the city's mythical characteristics but also the significance of certain topographical features. The first prominent expedition is Verloc's walk from his shop at 32 Brett Street, Soho, to his meeting with Vladimir at the Embassy at 10 Chesham Square, Belgravia. Verloc walks along Piccadilly towards "Hyde Park Corner" (SA 15), where he observes the following scene "[t]hrough the park railings" (SA 15):

> [M]en and women riding in the Row, couples cantering past harmoniously, others advancing sedately at a walk, loitering groups of three or four, solitary horsemen looking unsociable, and solitary women followed at a long distance by a groom [...]. Carriages went bowling by, mostly two horse broughams, with here and there a victoria [...]. (SA 15)

What Verloc sees has a number of important topographical, psychological, sociological, and historical implications. As regards the cityscape, Harkness and Reid point out that Conrad is here "aiming at an evocation of the district rather than topographical accuracy" because from Verloc's position at Hyde Park Corner "it is difficult to visualize his getting detailed glimpses of the fashionable in Rotten Row" (416). From a historical and sociological standpoint the vignette is, however, accurate. At the turn of the last century Hyde Park was still almost exclusively the preserve of the upper classes. What is remarkable, though, is that Verloc observes the members of this illustrious social stratum "[t]hrough the park railings" (SA 15), as if they were on display like a rare or endangered species in a zoo. Indeed, by virtue of his role as secret agent, Verloc sees himself as the protector of these "evidences of the town's opulence and luxury" (SA 15):

> They had to be protected; and their horses, carriages, houses, servants had to be protected; and the source of their wealth had to be protected in the heart of the city and the heart of the country; the whole social order favourable to their hygienic idleness had to be protected against the shallow enviousness of unhygienic labour. (SA 15-16)

This narrated monologue not only throws light on Verloc's vanity and complacency but also implicitly reflects the fears of the social elite that an unruly and violent working class might endanger its position. As Brian

Spittles (cf. 116-117) has noted, these anxieties were specifically connected to Hyde Park, where notable riots took place in 1866 and 1886, the year in which *The Secret Agent* is probably set. By the time Conrad started on the novel in 1906, the fear of social unrest or mob rule had no rational basis any more but nevertheless continued to exist. The choice of Hyde Park, therefore, as one of the London landmarks specified in the novel is not gratuitous but resonates with some of the novel's multi-layered themes.

The Assistant Commissioner's movements through London during one late afternoon and evening illustrate how the city may contain totally different worlds within a very small space. Starting out from the pillars of government, his Scotland Yard office and the Home Office off Whitehall (cf. Watts, Notes, *The Secret Agent* 249), he takes a cab from the Strand to get out "nowhere in particular, between two lamp posts before a large drapery establishment" (SA 114). Although we can assume that the "little Italian restaurant round the corner" (SA 114) is in Soho due to its closeness to Verloc's shop, it is essentially a 'nowhere' epitomizing urban anonymity. On entering, the Assistant Commissioner "lose[s] some more of his identity" (SA 115) and observes the same thing happening to the other patrons, who also "lost in the frequentation of fraudulent cookery all their national and private characteristics" (SA 115). The Italian restaurant is the most notable of a number of mysterious places of undefined location in *The Secret Agent*'s London. There is, for instance, the "triangular well of asphalt and bricks" (SA 207) that constitutes Brett Place, the Silenus Restaurant with its ghostly piano (cf. SA 51ff), and the second hand furniture dealer's shop in a derelict street that is described in terms of a rural idyll (cf. SA 67). According to Martin Ray, these locations are examples of the "discontinuities, [the] sudden and absurd black holes [...] which open up and fragment the physical fabric of the city" (206).

As Robert Hampson has pointed out the narrative in general "enacts a mapping that shades from specificities to indeterminacies" ("Mysteries" 169). This is also born out by Winnie's mother's last cab ride and Ossipon's frantic walkabout after his encounter with Winnie. The former takes us in a "hackney carriage" (SA 121) from Brett Street to Whitehall and the Houses of Parliament. However, after crossing "the bridge" (SA 122), which can only be Westminster Bridge, the journey becomes topographically indeterminate and – quite characteristically for the London of *The Secret Agent* – obscured by "the early dirty night, the sinister, noisy, hopeless and rowdy night of South London" (SA 123). Similarly, Ossipon's somnambulistic wanderings are also only partly traceable. As Ossipon leaves Winnie at Waterloo Station, "the bridge" (SA 224) he crosses afterwards could either be Waterloo or Westminster Bridge. He then passes "the towers of the Abbey" and walks along Victoria Street towards the "lights of Victoria [Station]" (SA 224). From there he probably continues down Buckingham Palace Road until he reaches "Sloane Square" (SA 224). His subsequent movements become increasingly indecipherable. The reference to "the railings of the park" (SA 224) might suggest that Ossipon walks north again, up Sloane Street, until he reaches Knightsbridge and Hyde Park. Assuming that the "clock tower" that 'boom[s] a brazen blast above his drooping head' (SA 224) is Big Ben, "the bridge" upon which he "once more [finds] himself" (SA 224) is Westminster Bridge. If Ossipon has indeed walked in a circle, this would fit his desperate and confused state of mind. As he continues his wanderings, the city transforms itself into an impersonal maze:

[His figure] was seen crossing the streets without life and sound, or diminishing in the interminable straight perspectives of shadowy houses bordering empty roadways lined by strings of glass lamps. He walked through monotonous streets with unknown names where the dust of humanity settles inert and helpless out of the stream of life. (SA 224)

The passage shows once again how the description of London in the novel moves towards a totalizing abstract by reducing, as Epstein has put it, "topographical detail to a geometric denotation deliberately removed from its sources in human endeavours, hopes, and fancies" ("Analogous Art" 122).

In *The Secret Agent*, as we have seen, London emerges as a protagonist in its own right. The town is not only represented as a monolithic immensity but also as "full of flashing discontinuities, irrational intrusions, bewildering fragments, absurd juxtapositions" (Kermode 135). It is both organic and inorganic, sometimes appearing as a voracious monster, sometimes as dead, impenetrable matter. It seems, on the one hand, deterministic in its indestructible totality and, on the other hand, indeterministic in its unpredictability and randomness.

7.2 The ambiguity of time

In *The Secret Agent* not just place but time, too, is portrayed as multi-faceted and ambiguous. If we, for instance, try to determine the exact year in which the novel is set, the dates seem precise only at first glance. The wedding ring that Winnie leaves behind her on the steamer before she kills herself has the date "24th June 1879" (SA 230) engraved on it. Mr Verloc has revealed earlier that he has been married for "seven years" (SA 180) and we know that the action takes place in "early spring" (SA 26). Most critics, therefore, claim that the year in which the novel is set is 1886 (cf. Fleishman, *Conrad's Politics* 205; Spittles 118; Watts, "Jews and Degenerates" 72ff). However, Bruce Harkness and S.W. Reid, the editors of the authoritative Cambridge edition of *The Secret Agent*, assert that "the 'official' time of the novel is 1887, the year of Queen Victoria's Jubilee and of the famous 'Bloody Sunday'"[14] (413). Harkness and Reid do not substantiate their claim but, as the novel specifies the action to take place in early spring and not in summer, it is true that in the spring of 1886 Verloc would not as yet be married a *full* seven years. This vagueness in the novel's temporal setting is amplified by a number of instances of anachronism. For instance, the automatic piano whose tunes accompany the meeting of the Professor and Ossipon in Chapter IV had only just being invented in 1887 (cf. Harkness and Reid 419). Another example is the short walking distance between the Assistant Commissioner's department and the Home Office, which suggests that the former is located in New Scotland Yard, to which police headquarters were only moved in 1891 (cf. Watts, Notes, *The Secret Agent* 249). Because of these indeterminacies it is probably better to think of *The Secret Agent* as set in a particular period rather than a particular year. Harkness and Reid (cf. 413) indeed claim that, in addition to the time of the novel's action, *The Secret Agent* is informed by two more time levels: that of the actual bombing of the Greenwich Observatory on 15 February 1894 and that of the novel's composition between 1906 and 1907. Conrad himself, however, seems intent on denying that *The Secret Agent* has contemporary relevance. In his "Author's Note" he refers to one his sources as "the *already old story* of the attempt to blow up the Greenwich Observatory" (5; my italics) and, in the novel's dedication to H.G. Wells, he emphatically calls *The Secret Agent* a "SIMPLE TALE OF THE XIX CENTURY" (SA 2). Consequently, the first paragraphs of the novel establish a distinction between story and discourse time, thus rooting the fictional events firmly in the past: "[Verloc's shop was housed] in one of those grimy brick houses which existed in large quantities *before the era of reconstruction* dawned upon London" (SA 9; my italics). According to Cedric Watts, "the era of reconstruction" set in with "the establishment of the London County Council in 1888" (Notes, *The Secret Agent* 240). Despite this narratorial strategy and Conrad's claims, the distance between the 1880s and the time of publication was certainly not great enough for the events of the novel to have no contemporary relevance. Therefore we should probably

---

[14]   A demonstration against unemployment, organized among others by Conrad's socialist friend Cunninghame Graham, which was violently suppressed.

agree with Harkness and Reid, who argue diplomatically that "Conrad is evoking the atmosphere of late Victorian times – the 1880s and 1890s – still felt in the early twentieth century" (413).

As regards the timing of the fictional events, we encounter a similar ambiguity due to chronological precision on the one hand and instances of anachrony on the other. Many critics have remarked upon the inexorability of the plot of *The Secret Agent*, which seems to proceed like clockwork. From the moment Vladimir instructs Verloc to target the first meridian, a remorseless chain of cause and effect is set in motion which can only have one outcome: the annihilation of the Verloc family. The relentless movement towards the tragic denouement is emphasized by the way the main action – the failed Greenwich bombing, the police investigation, Verloc's murder, and Winnie's flight – takes place within one day. For this reason R.W. Stallman has suggested viewing the first three chapters, which contain the interview with Vladimir and the meeting of the anarchists in Verloc's house, as a "Prologue to the drama" (245) that takes place about a month later. In analogy, the last chapter – in which Ossipon and the Professor return to the Silenus ten days after Winnie's suicide – can be regarded as an epilogue. The overall time span covered by the narrative is therefore about five and a half weeks. If the narrative is precise in the timing of its major fictional events, it displays a virtual obsession with temporal exactitude in certain minor scenes. For instance, when Mr Verloc leaves his house to walk to the Embassy, it is exactly "half past ten in the morning" (SA 15). When the Assistant Commissioner ends his "very full evening," it is precisely "half-past ten" (SA 173) at night. A pause in the conversation between Winnie and her husband is said to "last[..] for three ticks of the clock" (SA 49), whereas a sudden "utter stillness of [the Assistant Commissioner's] brain" covers a time-span of "about three seconds" (SA 80). Winnie kills her husband just before "ten minutes to nine" (SA 198) and drowns herself in the Channel a few minutes to "five o'clock in the morning" (SA 230). The insistence on chronological precision is emphasized by the ubiquity of clocks and the suggestion that they have a life of their own. For instance, at one point, the "lonely ticking of the clock on the [Verlocs'] landing [steals] into the room as if for the sake of company" (SA 137). Another notable timepiece is to be found in Sir Ethelred's office which, as befits the dignified environment, is "a heavy, glistening affair of massive scrolls in the same dark marble as the mantelpiece" and is characterized by "a ghostly, evanescent tick" (SA 106). At the end of the conversation between the Assistant Commissioner and the Home Secretary, the clock's tick has become "sly [and] feeble" and "the gilt hands [have] taken the opportunity to steal through no less than five and twenty minutes behind [Sir Ethelred's] back" (SA 111).

The emphasis on clocks, clock-time, and chronological precision also has a thematic function: after all, the plot revolves around the attempt to blow up the Greenwich Observatory, the very place from which clock time is measured. When Vladimir commands Verloc to "[g]o for the first meridian" (SA 33), his choice of target is made in full awareness of the location's symbolic significance. In 1884 the International Meridian Conference at Washington had determined that the basis for the coordination of the world's time zones should be the zero- or prime-meridian passing through Greenwich (cf. Watts, "Monstrous Town" 28). The Observatory thus became the keeper of Standard World Time and gained tremendous national and international prestige. For this reason Vladimir can assert that "[t]he whole civilized world has heard of Greenwich" (SA 32). According to Stallman, Vladimir understands that on a metaphorical level "all time – legal time, civil time, astronomical time, and Universal Time – emanates from Greenwich Observatory" (236). Thus the planned attack can be seen as an attempt to "destroy Time Now, Universal Time, or life itself" (Stallman 236). As Vladimir explains to Verloc, he, however, also wishes to attack what he regards as "the fetish of the hour that all the bourgeoisie recognise" (SA 29), science. Because he cannot "throw a bomb into pure mathematics" (SA 31), he orders Verloc to "have[..] a go at astronomy" (SA 31) instead, a science which the Greenwich Observatory embodies. As my discussion in Chapter 2 has shown, the claims Vladimir makes for the role of science in society, albeit polemically phrased, are not far off the mark. Although science might not have been the "fetish" of the middle class, it had replaced religion as a source of truth for many people. Vladimir also understands that the scientific-materialist world picture has been one of the main reasons for the increasing prosperity of the middle class since the Industrial Revolution. He also knows that a uniform international time system is in the commercial interests of the bourgeoisie and of the British Empire. Standard World Time is therefore not just a scientific but also a social and economic construction, which is reflected in Vladimir's statement that the prospected outrage should show the anarchists' determination to "make a clean sweep of the whole social creation" (SA 30).

The dismal failure of Vladimir's plan also suggests the impossibility to escape from or to destroy objective or clock-time, which the Greenwich Observatory after all embodies. Poignantly, however, time is 'exploded' on the discourse level through unchronological narration. A prominent example occurs at the very beginning of the novel. The opening sentence – "Mr

Verloc, going out in the morning, left his shop nominally in charge of his brother-in-law" (SA 9) – seems to throw us right into the middle of the action. However, what follows is an expository analepsis, providing information about Verloc's shop and his domestic situation. In chronological terms, Verloc only sets out on his walk to the Embassy at the beginning of Chapter II. Thus, between the start of the first and the beginning of the second chapter, time appears to be suspended. Another example of temporal dislocation is the ellipsis covering about a month between Chapters III and IV. The reader registers with surprise that the bomb outrage has already been committed and must believe, with the Professor and Ossipon, that the "man blown up in Greenwich Park this morning" (SA 58) is Verloc himself. Chapter V is chronologically continuous and follows the Professor as he walks home from the Silenus in the late afternoon. When he is accosted by Chief Inspector Heat "in a narrow and dusky alley" (SA 67), we expect the ensuing dialogue to follow straight away. Instead, a spectacular analepsis occurs, during which we learn about Heat's investigations since he received "the first telegram from Greenwich a little before eleven in the morning" (SA 68). In the course of eight pages the narrative performs a chronological loop, returning, finally, to the temporal starting point: the conversation between the policeman and the anarchist is resumed as if no interruption had taken place. Although the next two chapters (VI and VII) also contain a number of flashbacks, they proceed chronologically up to the point where the Assistant Commissioner is ready to enter Brett Street to question Verloc. Chapter VIII, however, interrupts the linear sequence of events and starts out with Winnie's mother's decision to move to an almshouse in South London in order to protect her son. It takes the reader some time to realize that now the time gap between Chapters III and IV – Verloc's return home from his conversation with Vladimir and the explosion in Greenwich Park – is being filled. Whereas Chapter VIII is mainly concerned with Winnie's mother's last cab ride, Chapter IX reveals how Verloc came up with the idea to use Stevie as his cat's-paw and how he managed to install him at Michaelis's cottage in the country. Thus the reader is able to answer some of the questions surrounding the outrage which, as yet, baffle the Assistant Commissioner and Heat. The most notable chronological feature of the main action's denouement is that the events of Chapter X occur simultaneously with those of Chapters XI and XII (cf. Stallman 246). Another ellipsis of ten days occurs between the action in Chapter XII and that of Chapter XIII which concludes the novel.

The power of objective time is, however, not only undermined by instances of anachrony but also by the frequent emphasis on the disparity between time as formally measured and time as personally experienced (cf.

Fleishman, "Symbolic World" 213ff). Chief Inspector Heat contemplates this phenomenon while pouring over Stevie's remains on a table in a hospital. He is beset by the "inexplicable mysteries of conscious existence" and thereby rises "above the vulgar conception of time" (SA 71). Looking at the "heap of nameless fragments" that Stevie's body has been reduced to, he "evolve[s] a horrible notion that ages of atrocious pain and mental torture could be contained between two successive winks of an eye" (SA 71). Subjective time may thus expand immeasurably while, according to clock-time, only a few seconds pass. A similar situation occurs during Winnie's mother's last cab ride. Due to the traffic in Whitehall and the infirm horse, the hackney carriage makes hardly any progress so that "time itself seem[s] to stand still" (SA 121). This 'frozen moment' appears to continue indefinitely and thus becomes emblematic of Winnie and her mother's suffering. Another scene that memorably dramatizes the contrast between the two concepts of time is Winnie's murder of her husband. Although the stabbing occurs in a matter of seconds and Verloc's death is instantaneous, he nevertheless manages to "take in the full meaning" (SA 197) of what is happening to him, determines "to come out victorious from the ghastly struggle with that armed lunatic" (SA 197), and "to elaborate a plan of defence" (SA 197). Directly after the murder, time seems to stand still for Winnie: she "[does] not think at all" and "enjoy[s] her complete irresponsibility and endless leisure" (SA 198). Finally, she becomes aware of a "ticking sound in the room" which confuses her as she remembers that "the clock on the wall was silent, had no audible tick" (SA 198). The ticking grows

> fast and furious like the pulse of an insane clock. At its highest speed this ticking changed into a continuous sound of trickling. Mrs Verloc watched that transformation with shadows of anxiety coming and going on her face. It was a trickle, dark, swift, thin. ... Blood! (SA 199)

Follwing time's apparent congealment, it then accelerates, reflecting Winnie's overwhelming sense of panic as she realizes what she has done. Once again, subjective time stands in stark contrast to objective time and expresses the state of mind of the character.

According to Fleishman, in addition to clock-time and experienced time, "the novel also proposes a vision of time beyond history" ("Symbolic World" 216). This a-historical or cosmic time is, for instance, invoked when the events and characters are seen in relation to an immense, non-human entity such as London or to indefinable places such as the Italian restaurant, Brett Place, or the second-hand furniture shop. The narrator's famous description of Winnie's murder (cf. SA 197) also brings into play cosmic time. The reader is not only made aware of Winnie's parental ancestry but also of that of her species, thus drawing attention to the inexorable forces of evolution and its gigantic time-scales. Another instance is Stevie's "mad art" – his drawing of "circles, circles, circles; innumerable circles" – which the narrator interprets as "a rendering of cosmic chaos" (SA 40). According to Hillis Miller, Stevie in this way intuits a Nietzschean view of the universe in which "the laws of time and space and the laws of logical thought are broken" (*Poets* 59). Nietzsche, as we have seen in Chapter 1, believed that the 'true' nature of the world is without structure, irrational, and indeterminist and that the ordering systems human beings impose upon the world – such as language, scientific laws, the coordinates of time and space – are therefore completely arbitrary. Stevie's drawings can thus be seen to offer us the intimation of a world that eludes our conceptualizing powers.

As Mark Hama has pointed out, it befits a novel that is concerned to such a significant extent with the multi-faceted nature of time that its last scene "juxtaposes three quite distinctive visions of time – Michaelis's, the Professor's, and Ossipon's" (138). Michaelis is a Marxist who is convinced that human beings' consciousness and behaviour are subject to an economic determinism that is also the driving force of history. He imagines the latter as a progressive process that will inevitably lead to the establishment of a socialist utopia where all class struggle will cease and where, as a consequence, history and historical time will be overcome. Although the Professor has nothing but contempt for Michaelis's naïve beliefs, he, too, dreams of "starting over in a suprahistorical world" (Hama 139). For the Professor this utopia is not the culminating point of an inevitable historical process but the result of the utter "destruction of what is" (SA 228). Paradoxically, however, the Professor's plan is dependent on what he wants to annihiliate, time. He seems to realize this himself when he cries out to Ossipon, "Give me time!" (SA 226), and refers to his other great enemy, the indifference of the human multitude. In contrast to the Professor, Ossipon has no hope of any kind for a world beyond time; for him "eternity is a damned hole" (SA 227). Human beings are mortal and determined by historical time; their only desire is "to live – to live" (SA 227). In Ossipon's vision of the future, therefore, "doctors will rule the world" because they will be in a position to "serve you out your time – if you are good" (SA 227). He is convinced that even the Professor would bow down to the person that "could give [him] for certain ten years of time" (SA 227). Ironically, there is no doubt that Ossipon, whose fanatical worship of science is repeatedly ridiculed in the novel, has reached the end of *his* time at the conclusion of the novel. Shattered by his betrayal of Winnie, "his robust form [...][is]

marching in the gutter as if in training for the task of an inevitable future" (SA 231). It seems that all of the characters in the novel who try to tamper with or overcome time – either symbolically as in the Greenwich outrage or more philosophically as in the examples above – fail in some way or other. It is only the narrator who manages to undermine successfully time's deterministic power.

7.3   Society and its control mechanisms

In *Heart of Darkness* Marlow disturbs his listeners' complacency by telling them that they would degenerate just as quickly as Kurtz if exposed to similar circumstances. He then mentions two professions that ensure that this does not happen in European societies, "the butcher and the policeman" (HD 116). Revealingly, representatives of both professions abound in *The Secret Agent*. As a large part of the novel is concerned with a police investigation, the frequent reference to the forces of law and order is to be expected. What is remarkable, however, is the sheer omnipresence of police officers and plain-clothes detectives on the streets of London. There is, for instance, the already mentioned "thick police constable looking a stranger to every emotion" who suddenly "surg[es] [...] out of a lamp post" (SA 17) as if endowed with supernatural qualities. When Verloc decides to demonstrate the power of his voice to Vladimir, there is a policeman ready to answer his call just "across the courtyard" (SA 24). In Chapter VII Toodles reveals that to ensure the safety of his employer and the other MPs "[t]here's a constable stuck by every lamp-post, and every second person we meet between this and Palace Yard is an obvious 'tec'" (SA 112). When the Assistant Commissioner and Chief Inspector Heat pay a visit to Verloc as 'private citizens' on the night of the bombing, they have to take "especial pains to avoid all the police constables on point and patrol duty in the vicinity of Brett Street" (SA 153). The police's aim in *The Secret Agent* is, however, not just omnipresence but also omniscience, which they attempt to achieve by means of a sophisticated and comprehensive system of surveillance. The initial phase of the investigation into the failed bombing illustrates how the whole populace comes under the police's panoptic gaze. At Greenwich the "first man on the spot" (SA 70) is a local constable who, at the time of the explosion, "was standing at the door of the King William Street Lodge talking to the [park] keeper" (SA 70-71). A telegram is immediately dispatched to Scotland Yard and witnesses are sought for and questioned. An "old woman" (SA 72) is found who, according to the constable, "noticed two men coming out of the station after the up train had gone on [...]. [...] She took no particular notice of the big one, but the other was a fair, slight chap, carrying a tin varnish can in one hand" (SA 72). As if she had been trained to the job of a surveillance officer or detective, the woman even noticed that Stevie was wearing a "[d]ark blue overcoat with a velvet collar" (SA 73). Indeed, the latter will prove to be the most important piece of evidence later as it contains Stevie's address. When Chief Inspector Heat wants to know more about the witness, the officer has all the information at hand. He replies "weightily" that "[s]he's housekeeper to a retired publican, and attends the chapel in Park Place sometimes" (SA 72). In Chapter V the Assistant Commissioner imagines how the investigation would have proceeded further as a matter of routine: "A few inquiries amongst the ticket collectors and the porters of the two small railway stations would give additional details as to the appearance of the two men; the inspection of the collected tickets would show at once where they came from that morning" (SA 81). Heat, indeed, confirms that all of this has been done. The deposition of the porter at Maze Hill Station corresponds to that of the old woman and is similarly astounding in its accuracy (cf. SA 81). Heat further reveals that the inspection of the collected tickets has left no doubt that the two suspects boarded the train at a "little country station" (SA 81) in the vicinity of Michaelis's cottage. As these examples illustrate, it is not just the police who keep a close watch on everything that goes on around them. The system of surveillance is so pervasive that members of the public automatically continue it. For these reasons William Moseley Jr. sees the society portrayed in *The Secret Agent* as an illustration of Michel Foucault's claim that "the power of social organization is based on the panoptic principle" (59). It enables a small number of individuals to impose order on a vast number of people so that "the system of surveillance – the belief that a "guard" is watching – [...] become[s] ingrained in each member [of society] in order to regulate individuals within the modern state" (Moseley 60).

The investigation into the Greenwich outrage concerns the prosecution of actual *criminal* activity. However, there are also instances in the novel where a policeman immediately thwarts the mere possibility of disorder among ordinary citizens. In Chapter I we, for instance, learn that Stevie failed as an errand-boy because he was mesmerized by the attractions of street-life, such as "the dramas of fallen horses, whose pathos and violence induced him sometimes to shriek piercingly in a crowd" (SA 13). To keep the latter from being disturbed "by sounds of distress in its quiet enjoyment of the national spectacle [...] a grave and protecting policeman" (SA 13) is immediately at hand to lead Stevie away. In another memorable scene Winnie's mother all of a sudden loses heart on seeing that she is to be conveyed to the almshouse by "a maimed driver" commanding an "infirm horse" (SA 121). When the cabman notices her hesitation, he flies into a rage of "passionate expostulations" (SA 121). At that moment the "police-constable of the locality" appears as if by magic and "quiet[s] him by a friendly glance" (SA 121). He then turns to Winnie and her mother and says, "He's been driving a cab for twenty years. I never knew him to have an accident" (SA 121). Not only is the length of acquaintance astonishing but also the implication that the decrepit but innocent cabman has been under the officer's intimate observation for such a long time. According to Moseley, this kind of surveillance "exercised not only a physical control over the lives of working-class and poor Londoners, but [...] also penetrated the individual's psyche to the point of instilling in the populace a sense of moral control over their lives, constituting an effective political technology" (65). Mrs Verloc's thoughts and behaviour after her murder are a good example of this claim. As soon as she realizes that she has committed a capital offence, the punishment exacted for such crimes looms up threateningly in her mind, namely "the gallows" (SA 201). She starts to imagine "the business of hanging her by the neck" (SA 201) in vivid images informed by newspaper articles and "illustrative woodcuts to a certain type of tale" (SA 201). Winnie is surprisingly well informed as to the details of executions and can even remember verbatim phrases from reports in the press (cf. SA 201). This is not entirely surprising as, for instance, *The Times* of the late nineteenth-century featured daily reports about the capture, sentencing, and execution of criminals (cf. Moseley 65 ff). The press, therefore, had become another "policing agency" (Mallios 162) and vehicle for the dissemination of the surveillance system. By making visible the legal and penal procedures newspapers not only put their readers into the positions of 'surveillers' and potential 'surveillants' but by holding up the convicts as examples of exacted punishments they also implicitly transmitted the desired rules of social behaviour. This is reflected in the way Winnie's execution takes place, as it were, in her imagination (cf. Conroy 216ff) before she sentences herself to death by drowning in the Channel.

Ossipon may serve as another illustration of the power of the surveillance system and of how it may infiltrate an individual's mind. Certainly, as an anarchist and "special delegate of the more or less mysterious Red Committee [...] for the work of literary propaganda" (SA 41) he has more reason to be concerned about being watched than Winnie Verloc. Indeed, his actions and movements are informed by the wish that the police should not "form an exaggerated notion of his revolutionary sympathies" (SA 204).

Therefore, although he should theoretically welcome the Greenwich outrage, he panics and calls it "nothing short of criminal" (SA 59). When Ossipon anxiously wonders what he had better do now, the Professor sardonically suggests turning to the police for protection: "They know where every one of you slept last night. Perhaps if you asked them they would consent to publish some sort of official statement" (SA 63-64). Ossipon feels "virtuous indignation [that] the even tenor of his revolutionary life [is] menaced by no fault of his" (SA 64) and worries about the next steps the police might take. He believes they "will be bound to make some arrests," turn Verloc's shop into "a police trap" and increase their surveillance of "marked anarchists" (SA 64). When Ossipon bumps into Mrs Verloc late at night and realizes that she has murdered her husband, he is scared of being "saddle[d] [...] with complicity" and is "terrified at the thought that he [cannot] prove the use he [has] made of his time since seven o'clock" (SA 216). The elaborate precautions he asks Winnie to take before boarding the train is further evidence of his fears of the all-seeing police. During Ossipon's later aimless walks through the streets of London the very city becomes the panopticum (cf. Conroy 214), the embodiment of Ossipon's paranoia: "[T]he towers of the Abbey *saw* in their massive immobility the yellow bush of his hair passing under the lamps. The lights of Victoria *saw* him too, and Sloane Square, and the railings of the park" (SA, 224; my italics). Although Ossipon's fear of being caught up in the penal and justice system seems excessive, the fate of Michaelis illustrates that it is not unjustified. Michaelis certainly confirms Karl Yundt's definition of the law as a "pretty branding instrument" (SA 41) as his "own skin [has] sizzled under the red hot brand" (SA 42). He was passed a life-sentence for his minor role "in a rather mad attempt to rescue some prisoners from a police van" (SA 84) during which an officer was killed. After fifteen years he was liberated on a so-called "ticket-of-leave" and, since then, has been at the beck and call of the police. As a result of his solitary confinement he has developed a "grotesque and incurable obesity" (SA 85) and can no longer work or interact meaningfully with other people. Although he is theoretically at liberty, his existence remains determined by his prison experience.

The doubts Michaelis's example raises as to the fairness of the penal and justice system are reinforced by what we learn about Chief Inspector Heat and his attempt to turn him into the scapegoat for the failed bombing. For Heat the Greenwich outrage is particularly annoying due to its occurrence "less than a week after he [has] assured a high official that no outbreak of anarchist activity [is] to be apprehended" (SA 68). He has made this assertion not because of its factual truth but because "the high official desired greatly to hear that very thing" (SA 69). The narrator comments that Heat's knowledge and experience should have taught him to be more cautious. On the other hand "[t]rue wisdom, which is not certain of anything in this world of contradictions, would have prevented him from attaining his present position. It would have alarmed his superiors, and done away with his chances of promotion. His promotion had been very rapid" (SA 69). This implies that to 'get on' in the police apparatus and, possibly, in society as a whole, it is better to steer away from the truth or to convert it into the version most palatable to one's superiors. When Heat enters the office of his immediate superior, the Assistant Commissioner, to inform him about the Greenwich bombing, he is again determined to rely on a trusted principle, namely that "[i]t would not be good for [the department's] efficiency to know too much" (SA 73). He has decided to conceal his knowledge of the address written on the "square piece of calico" (SA 98) he found among Stevie's remains. After all, this would clearly establish a link to Verloc, who is – among many other things – Heat's informer. Although it seems obvious that the police investigation should include the Professor, a known fabricator of bombs, Heat cannot overcome his "dislike of being compelled by events to meddle with [his] desperate ferocity" (SA 96). For Heat the most expedient way of dealing with the affair is to arrest another notable anarchist, Michaelis. After all, he is an ex-convict and therefore "the rules of the game [do] not protect [him] so much" as other individuals "whose arrest [would be] a more complicated matter" (SA 95). The evidence he has for Michaelis's involvement in the bombing is merely circumstantial but "enough to go upon" (SA 90), especially because it is "perfectly legal to arrest that man on the barest suspicion" (SA 95). The Assistant Commissioner, however, is not so easily convinced and observes that Heat "will want some [more] conclusive evidence" (SA, 90). The Inspector's reply is shocking in its careless nonchalance: "There will be no difficulty in getting up sufficient evidence against *him* […]. You may trust me for that, sir […]" (SA 90). The implication is that Heat would even stoop to manufacture evidence in order to bring the case to a satisfactory conclusion. Troublesome is not just Heat's *own* idea of legality but his evident belief that his superiors share it. This becomes clear when he contemplates regretfully that, in contrast to the present Assistant Commissioner, his "two former chiefs would have seen the point [of arresting Michaelis] at once" (SA 95). Heat is genuinely convinced that his planned course of action is not just in accordance with Scotland Yard's established traditions but also in its best interests. After all, blaming Michaelis would have the additional advantage of taking from Heat and the department the expected pressure from the press and public opinion, especially if the affair remained unresolved. To Heat it seems "an excellent thing to have that man in hand to be thrown down to the public should it think fit to roar with any special indignation in this case" (SA 90). He knows that "in the last instance [this] depend[s], of course, on the newspaper press" (SA 90) but he is convinced that "the journalists who [have] written [Michaelis] up with emotional gush would be ready to write him down with emotional indignation" (SA 95-96). The so-called "ticket-of-leave-apostle" (SA 37) is therefore in danger of becoming – for the third time in his life – the helpless toy of the shifting alliances between the public, the press, and the justice system. Just as initially the "ferocity of the life sentence passed upon him" (SA 84) was partly due to "public sentiment" (SA 84), his release on parole was also prepared "by people who wished to exploit the sentimental aspect of his imprisonment" (SA 85). It is especially the "celebrity bestowed upon Michaelis on his release two years ago by some emotional journalists in want of special copy [which has] rankled ever since in [Heat's] breast" (SA 95). Buried beneath all the other motives for having the anarchist detained there is therefore also a very personal one: Heat regards Michaelis's arrest as an opportunity to revenge himself and to have his maxim vindicated that "incarceration [is] the proper fate for every declared enemy of the law" (SA 90). Inspector Heat's egoism and spitefulness are confirmed later by his inability to accept that the Assistant Commissioner has taken over the investigation. Although he realizes that he has effectively been "chucked out of that case" (SA 153), he cannot resist turning up at 32 Brett Street himself in the hope that "Mr Verloc's talk would be of a nature to incriminate Michaelis" (SA 153). When it emerges that Verloc has agreed to a full confession, Heat deliberately undermines his superior's arrangements by telling the secret agent not to "trust too much the gentleman who's been talking to you" (SA 159) and "to clear out while you may" (SA 160). As Verloc's determination to "tell the whole story" (SA 159) might make life difficult for Heat as well, his advice primarily serves his own interests.

Although the Assistant Commissioner cannot be classed with the Chief Inspector, his impulse to protect Michaelis and to take over the case himself also springs from self-interest. When Heat mentions the ticket-of-leave-apostle, the Assistant Commissioner is overcome by "a special kind of interest in his work of social protection – an improper sort of interest, which may be defined best as a sudden and alert mistrust of the weapon in his hand" (SA 82). This suspicion is not primarily aroused by a concern for the Chief Inspector's idea of legality, by the fear of a possible miscarriage of justice, or the need to save an innocent man from imprisonment but by the "instinct of self preservation" (SA 89), which tells him to safeguard at all costs the peace and quiet of his domestic situation. One of the few details we learn about the Assistant Commissioner's background is that, subsequent to his employment in "a tropical colony" (SA 79), he "got married rather impulsively" (SA 80). It is "a good match from a worldly point of view," especially because of his wife's "influential connections" (SA 80). Principal among the latter is the so-called Lady Patroness, a renowned aristocratic society hostess, who has made the Assistant Commissioner's "married life much easier than it would have been without her generously full recognition of his rights as Annie's husband. Her influence upon his wife, a woman devoured by all sorts of small selfishnesses, small envies, small jealousies, was excellent" (SA 88). The Lady Patroness, however, does not just extend her patronage to members of her own class but prides herself on "attracting within her ken [...] everything that [rises] above the dead level of mankind" (SA 83). Thus she has also received Michaelis in her drawing room and has judged him to be "inoffensive" (SA 87). She has even "come to believe, almost, [Michaelis's] theory of the future" and her sympathy for the revolutionist is described as "a deep, calm, convinced infatuation" (SA 87). The Assistant Commissioner knows that if Michaelis is arrested for complicity in the outrage, he will be "sent back to finish his sentence" and will "never come out alive" (SA 89). He is also aware that the Lady Patroness's "arbitrary kindness would not brook patiently any interference with Michaelis' freedom" (SA 87), which, in turn, would have an adverse influence on his marriage. He therefore comes to a conclusion "extremely unbecoming his official position without being really creditable to his humanity. "If the fellow is laid hold of again, [...] she will never forgive me"" (SA 89). It is from this moment onward that the Assistant Commissioner proceeds to "turn [the Chief Inspector] inside out like an old glove" (SA 93) and – due to the unexpected information Heat divulges – "succumb[s] to a fascinating temptation" (SA 103), namely to take on the case himself. Although partly motivated by the desire to give justice its due, his decision is nevertheless grounded in egoism and, furthermore, smacks of self-indulgence. After all, the Assistant Commissioner is not only unhappy with his marriage but also with his job. He is annoyed with his dependence "on too many subordinates and too many masters" (SA 80) and feels that the office work that he is now forced to do is "the bane of his existence because of its confined nature and apparent lack of reality" (SA 104). Because he is really "a born detective" (SA 92) and possesses "an adventurous disposition" (SA 89), he cannot resist the chance to escape the "futility of office work" (SA 80). Despite the Assistant Commissioner's problematic reasons for his action, he should not be judged too harshly. In contrast to Chief Inspector Heat he is, for instance, not prone to vanity and self-satisfaction. He has not "preserve[d] many saving illusions about himself" and is therefore capable of "some derisive self-criticism" (SA 89), not least with regard to the true motives for his intercession on behalf of Michaelis. Furthermore, his manner of dealing with Heat, Verloc, and the Home Secretary proves the narrator's comment that he "has really some qualifications for his post" (SA 90). Nevertheless it is doubtful whether the fact that the Assistant Commissioner does, as it were, the right thing for the wrong reasons is likely to restore the reader's trust in the police and justice system as it is portrayed in *The Secret Agent*.

Certainly, the character at the pinnacle of the police hierarchy, the Home Secretary, does not inspire much confidence either. In the two scenes featuring Sir Ethelred he is only referred to as the "great Personage" (SA 107) or the "great Presence" (SA 162) and it is suggested that his greatness is confined to his physical size. He appears "[v]ast in bulk and stature, with a big white face [...] broadened at the base by a big double chin" (SA 105) and "[f]rom the head, set upwards on a thick neck, the eyes, with puffy lower lids, [stare] with a haughty droop on each side of a hooked aggressive nose, nobly salient in the vast pale circumference of the face" (SA 105-106). Indeed, the "haughty eyes [are] physically the great man's weak point" (SA 164) and the reader suspects that this defect has metaphoric significance as well. After all, during the two interviews with the Assistant Commissioner, Sir Ethelred constantly asks him to "[b]e lucid" (SA 108) and to "[s]pare [him] the details" (SA 106), as if the complexity of human affairs were simply too much for him. The portrayal of the Home Secretary turns into caricature when we learn that his most pressing concern at present is his "Bill for the Nationalisation of Fisheries" (SA 112) and that his private secretary with the Dickensian nickname Toodles regards this as a "revolutionary measure" (SA 112).

As we have seen, the significance of the police in *The Secret Agent* can hardly be overestimated. Due to their ubiquitous presence and their sophisticated system of surveillance the forces of law and order are capable of wielding enormous power not just over the life of the individual but over society as a whole. What we learn about the internal mechanisms of the police apparatus certainly does not confirm Vladimir's and the Professor's claims that Britain's institutions are characterized by a "sentimental regard for individual liberty" (SA 28) or an "idealistic conception of legality" (SA 60). Indeed, as John Lyon has put it, "[i]n the hard-headed logic of *The Secret Agent*, the London police are not the measure of a civilized society but an indication of just how far short of civilization that society falls" (*The Secret Agent* xx). The most subversive suggestion about the police in the novel, however, is that the policeman and the criminal exist in a symbiotic relationship so that we can no longer distinguish between them. During his conversation with Ossipon in the Silenus the Professor expresses this idea in respect to the relation between the police officer and the revolutionary terrorist: "The terrorist and the policeman both come from the same basket. Revolution, legality – counter moves in the same game; forms of idleness at bottom identical" (SA 58). Surprisingly, the complacent and uncritical Chief Inspector Heat puts forward a somewhat similar notion. His contempt for the anarchists makes him feel nostalgic about the beginning of his career when he was concerned with "the more energetic forms of thieving" (SA 74). Unlike anarchism, robbery is to him "not a sheer absurdity. It [is] a form of industry, perverse indeed, but still an industry exercised in an industrious world; it [is] work undertaken for the same reason as the work in potteries, in coal mines, in fields, in tool-grinding shops" (SA 74). According to Heat, therefore, the difference between respectable forms of labour and criminal activity merely lies in the possible risk entailed: in the case of the former this might be "ankylosis, or lead poisoning, or fire damp, or gritty dust," in the case of the latter "[s]even years hard" (SA 74). Because to the Chief Inspector "the idea of thieving appear[s] [...] as normal as the idea of property" (SA 75), he is not bothered by the question whether it is fair that society should punish a working man for his life of toil as severely as a thief for his crimes. Neither does Heat realize that his train of thought thoroughly undermines his own professional, social, and moral position, which no longer appears superior or essentially different to that of the criminal. The sardonic narrator, however, enjoys pointing this out to the reader:

> [T]he mind and the instincts of a burglar are of the same kind as the mind and instincts of a police officer. Both recognise the same conventions [...]. [...] Products of the same machine, one classed as useful and the other as noxious, they take the machine for granted in different ways, but with a seriousness essentially the same. (SA 74-75)

The observation at the beginning of the quote is borne out later in the novel when both the Assistant Commissioner and the Chief Inspector behave like criminals when they avoid police officers on their way to Verloc's shop. The comparison of the relationship between society and the individual to a machine that arbitrarily labels its products reminds us of similar deterministic passages in *Heart of Darkness* and *Nostromo* and of Conrad's famous description of the universe as an indifferent "knitting machine." As regards *The Secret Agent*, the metaphor underlines the blurring of distinctions between the legal and the illegal, the criminal and the law-abiding. As the meaning of these words is eroded, we are left to wonder whether we should, as a consequence, regard all characters in the narrative as equally innocent or equally criminal. Judging from a well-known passage in a letter already quoted in Chapter 3, Conrad would probably have wanted us to choose the second option: "Man is a vicious animal. His viciousness must be organised. Crime is a necessary condition of organised existence. Society is fundamentally criminal – or it would not exist" (*CL2*: 160).

7.4   Society and economic determinism

Even if there is no silver mine in *The Secret Agent*'s London, material interests are just as ubiquitous as in *Nostromo*'s Sulaco. As Margarete Holubetz has emphasized "[t]he fates of all characters [in *The Secret Agent*] are influenced by money. Money decides upon their positions in society and their well-being; it motivates their marriages and the choice of their professions, their heroic decisions and their base betrayals" (15). The uneven distribution of wealth in this society produces glaring social inequality, which is aggravated by the bias of the justice and penal system in favour of those at the top of the social hierarchy. In the novel we encounter many instances of the immense gap between the rich and the poor. The glimpses we are afforded of the lives of the well-to-do include the "majesty" (SA 17) of private streets such as the one leading to Vladimir's Embassy, the social rituals of the upper classes in Hyde Park, the exclusive but shallow gatherings of the moneyed and/or fashionable at the Lady Patroness's receptions, the complacent behaviour of eminent politicians like Sir Ethelred, and poignant vignettes such as that of a "gorgeous perambulator of a wealthy baby being wheeled in state across [a] Square" (SA 24). These scenes are juxtaposed to those that reveal the social deprivation, poverty, and suffering of the majority of Londoners. The city may thus also appear as a wasteland full of "low brick houses [that have] in their dusty windows the sightless, moribund look of incurable decay" (SA 67), or as consisting of "monotonous streets with unknown names where the dust of humanity settles inert and hopeless out of the stream of life" (SA 224). There are the depressing charity cottages in South London to which Winnie's mother retires, the Professor's small house in Islington down a "shabby street, littered with straw and dirty paper" (SA 53), or the "dismal row of newspaper sellers" outside the Silenus, who "deal[.] out their wares from the gutter" (SA 65). The two representatives of the working class that put in brief but memorable appearances – Mrs Neale and the cabdriver – exemplify the inescapable hardships and humiliating constraints of poverty. Mrs Neale, the "charwoman of Brett Street," is the "[v]ictim of her marriage with a debauched joiner [and is] oppressed by the needs of many infant children" (SA 138). Her misery has turned her into a sub-human creature, "a sort of amphibious and domestic animal living in ash-bins and dirty water" (SA 140) that "exhale[s] the anguish of the poor in a breath of soapsuds and rum" (SA 138). Aaron Fogel has drawn attention to the "uncompromisingly allegorical note" of the character's speaking name, which "refers to the plainest servitude or slavery" (180). Like Mrs Neale, the cabman who takes Winnie's mother on her last ride suffers from social and economic destitution: he, too, is an alcoholic and seems hardly human. Instead of an arm, a "hooked iron contrivance protrude[s] out of [his] coat," his voice seems to be "squeezed out of a blocked throat," and his "enormous and unwashed countenance flame[s] red in the muddy stretch of the street" (SA 121). Even more pathetic and pitiable than the maimed driver is his infirm and emaciated horse, "the steed of apocalyptic misery" (SA 128). The cabby's refusal to heed Stevie's emotional entreaty not to hurt the suffering horse prompts an irrefutable narratorial comment on economic necessity: the driver whips the animal *not* because "his soul [is] cruel and his heart evil, but because he [has] to earn his fare" (SA 122). The cabman explains to Stevie that he has no choice but to sit behind his horse "[t]ill three or four o'clock in the morning" because he has "got [his] missus and four kids at 'ome" (SA 128). Stevie is struck dumb by the "monstrous nature of that declaration of paternity" (SA 128) and feels "indignation and horror at one sort of wretchedness having to feed upon the anguish of the other – at the poor cabman beating the poor horse in the name, as it were, of his poor kids at home" (SA 132). According to Jacques Berthoud, the conclusion Stevie laboriously arrives at – ""Bad world for poor people"" (SA 132) – shows how he "manages to conceive of the poor as part of a veritable system of suffering, in which the relief of misery requires the infliction of misery" (*Conrad* 140). This insight into the nature of society and its economic necessities is comparable to Marlow's sudden comprehension of the mechanics of imperialism in the "grove of death" in *Heart of Darkness*. What Berthoud calls "Stevie's momentary lifting of the veil" (*Conrad* 140) is therefore another Schopenhaueran moment of true understanding. Berthoud, however, adds the caveat that the "vision of society as some kind of pain generator is clearly not one in terms of which normal life can be led" (*Conrad* 140). This might explain why virtually all characters in *The Secret Agent* follow Winnie's dictum that "things do not stand much looking into" (SA 136). The cabman is certainly no exception and, as soon as he has pocketed his fare, seeks forgetfulness in the "pub down the street" (SA 130).

As we have seen, the lives of Mrs Neale and the cabman are completely determined by the brutal social and economic system of which they form a helpless part. However, not only members of the working class find themselves in such a situation. Winnie, Stevie, and their mother, too, are uncomfortably close to destitution and are themselves part of the "system of suffering" that Stevie has revealed to lie at the heart of society. Mrs Verloc's mother is "a stout, wheezy woman, with a large brown face" and "swollen legs [which] render[.] her inactive" (SA 11). Her "dark, dusty wig, and ancient silk dress festooned with dingy white cotton lace" (SA 124) reveal both her pretence at gentility and her straitened circumstances. Physically and mentally Winnie's mother has been shaped by "the fires of adversity" and "the trials of a difficult and worried existence, first as wife, then as widow" (SA 123). After the death of her brutal husband she "provided for the years of widowhood by letting furnished apartments for gentlemen near Vauxhall Bridge Road in a square once of some splendour" (SA 11). Among her patrons, who were in general "not exactly of the fashionable kind" (SA 11), was also one Mr Verloc, whom she regarded as "a very nice gentleman" (SA 12). To Winnie's mother, Verloc's subsequent marriage to her daughter seemed "clearly providential" (SA 36) because it assured not only her daughter's but also her son's future – at least for the time being. The downside was that Winnie's mother lost her precarious financial independence as Verloc did not want to continue running the lodging house and took her and Stevie "over with the furniture" (SA 12). At the time of the novel's main action Winnie's mother has started to worry once again about her son's future and is haunted by the "vision of a workhouse infirmary for poor Stevie" (SA 127). As she has virtually no material possessions left, her desperate "arrangement for settling her son permanently in life" (SA 125) forces her to undergo what Berthoud calls "the contradictory paradoxes of poverty" (*Conrad* 142). First of all, what is really an act of maternal devotion has to take the form of an act of abandonment: she leaves Brett Street and her children for a charity almshouse in order to strengthen Stevie's "moral claim" (SA 125) on Winnie and her husband. Secondly, the welfare of her son requires her to sacrifice not just herself but also her daughter: in order to be allocated a place she has to convince the trustees of the charity that Winnie has driven her out. Thirdly, her heroic selflessness exposes her to the charge of ingratitude: Winnie suspects her of leaving out of dissatisfaction with her treatment in the Verloc houshold. The climax of Winnie's mother's suffering is reached when she is taken to South London in the aptly named "Cab of Death" (SA 131). During the agonizingly slow journey Winnie's mother's life of deprivation and misery seems to be condensed into one timeless moment of unbearable pain:

> The cab rattled, jingled, jolted [...]. By its disproportionate violence and magnitude it obliterated every sensation of onward movement; and the effect was of being shaken in a stationary apparatus like a mediaeval device for the punishment of crime [...]. [...] and the raising of Mrs Verloc's mother's voice sounded like a wail of pain. (SA 126)

The passage describes not only Winnie's mother's experience but also that of her two children who share the cab with her. The quote can, however, also be read as a general comment on what existence in this society is like. According to Jacques Berthoud, it is one of Conrad's "most suggestive symbols" and presents "the experience of unremitting hardship as a passage through life in which the travellers are isolated from one another in an endlessly distorting succession of shocks, strains, jolts, buffets, and dislocations" (*Conrad* 142). The cab ride thus forms a link in the pattern of pain that Stevie reveals to run through the whole of society. How remorseless this pattern can be is disclosed in the irony that shadows the entire sequence under discussion: the mother's very efforts to safeguard her son only bring about his destruction. As Berthoud puts it, "in her inevitable ignorance of the true thoughts of others, she initiates a causal chain the outcome of which she can neither foresee nor control" (*Conrad* 143). The first link in this chain is Winnie herself. While her mother does not doubt Winnie's devotion to Stevie, she nevertheless believes that "by making him over to his sister" she will give him "the advantage of a directly dependent position" (SA 125). What she considers to be a "move of deep policy" (SA 125) is tragically successful. Winnie's "quasi-maternal affection" (SA 13) for her brother is indeed intensified and she redoubles her efforts to recommend his usefulness and devotion to her husband. She even tells him, ""*You* could do anything with that boy, Adolf [...]. He would go through fire for you"" (SA 140). This is hardly an exaggeration: in her "endeavour to keep him from making himself objectionable in any way to the master of the house" (SA 35) Winnie, backed by her mother, has instilled in Stevie the "ethical fact" that "Mr Verloc [is] *good*" (SA 135). The latter, of course, has "no notion of appearing good to Stevie" (SA 135) and has hitherto "extended as much recognition to [him] as a man not particularly fond of animals may give to his wife's beloved cat" (SA 35). Now, however, he starts to feel flattered by "the extraordinary character of the influence he [apparently has] over Stevie" (SA 178) and even agrees to let him come along on his walks. While Winnie believes that "the supreme illusion of her life" (SA 184) is about to be realized – that Verloc should behave like the loving father Stevie never had –, the reader already knows that Verloc's kindness is in fact irresponsible selfishness. Driven to desperation by Vladimir's threats, he has decided to use Stevie as an unwitting accomplice in the bomb plot.

For Winnie the news of Stevie's death is a shock greater than "the most violent earthquake in history" (SA 192) and she starts "to perceive certain consequences which would have surprised Mr Verloc" (SA 189). They reveal her marriage to have been a sacrifice at least as painful as that of her mother:

> There was no need for her now to stay there, in that kitchen, in that house, with that man – since the boy was gone for ever. [...] Mrs Verloc began to look upon herself as released from all earthly ties. She had her freedom. Her contract with existence, as represented by that man standing over there, was at an end. (SA 189)

It transpires that Winnie has regarded her marriage as a trade-off: she has, as it were, sold herself to the lascivious and comparatively well-off Verloc in order to win financial support and protection for her two closest relatives. John Lyon uses drastic terms to describe the decision Winnie was driven to take:

> Given that we are left in no doubt that economic necessity [...] is the sole rationale for the Verlocs' relationship, what often seems merely a cliché – the notion of marriage as institutionalised prostitution – is here rendered particular and meaningful. (*The Secret Agent* xxxiii)

Winnie herself reveals the economic nature of her union with Verloc when she assesses it in terms of "seven years' security for Stevie, *loyally paid for on her part*" (SA 184; my italics). There is no doubt that the 'payments' Winnie believes Verloc to be entitled to by the terms of the 'contract' also include sexual services. It is therefore fitting that Verloc's veiled invitation to copulation should complete Winnie's transformation into a murderess:

> "Come here," he said in a peculiar tone, which might have been the tone of brutality, but, was intimately known to Mrs Verloc as the note of wooing.
> She started forward at once, as if she were still a loyal woman bound to that man by an unbroken contract. (SA 196-197)

Because, according to Winnie's logic, the contract has been broken by Verloc's murder of Stevie, she now feels free to kill him. In fact, her homicide is what has been "wanting on her part for the formal closing of the transaction" (SA 195). As we have seen, it is primarily economic circumstances that force Winnie and her mother to sacrifice their own right to happiness for the sake of a loved one. Partly due to society's structures, partly due to a tragic chain of cause and effect their acts of self-abnegation lead to the destruction of the very person they wanted to protect.

Jeremy Hawthorn has linked Stevie's total annihilation in the novel to the capitalist nature of the society in which he lives. He regards his fate as an extreme example of the process of alienation, "part of which involves the treatment of people as if they were merely things" (*Language* 74). This tendency seems ubiquitous in *The Secret Agent* and reminds us of *Nostromo*, where everyone is 'our man' to everyone else. Thus, Vladimir uses Verloc to implement his bombing plan, while Verloc, in turn, uses Stevie to carry it out; Karl Yundt and Ossipon exploit their female companions to survive financially; the Assistant Commissioner uses his wife to gain access to the highest levels of society, whereas Winnie has married Verloc to protect her mother and Stevie; Inspector Heat proposes to use Michaelis as a scapegoat to bring the investigation to a quick conclusion, while Michaelis himself uses the Lady Patroness to enable him to write his autobiography. Fittingly, people are frequently referred to as objects rather than as individualized human beings. Michaelis's extremities, for instance, are likened to "a dummy's limb[s]" (SA 37); Sir Ethelred "might have been the statue of one of his own princely ancestors" (SA 107); the Assistant Commissioner's face looks "wooden" (SA 162) and Ossipon's appears "like a fresh plaster cast" (SA 219); Winnie is compared to "a figure half chiselled out of a block of black stone" (SA 209). While Mrs Verloc gets up "as if raised by a spring" (SA 189), her husband obeys her command "woodenly, stony-eyed, like an automaton whose face [has] been painted red" (SA 149). According to Hawthorn, however, we not only come across a "reduction of the animate or living to the status of a thing" but also "a contrasting animism: objects not possessed of life are treated as if they were alive" (Hawthorn, *Language* 73). John Lyon, who has also noted this technique, regards it as expressive of the effects of the inordinate "valorization of property" (*The Secret Agent* xxi) that capitalism produces. Examples are the Verlocs' aggressive shop bell which "clatter[s] behind customer[s] with impudent virulence" (SA 10); Vladimir's "old fashioned bow-necktie [which] bristle[s] with unspeakable menaces" (SA 24); the Professor's "round black rimmed spectacles" which Ossipon envisages "progressing along the streets" independent of their bearer; Mr Verloc's hat which "as if accustomed to take care of itself, [makes] for a safe shelter under the table" (SA 195); or the mechanical piano in the Silenus which is able to "execute[...] suddenly all by itself a valse tune with aggressive virtuosity" (SA 52). Another aspect of the process of alienation that Robert Hampson has pointed out is the way the novel's society is "characterised by atomised individuals and the clash of individual interests" (*Joseph Conrad* 166). According to Hampson, this illustrates what Friedrich Engels regards "as the starkest revelation of the essence of capitalism: 'the unfeeling isolation of each in his private interest'" (*Joseph Conrad* 166). Although all of the characters in the novel are shown to be connected with each other in one way or another, these connections are only superficial and fleeting. Surrounded by what Hugh Epstein has called "deadening self-enclosure" (Introduction viii), genuine communication between the figures seems impossible. The anarchists, for instance, are only interested in grinding their ideological axes and do not listen to each other. Michaelis, in particular, is unable to converse with other people and only "talk[s] to himself, indifferent to the sympathy or hostility of his hearers, indifferent indeed to their presence" (SA 39). The Verlocs' marriage is based on silence, "unfathomable reserve" (SA 11), and the avoidance of communication. When Winnie tries to speak to her husband at the end of Chapter III, it is "as if her voice [is] talking on the other side of a very thick wall" (SA 49), and when Verloc attempts to explain himself after the Greenwich incident, he finds "it extremely difficult to get into contact with [his wife], now this tragic necessity had arisen" (SA 179). The Verlocs' failure to communicate and the misunderstandings and cross-purposes this engenders directly contribute to their own and Stevie's destruction. As Hugh Epstein has pointed out, this is a society in which words have become "a currency to be cashed for particular returns" (Introduction x). The result is an insincere use of language which is everywhere apparent in the novel. The anarchists talk in blood-curdling terms about revolution but would not dream of taking the smallest active step towards realizing their goals. At the Lady Patroness's receptions the guests engage in meaningless small talk and say what they think their hostess wants to hear. During the two long interview scenes between Vladimir and Verloc on the one hand, and the Assistant Commissioner and Chief Inspector Heat on the other the narrator constantly highlights the disparity between what the protagonists say and what they actually think. Ossipon is certain that although the police know that the anarchists have nothing to do with the bombing, they might say something completely different (cf. SA 64). For this reason he wants Michaelis, who is currently in favour with journalists, to make a public statement. Despite the fact that "[w]hat he would say would be utter bosh, [...] he has a turn of talk that makes it go down all the same" (SA 64). That Ossipon regards newspapers to be particularly susceptive to linguistic insincerity chimes with the sceptical view the novel in general takes of journalism. For the press language is indeed a currency and words possess particular exchange value. As Michaelis's fate illustrates, journalists may arbitrarily write an individual 'up' or 'down' in order to manipulate public opinion and to increase the sale of copies. For Jeremy Hawthorn the effect of the newspaper press on its readers is therefore a significant part of the process of alienation: "The person who gets his or her opinions in the form of prefabricated phrases from the popular press is in a real sense dehumanized, operated as a ventriloquist's dummy by other people's insincere words" (*Language* 88). Hawthorn's analysis is supported by the way newspaper phrases run through Winnie's and Ossipon's minds in interminable loops at the end of the novel and seem to turn the two characters into conscious automata.

7.5   Society and variants of Darwinian determinism

As we have seen, in *The Secret Agent* economic forces determine individual lives and society as a whole to an astonishing degree. However, just as in *Heart of Darkness* and *Nostromo*, Conrad insists in *The Secret Agent*, too, that the ubiquitous lack of freedom has its roots not only in a particular economic system but also in human nature. This draws our attention to the presence of Darwinism in the novel. Conspicuous are for instance the frequent comparisons of human beings to animals and the implied invocation of atavism, the idea that human beings might revert to earlier evolutionary stages. Verloc, for instance, is variously referred to as a "fat pig" (SA 16), a "bear" (SA 136), or a "domestic dog" (SA 31). He has the "air of a large animal in a cage" (SA 179) and is able to "bare[.] his teeth wolfishly" (SA 185). Directly after he has assured his wife that he is "a human being – and not a monster" (SA 193), he is described as a "reflective beast, not very dangerous – a slow beast with a sleek head, gloomier than a seal, and with a husky voice" (SA 193). Stevie, too, is sometimes likened to an animal: he "prowl[s] [...] like an excited animal in a cage" (SA 47) and "mope[s] in the striking fashion of an unhappy domestic animal" (SA 141). Vladimir refers to Verloc as an "animal" (SA 20) and the latter retorts by calling the First Secretary a "Hyperborean swine" (SA 160). Heat refers to the Professor as a "mad dog" (SA 96), while the terrorist himself compares the "immense multitude" (SA 66) of Londoners to "locusts" and "ants" (SA 67). As Avrom Fleishman argues the effect of the pervasive use of animal imagery is that "[t]he entire society comes to be seen as a jungle of animal forms obeying the laws of predatory survival. Alien to this world, forced to live in it yet inevitably devoured, men acquire the characters of beasts" ("Symbolic World" 209). These creatures are presented as largely controlled by their instincts and as hiding a brutal animal nature beneath an ordinary or even elegant exterior. Verloc, for instance, appears to strangers as if he were a respectable labourer: "a well to do mechanic," "picture-frame maker," or "locksmith" (SA 16). He seems "thoroughly domesticated" (SA 11) and his mother-in-law believes him to possess a "heavy good nature" (SA 12). His ordinariness is, however, undermined by the fact that he sells his wares "[w]ith a firm, steady eyed impudence, which seem[s] to hold back the threat of some abominable menace" (SA 10). Even more ominous is the way he is credited with "the air common to men who live on the vices, the follies, or the baser fears of mankind" (SA 16). This reminds us that Verloc is not any kind of shopkeeper but a pornographer and that his own sexual instincts are pronounced. He, for example, conveys the impression of "having wallowed, fully dressed, all day on an unmade bed" (SA 10), his eyes are wont to "roll[.] sideways amorously and languidly" and his "thick lips [are] capable of much honeyed banter" (SA 12). His "note[s] of wooing" are, however, expressed in the "tone of brutality" (SA 197). His barely repressed violence also manifests itself in his dreams of revenge on Vladimir and the "Embassy people" (SA 152). He wishes to be let "loose in there with a cudgel for half an hour [and to] keep on hitting till there [isn't] a single unbroken bone left amongst the whole lot" (SA 185). More than that, he would also like to "cut their hearts out one after another" (SA 152). The most notable example of Verloc's callousness and selfishness, however, is his use of Stevie to carry out the bomb plot, which shows his complete inability to empathize and to understand the value a human being might have to another person.

Whereas Verloc does not openly resort to violence in the course of the novel, his wife most spectacularly does. Winnie is the character in *The Secret Agent* who most powerfully illustrates how closely the ordinary and the savage may be intertwined. Although to a first-time reader Winnie's homicide might come as a shock, her transformation into a murderess is, in fact, carefully prepared; in particular by the way her behaviour is presented as instinct-driven. Her "unfathomable indifference" (SA 10) and "stony reserve" (SA 50), for instance, are more than assumed attitudes; they are the means of surviving a hardly bearable domestic situation. Indeed, her belief that "things don't bear looking into very much" (SA 138) is referred to as an "*instinctive* conviction" (SA 138; my italics). The suspicion that Winnie is repressing something beneath her outward complacency and incuriosity is confirmed by the narrator's revelation that "Mrs Verloc's temperament, [...] when stripped of its philosophical reserve, [is] maternal and violent" (SA 182). Certainly, her "militant love" (SA 186) for Stevie is rooted more deeply than in a pious commitment to altruism or to accepting responsibility for a relative: it has "the unerring nature and the force of an instinct" (SA 137). When Stevie is killed, Winnie regards her 'contract' with Verloc to be at an end and feels – for a moment at least – released from all bonds. Then, however, her instincts take control again and turn her into a killer: she becomes what Ossipon calls a "savage woman" (SA 216).

Not surprisingly, other characters, too, veer between the civilized and the instinctual-animalistic. Vladimir, for instance, has "a drawing room reputation as an agreeable and entertaining man" (SA 20), which, however, stands in stark contrast to his cynical talk of murder, butchery, destruction, and bombing campaigns during his interview with Verloc. He is also able to switch with perfect ease between a refined and a savage mode of speaking and behaving. At one moment he talks in French or "idiomatic English without the slightest trace of a foreign accent" (SA 21), at another he avails himself of "an amazingly guttural intonation not only utterly un-English, but absolutely un-European" (SA 24). During one part of the interview he is "[l]ying far back in the armchair, with squarely spread elbows, [...] throwing one leg over a thick knee" (SA 21), during another he "advance[s] into the room with such determination that the very ends of his [...] bow-necktie [seem] to bristle with unspeakable menaces" (SA 24). What Vladimir orders Verloc to do and the reasons he gives confirm his unscrupulousness and inhumanity.

As we have already seen, Chief Inspector Heat's brutality is also barely hidden beneath his official demeanour as a police officer. His "business" is described as "man hunting" (SA 80) and he regards "[c]atching thieves" as a "form of open sport where the best man wins" (SA 78). He views the Professor as "obviously not fit to live" (SA 76) and tells him openly that "some of you ought to be shot at sight like mad dogs" (SA 76). It is among other things his "*instinct* of a successful man" (SA 69; my italics), which drives him to abuse his powers to seek revenge on Michaelis. Although superior to Heat in more than a hierarchical sense, the Assistant Commissioner is also not free from being controlled by primal desires. As has already been shown, his intercession in favour of Michaelis is motivated by his basic "instinct of self-preservation" (SA 89). Revealingly, his particular aptitude "for the detection of incriminating truth" is also referred to as "a peculiar *instinct*" (SA 92; my italics), which has, moreover, "*unconsciously* governed his choice of career" (SA 92; my italics). Poignantly, the Assistant Commissioner thinks about his first job – colonial "police work" (SA 89) – in similar terms as Heat: "[It] had the saving character of an irregular sort of warfare or at least the risk and excitement of open air sport" (SA 89). Although he is now chained to a desk in London, his instinct of detection cannot be repressed: "It fed, since it could not roam abroad, upon the human material which was brought to it in its official seclusion" (SA 92). The instinct is here personified and likened to a voracious parasite. The phrasing suggests that it is the instinct that controls the human being and not the other way round.

Other examples of atavistic discourse in the novel are the many references to anthropophagy and butchery. For Karl Yundt, for instance, the "nature of the present economic conditions [is] cannibalistic" (SA 44); the capitalists are "nourishing their greed on the quivering flesh and the warm blood of the people" (SA 44). This analysis seems to be confirmed by the narrator's comment that this is a society in which "one sort of wretchedness [has] *to feed* upon the anguish of the other" (SA 132; my italics). Stevie becomes the victim of socio-economic man-eating as the bomb explosion reduces him to "raw material for a cannibal feast" (SA 70). His blood-scorched remains are presented to the 'cannibal', Chief Inspector Heat, on a "waterproof sheet" spread over a hospital table "in the manner of a table cloth" (SA 70). Fittingly, Heat, who "[has] not managed to get anything to eat" (SA 70) since morning, peers at the fragments of Stevie's body "with a calm face and the slightly anxious attention of an indigent customer bending over what may be called the by-products of a butcher's shop with a view to an inexpensive Sunday dinner" (SA 71). The idea that Stevie has been, as Gill calls it, "reified to food" (24) is taken up again when Verloc returns home on the night of the failed Greenwich bombing and is overcome by the "sensation of unappeasable hunger" (SA 190). When he notices the "piece of roast beef" on the table, which is "laid out in the likeness of funereal baked meats for Stevie's obsequies" (SA 190), he falls to "ravenously, without restraint and decency, cutting thick slices with the sharp carving knife, and swallowing them without bread" (SA 190-191). As Fleishman notes, it seems that Verloc "is eating the very flesh of Stevie" ("Symbolic World" 210). Ironically, Verloc, in *his* turn, will be reduced to mere meat with the help of the very carving knife he has used to cut the beef (cf. Fleishman, "Symbolic World" 210). As the examples above show, the references to cannibalism in the novel are frequently accompanied and amplified by allusions to meat, butchers, and butchery. To be sure, next to the police officer, the second most frequently mentioned occupation in *The Secret Agent* must be that of the butcher. It is worthwhile recalling that these are also the two professions Marlow in *Heart of Darkness* singles out as being typical of the way restraint is ensured in European societies (cf. HD 116). Thus, when Verloc walks to the Embassy, he notices in symbolic succession: "a doctor's brougham," serving as a "reminder of mortality" (SA 17); a "guilty looking cat" (SA 17), representing predatory instincts; and "a thick police constable" and "a butcher boy" (SA 17), who stand for the manner in which these instincts are held in check in

Western civilization. Another butcher who is mentioned a number of times is Winnie's first lover, whom she could not marry for financial reasons. Surprisingly, the meek Stevie, too, has "butcherly ambitions" (Lyon, *The Secret Agent* xxii): after hearing about cruelty in the German army, he flies into such a rage that Winnie has to take the carving knife from him. According to her, "[h]e would have stuck that officer like a pig if he had seen him then" (SA 51). Stevie, of course, will be butchered himself and Winnie will butcher her husband in turn.

The references to anthropophagy and butchery, the use of animal imagery, and the insistence on the way mankind is determined by the instincts of survival and reproduction reveal the novel's debts to Darwin and Freud. *The Secret Agent*, however, also makes use of pseudo-Darwinian theories, such as those propounded by Max Nordau and his predecessor, the Italian physician, psychiatrist, and criminologist Cesare Lombroso. Due to Lombroso's belief that "'criminal degenerates', epileptics, and 'idiots' could be recognized and categorized by such physical features as the shape of their ears or lips," he set up a classification of "various criminal types by means of physical anthropology" ("Lomboros, Cesare"). In *The Secret Agent* it is the anarchist and "ex-medical student without a degree" (SA 40), Alexander Ossipon, who is saturated with Lombroso's theories. He appears to be on the constant lookout for Lombrosan types. When he, for instance, observes Stevie at the kitchen table drawing circles, he classifies him as follows: "Very good type too, altogether, of that sort of degenerate. It's enough to glance at the lobes of his ears. If you read Lombroso –" (SA 41). At the end of the novel, sitting on the train to Southampton with Winnie, Ossipon once again "invoke[s] Lombroso" (SA 222) and notes the resemblance between her and her brother: "[T]he sister of a degenerate, a degenerate herself – of a murdering type" (SA 222). He goes on to make a mental list of her physical characteristics: "He gazed at her cheeks, at her nose, at her eyes, at her ears.... Bad!...Fatal! Mrs Verloc's lips parting, slightly relaxed under his passionately attentive gaze, he gazed also at her teeth....Not a doubt remained...a murdering type...." (SA 222). Ossipon's fanatical belief in criminal typologies is, however, ironically undermined by his own vulnerability to his Lombrosan diagnosis. After all, his physical characteristics are conspicuous: "A bush of crinkly yellow hair topped his red, freckled face, with a flattened nose and prominent mouth cast in the rough mould of the negro type. His almond-shaped eyes leered languidly over the high cheek bones" (SA 39). Cedric Watts has compared Ossipon's portrait to the typologies of Lombroso and has come across a surprising number of parallels:

[T]he nose of the born thief [says Lombroso] is often 'of a flattened, negroid character'; violators of women have lips 'protruding, as in negroes'; swindlers have 'curly and woolly hair'; many congenital criminals also have such mongoloid facial features as prominent cheek-bones and oblique eyes; and a high proportion of anarchists [...] are congenital criminals. (Notes, *The Secret Agent* 245)

According to this analysis, Ossipon would without doubt qualify not only as a degenerate but also as a congenital criminal.

Another possible degenerate in the novel who does not see that he is a potential victim of his own theories is the Professor. Physically he is of "lamentable inferiority" (SA 52): he is "frail, insignificant, shabby, miserable" (SA 231), "unwholesome looking" (SA 68), and speaks with a weak voice. His most conspicuous external characteristics are "large ears, thin like membranes, [...] standing far out from the sides of his frail skull" (SA 226). His physical wretchedness is ironically contrasted to his exalted view of himself as a Nietzschean superman, whose time will come after the world has been purged of all weakness: "Exterminate, exterminate! That is the only way of progress. [...] First the great multitude of the weak must go, then the only relatively strong. [...] First the blind, then the deaf and the dumb, then the halt and the lame – and so on. [...]" (SA 226). To Ossipon's anxious question as to what or who will remain, the Professor's megalomaniac answer is, ""I remain – if I am strong enough"" (SA 226). As Robert Hampson points out, the Professor here "unconsciously advocates an extreme version of Lombroso's ideas" ("Lombroso" 322) and does not see that he himself would be one of the first to be exterminated. Certainly, the narrative's insistence on his physical weakness and the repeated references to the extraordinary shape of his ears identify him as a Lombrosan type. As Cedric Watts notes, Lombroso indeed claimed that "[t]wenty-eight per cent. [sic] of criminals have handle-shaped ears standing out from the face as in the chimpanzee" (Notes, *The Secret Agent* 247). In addition, as Norman Sherry has shown (cf. 276-277), the Professor also conforms to one of Max Nordau's types of degenerates, the egomaniac, who is "in constant revolt against all that exists, and contrives how he may destroy it, or at least, dreams of destruction" (Nordau, quoted in Sherry 277).

In the case of Ossipon and the Professor Lombrosan typology is used to undermine the characters and to expose their arrogance and vanity. What their presentation, however, does not imply is that the theories of criminal anthropology and degeneration are invalid. In fact, while Ossipon and the Professor do not realize that they could themselves be classified as degenerates, the narrative, by emphasizing their physical abnormalities, insists that they can. Similarly, the portrayal of the other anarchists also suggests a correlation between extraordinary bodily characteristics and character qualities, such as hypocrisy, indolence, sensuality, immorality, or a predilection for radical political opinions. Poignantly, Lombroso indeed claimed that "between 31-40% of anarchists are conspicuously "the criminal type"" (Watts, "Jews and Degenerates" 78).[15] Not surprisingly, therefore, Michaelis, the Marxist, is "round like a tub, with an enormous stomach" (SA 85) and almost immobile due to his "grotesque and incurable obesity" (SA 85). Karl Yundt is old and decrepit with a "toothless mouth" and an "extraordinary expression of underhand malevolence [...] in his extinguished eyes" (SA 38). His movements resemble that of "a moribund murderer summoning all his remaining strength for a last stab" (SA 38). Like Ossipon and Michaelis, Yundt, too, lives parasitically off a lady friend and there is more than a hint at perverse sexuality in the description of his "worn out passion [...] resembling in its impotent fierceness the excitement of a senile sensualist" (SA 38). Just as in the case of the Professor, Michaelis's and Yundt's physical decrepitude is contrasted to their fiery talk of an overthrow of the current socio-economic system. Unlike the "perfect anarchist" (SA 67), however, the others are hypocrites: they do nothing but talk and would never dream of "rais[ing] personally as much as [their] little finger against the social edifice" (SA 42).

Even though the narrator does not use the term degenerates for Winnie and Stevie, he endorses Ossipon's Lombrosan analysis to some extent by highlighting certain tell-tale physical and behavioural characteristics. There are, for instance, Stevie's "vacant droop of his lower lip" (SA 13) and his "incapable weak hands" (SA 130). A brusque question causes him "to stutter to the point of suffocation" and, when startled by anything perplexing, he "squint[s] horribly" (SA 13). One moment he is given to "futile bodily agitation" (SA 130), another he appears "sunk in hebetude" (SA 43). Stevie's peculiarity and retardedness are further underlined by the way he is constantly referred to as a boy or child, whereas, in fact, he is at least twenty-one (cf. Fogel 169). According to Rebecca Stott, *The Secret Agent* "immediately evokes popular diagnoses of degeneracy in the creation of Winnie as the daughter of an alcoholic and the sister of a 'degenerate type'" (203). Like Ossipon, the narrator, too, notes the resemblance between her and her brother. When Winnie approaches her husband with the carving knife, her temporary madness is reflected in the way "the resemblance of her face with that of her brother [grows] at every step, even to the droop of the lower

---

[15]   Watts even argues that "in an elaborate covert plot, the unsavoury characters in *The Secret Agent* combine traits of criminal degeneracy [...] with a largely Jewish heritage" ("Jews and Degenerates" 78-79).

lip, even to the slight divergence of the eyes" (SA 197). As Robert Hampson has argued, the increased physical similarity to Stevie "signifies that, under pressure, Winnie reverts to type, and that reversion is emphasised by the addition of new details (in particular the strabismus) which feature in Lombroso's description of 'degenerates'" (*Joseph Conrad* 161). The climax is reached in the description of the "plunging blow" (SA 197) with which Winnie Verloc expertly dispatches her husband. She has put into it "all the inheritance of her immemorial and obscure descent, the simple ferocity of the age of caverns, and the unbalanced nervous fury of the age of barrooms" (SA 197). The first part of the quote explicitly invokes the concept of atavism, which is central to the theories of degeneration. Winnie reverts to savagery, that is, she regresses to earlier stages of evolutionary development. The last phrase of the quote reminds us of Winnie's more specific parental inheritance: as the daughter of a "licensed victualler" (SA 34) given to alcoholism and brutality she would have been – according to Lombroso and Nordau – prone to degeneracy and crime. Hampson even claims that "Winnie corresponds precisely to the sub-group of 'born criminals' that Lombroso calls 'mattoids'" (*Joseph Conrad* 161). This is a type "'whose lunacy has so long concealed itself behind an habitual calm' until it suddenly emerges in the form of 'transitory madness'" (Lombroso, quoted in Hampson, *Joseph Conrad* 161-162). Fitting this descripton, one of Winnie's major characteristics is her "unfathomable reserve" (SA 11), which she stubbornly holds on to until the night of her homicide when she goes "raving mad – murdering mad" (SA 197).

As we have seen, the character portrayals in *The Secret Agent* inevitably call up degenerationist typologies, thus creating an additional determinist sub-text. Nevertheless, the conclusion that the narrator is a full-fledged degenerationist is not warranted. This is due to his trenchant scepticism in general and his questioning of scientific fanaticism in particular. Ossipon, for instance, is blamed less for the *particular* theories he believes in but for the way they induce him to regard his fellow human beings with "that glance of insufferable, hopelessly dense sufficiency which nothing but the frequentation of science can give to the dullness of common mortals" (SA 41). The inhumanity of this view stands revealed in the contrast between Ossipon's and Winnie's perspective of Stevie: to the former he is merely a "[v]ery good type [...] of that sort of degenerate" (SA 41), whereas the latter sees him as "amiable, attractive, affectionate, and only a little, a very little, peculiar" (SA 134). Ossipon's scientific fanaticism illustrates what Vladimir attributes to the middle classes as a whole, namely that science is worshipped like a "sacro-sanct fetish" and treated as a "wooden faced panjandrum" (SA

29). The way Ossipon "*invok[es]* Lombroso" (SA 222; my italics) in the manner of "an Italian peasant [who] recommends himself to his favourite saint" (SA 222) illustrates that science is indeed Ossipon's religion. Karl Yundt's polemical Marxist reply to Ossipon's praise of Lombroso also shows that we should be wary of regarding one particular system of belief as the only true view of the world:

> Teeth and ears mark the criminal? Do they? And what about the law that marks him still better – the pretty branding instrument invented by the overfed to protect themselves against the hungry? Red hot applications on their vile skins – hey? [...] That's how your criminals are made for your Lombrosos to write their silly stuff about. (SA 41)

By thus juxtaposing two systems of belief – the Lombrosan and the Marxist one – both are revealed as ideologically biased. The implication is that they are 'merely' two types of discourse or, put differently, two possible descriptions of the world that may contain some truth but are not *the* truth.

The narrator's apparent degenerationist stance must also be qualified by the fact that not only the anarchists and Winnie and Stevie are endowed with exaggerated physical characteristics but most of the other characters as well. Noticeable is, for instance, the almost ubiquitous obesity. According to Hillis Miller, the reader realizes "[w]ith something of a shock [...] how many characters in *The Secret Agent* are fat. Conrad seems to be insisting on their gross bodies, as if their fatness were connected with the central theme of the novel" (50). Winnie, for instance, is a "young woman with a full bust, in a tight bodice, and with broad hips" (SA 10). Her mother is "a stout, wheezy woman, with a large brown face" and "swollen legs" (SA 11). Vladimir has a "large, white, plump hand" (SA 22) and Chief Inspector Heat's "full and pale physiognomy [is] marred by too much flesh" (SA 91). The cabman has an "enormous and unwashed countenance" (SA 121) and Sir Ethelred is "[v]ast in bulk and stature [...] an expanding man" (SA 105). An exception is the Assistant Commissioner who is, however, unusually thin. He has a "long, meagre face" (SA 91) and compared to the Home Secretary he has the "frail slenderness of a reed addressing an oak" (SA 106). We will be hard put to find in *The Secret Agent* a character that might be called physically 'normal'. The conclusion that therefore obtrudes itself is that in the novel everyone is in one way or another a degenerate or savage.

If we look at the novel's society from the point of view of the control mechanisms it has set up, such as the police and the surveillance system, it appears static and inert. The same thing holds true if we take an economic perspective and view the position of each individual as fixed in the social hierarchy by materialist determinants. These readings suggest that *The Secret Agent*'s society is completely deterministic. As Hillis Miller puts it,

[s]ociety [in the novel] is a machine, a man-made system of conventions [...]. The man-made machine has ended by making men, and by determining their existence within a framework of which many of them are not aware and which they do not wish to question. (42)

However, a somewhat different picture emerges, if we see the members of this society as not just controlled by forces outside but also inside themselves, such as biological or evolutionary ones. In *The Secret Agent* the latter are shown to manifest themselves in the dominance of the instincts, in particular egoism, which can be understood as a variant of the all-powerful survival instinct. If, as the novel insists, everyone's decisions and actions are motivated by self-interest, then society as a whole cannot be truly stable or immobile: concealed beneath a deceptive surface there is an ongoing anarchic struggle for individual advantage. This view, which seems diametrically opposed to Hillis Miller's, is taken by Avrom Fleishman: "*The Secret Agent* is [...] a novel about social anarchy. It is a dramatic portrayal of the sociological concept of *anomie* – radical disorder in the social structure and consequent personal dislocation" (Fleishman, "Symbolic World" 218). A reading which foregrounds the individual as biologically determined may therefore lead us to regard this society as shifting, unpredictable, and indeterministic. Without doubt, both Hillis Miller's and Fleishman's views of the novel's society are justified. Just as the representation of London and of time in *The Secret Agent* suggests that they contain both deterministic and indeterministic elements the same holds true for the portrayal of society.

7.6   The individual, freedom, and morality

As we have seen, the characters in *The Secret Agent* are subjected to a number of impersonal forces that leave little room for indiviudal control and free will. Most of the characters' reaction to this predicament is to try and adhere to Winnie's maxim that "things do not stand much looking into" (SA 136). Nevertheless, as Hillis Miller has noted, in the course of the story "[o]ne by one [the] characters are wrested from their complacency and put in a situation which is outside everything they have known, a situation which is, one might say, out of this world" (*Poets* 45). The intervention of chance in their lives does not, however, give the characters more freedom but throws their lack of it into even sharper relief. Verloc may be said to be the first victim of the "sequence of disenchantments" that Hillis Miller (*Poets* 45) sees as central to the plot. Although we might suppose that Verloc's multiple professions and identities as an embassy spy, unofficial informer to the British police, anarchist, and dealer in pornography give him more elbow-room than is granted to others, the opposite is the case. As the narrator insists, Verloc's primary characteristic is not adventurousness but indolence, to which he is devoted "with a sort of inert fanaticism, or perhaps rather with a fanatical inertness" (SA 16). Thus he is "thoroughly domesticated" (SA 11) and, after eleven years as a secret agent, "dwell[s] secure in the consciousness of his high value" (SA 187). At the beginning of the action, however, he is in for "an extremely rude awakening" (SA 166) when Vladimir accuses him of incompetence and threatens him with dismissal, if he does not commit himself to the Greenwich bomb plot. In the aftermath of the interview Verloc finds himself "struggling like a man in a nightmare for the preservation of his position" (SA 179). Driven to desperation, Verloc carries out Vladimir's orders but only finds, at the end of the day of the bombing, that "all action [is] over and his fate taken out of his hands with unexpected swiftness" (SA 176). That the affair has "[come] home to roost in Brett Street" (SA 179) so rapidly is due to the "small, tiny fact" (SA 179) of the address sewn into the lapel of Stevie's coat. To Verloc this appears like arbitrary chance and he "accept[s] the blow in the spirit of a convinced fatalist. The position [of secret agent] was gone through no one's fault really. [...] It was like slipping on a bit of orange peel in the dark and breaking your leg" (SA 179). Directly his professional complacency has been destroyed, his domestic situation explodes as well. His marriage, as we have seen, is based on a fatal misunderstanding. While he has "imagined himself loved by that woman" (SA 180) and, furthermore, "loved for his own sake" (SA 190), Winnie has looked upon Verloc merely as part of a "bargain" (SA 196) which has allowed her to 'buy' seven years' security and protection for her brother. Although the narrator condemns Verloc's selfish and irresponsible use of his brother-in-law to carry out the bombing, he makes some allowance for his lack of comprehension for the value Stevie has for his wife: '[I]n this he was excusable, since it was impossible for him to understand it *without ceasing to be himself*' (SA 176-177; my italics). The statement throws a tragic light on the Verlocs' marriage: their very natures have made genuine communication between them impossible.

Winnie's own "unfathomable reserve" (SA 11) and willed complacency receive their first upset when her mother, quite unexpectedly, tells her that she has decided to leave Brett Street. The shock of this information is so severe that it makes Winnie "depart from that distant and uninquiring acceptance of facts which [is] her force and her safeguard in life" (SA 119). ""Whatever did you want to do that for?"" she exclaims in spite of herself "in scandalised astonishment" (SA 119). After this outbreak she, however, immediately takes up her old attitude again. When she learns of Stevie's violent death, however, this is no longer possible as it shatters her "life of single purpose and of [...] noble unity of inspiration" (SA 183). As a consequence, she considers her "contract with existence, as represented by that man [i.e. Verloc] standing over there, [to be] at an end" (SA 189) and regards herself as "a free woman" (SA 189). In a novel in which most characters appear to be anything but free this is a remarkable statement. The epithet "free woman" is used for Winnie five times before and once after her murder. Only when Winnie surrenders herself to Ossipon is she said to be "no longer a free woman" (SA 218). The question, of course, arises whether Winnie, in the short time span before and after her murder, is genuinely free. After all, as determinists have warned us, *feeling* free in no way proves that we are free in an objective sense of the word. Indeed, Winnie's freedom seems to resemble more a state of uncertainty: she "[does] not exactly know what use to make of her freedom" (SA 191) and "enjoy[s] her complete irresponsibility and endless leisure [...] almost in the manner of a corpse" (SA 198). Furthermore, she is "at the mercy of mere trifles, of casual contacts" (SA 192) and her reasoning has "all the force of insane logic" (SA 192). When Verloc settles down on the sofa and tells his wife ominously to ""Come here"" (SA 196), Winnie seemingly obeys: ""Yes," answered obediently Mrs Verloc the free woman. She commanded her wits now, her vocal organs; she felt herself to be in an almost preternaturally perfect control of every fibre of her body" (SA 196). However, just as her feeling of freedom, her sense of absolute control, too, is an illusion. What *has* taken control of her are her murderous instincts. This becomes clear from the description of her savage "plunging blow" (SA 197) that evokes not only her direct parental inheritance but also her evolutionary ancestry. After her murder Winnie is – at least theoretically – in a position to *buy* a little freedom for herself with Verloc's money. However, she immediately hands it over to Ossipon and is prepared to enter into a 'bargain' which is even worse than her former marital arrangement: if Ossipon helps her flee the country, she will become his mistress. Winnie, apparently, is not able to imagine a relationship on any other terms or simply acts by force of habit.

Although less dramatically than in the cases discussed above, Chief Inspector Heat and Vladimir also have their wonted assumptions of control over their lives upset by the course of events. On the night of the bombing

Vladimir holds forth with immense self-satisfaction to the Lady Patroness about the lessons the British should draw from the Greenwich outrage. His smugness, however, evaporates when he suddenly finds himself face to face with the Assistant Commissioner, who confronts him with the results of the investigation. Vladimir's nervous reaction is enough to convince the police officer "that there must be some truth in the summary statements of Mr Verloc" (SA 171). Vladimir, who has only minutes before felt so secure in "his immense contempt for the English police" (SA 169), is now "almost awed by [the latter's] miraculous cleverness" (SA 171). Indeed, the "change of his opinion on the subject [is] so violent that it [makes] him for a moment feel slightly sick" (SA 171). When the Assistant Commissioner warns him in even more explicit terms, Vladimir escapes into a hansom "stony-eyed" and "[drives] off without a word" (SA 172).

Chief Inspector Heat's "sense of the fitness of things" (SA 69) is also seriously upset by the Greenwich outrage. After all, less than a week before the attack he assured the Home Secretary "with infinite satisfaction to himself [that] nothing of the sort could even be thought of without the department being aware of it within twenty four hours" (SA 69). However, because his "wisdom [is] of the official kind" he has deliberately neglected "a matter not of theory but of experience that in the close-woven stuff of relations between conspirator and police there occur unexpected solutions of continuity, sudden holes in space and time" (SA 69). Chance may reduce to nought even the most intricate system of supervision. Heat, however, is not just the victim of accident but also its beneficiary. When he inspects the blown-up body at Greenwich he finds a "singed piece of cloth" (SA 73) containing Stevie's Brett Street address, which is familiar to Heat. He is astonished "at the casual manner" in which it has come into his possession and therefore "after the manner of the average man, *whose ambition is to command events*, he began to mistrust such a gratuitous and accidental success – just because it seemed forced upon him" (SA 73; my italics). The interference of chance – even if beneficial – is annoying because it destroys the illusion of being in control. Partly because of Heat's suspicion of his apparent good luck and partly because of the motives discussed earlier, Heat does not at first tell his superior about his find but suggests pursuing the investigation in the direction of Michaelis. What follows, however, is the Chief Inspector's second comeuppance of the day. Instead of recognizing the advantages of arresting Michaelis, the Assistant Commissioner attacks him with the question, ""Now what is it you've got up your sleeve?"" (SA 91). Heat, who is not used to being addressed in this manner, senses that his professional expertise is being undermined and feels "like a tight rope artist

[...] if suddenly, in the middle of the performance, the manager of the Music Hall were to rush out of the proper managerial seclusion and begin to shake the rope" (SA 92). The Assistant Commissioner indeed proceeds to "turn him inside out like an old glove" (SA 93). Although it would be an exaggeration to say that the Chief Inspector's world is shattered by the unexpected turn of events, he nevertheless "[has] his performance spoiled" (SA 97) by finding himself, at the end of the interview, "chucked out of that case" (SA 153).

In contrast to the other characters, the Assistant Commissioner is very much aware of his lack of freedom – perhaps because "[h]is nature [is] one that is not easily accessible to illusions" (SA 79). He considers himself the "victim of an ironic fate" which has not only "chained [him] to a desk in the thick of four millions of men" but has also "brought about his [unhappy] marriage" (SA 89). Rather pathetically, he only feels free during "his daily whist party at his club" (SA 82), which allows him the "successful display of his skill without the assistance of any subordinate" and lets him forget for two hours "whatever was distasteful in his life" (SA 82). Again unlike the other characters he sees in the occurrence of the unexpected not a threat to his wonted ways but a welcome opportunity to escape the treadmill of day-to-day existence. Whether his transformation into an active investigator involves genuine free choice is, however, to be doubted. First of all, as has been noted earlier, his intercession on behalf of Michaelis does not spring from moral or professional considerations but from his "instinct of self preservation" (SA 89). Furthermore, when he starts sounding out his Chief Inspector, he is again guided by his "peculiar instinct" for the "detection of incriminating truth" (SA 92). Finally, when he decides to go after Verloc himself, this is not the result of calm reasoning but of "sccumb[ing] to a fascinating temptation" (SA 103).

Because the characters are represented as having so little freedom, the question as to the status of altruism and moral responsibility in the novel naturally arises. After all, these concepts can only have genuine value if free will and free choice exist. *The Secret Agent* is probably Conrad's most pessimistic novel as regards the possibility of unambiguous moral action in a materialist-Darwinian world. For instance, as Martin Seymour-Smith has pointed out, there is in the novel "no 'saved character', as in *Nostromo*, where there may even be two – Monygham, as well as the more obvious figure of Mrs Gould" (23). We could add Marlow of *Heart of Darkness* to this list. Although the respective narratives do not take completely uncritical views of Mrs Gould, Monygham, or Marlow, the undeniable integrity of these characters gives weight to their belief in moral principles and action. The only figure in *The Secret Agent* whose intelligence and capacity for self-criticism is comparable to the afore-mentioned characters is the Assistant Commissioner. His probity, however, is severely undermined by the way his ostensibly moral decision not to arrest Michaelis is revealed to be motivated not by ethical, legal, or professional principles but by petty private interests. It has been argued that in a novel in which all of the 'normal' characters are shown to be corrupted by egoism the moral alternative is embodied in the 'fool' Stevie. Jacques Berthoud, for instance, refers to him as "a variant of the traditional 'holy idiot'" (*Conrad* 141) and Avrom Fleishman sees him "in the tradition of the comic jester [...] who is out of touch with the practical realities of the world but who reaches the heart of its moral condition by his awareness of its divergence from a lost ideal state" ("Symbolic World" 204). It is without doubt of great moral significance that Stevie's cruel fate illustrates his own instinctive analysis of society as a "system of suffering" (cf. Berthoud, *Conrad* 140). Nevertheless, this does not turn Stevie into the moral centre of the narrative. What should make us wary of attributing to him the status of 'holy idiot' is, for instance, that he is not exempt from the materialist/Darwinian perspective the narrator takes of his characters. Thus we learn, for instance, that "[t]he tenderness of [Stevie's] universal charity had two phases as indissolubly joined and connected as the reverse and obverse sides of a medal. The anguish of immoderate compassion was succeeded by the pain of an innocent but pitiless rage" (SA 130). Stevie's moral qualities are therefore not informed by the Christian principle of 'turning the other cheek' but are part of a chain of instinctive, uncontrollable reflexes. It is also doubtful whether Stevie's morality is something naturally given or whether it is merely the result of his mother's and sister's efforts at 'conditioning' him. Thus Stevie's belief that Mr Verloc is "*good*" (SA 135) is an "ethical fact" which his mother and sister have "established, erected, consecrated [...] behind Mr Verloc's back, for reasons that [have] nothing to do with abstract morality" (SA 135). Furthermore, we learn that the "sanctions of Stevie's self restraint" have been "[h]is father's anger, the irritability of gentlemen lodgers, and Mr Verloc's predisposition to immoderate grief" (SA 135). John Lyon (cf. Introduction, *The Secret Agent* xii) also argues that Stevie's compassion is not entirely altruistic because it is so intricately bound up with what the narrator calls Stevie's "morbid horror and dread of physical pain" (SA 42). The idea that altruism is informed by fear for one's own well-being and is therefore to some extent egoism in disguise is expressed explicitly in a narratorial comment in the scene where Chief Inspector Heat contemplates Stevie's remains in the hospital. He is so affected by what he sees that he rises "by the force of sympathy, *which is a form of fear*, above the vulgar conceptions of time" (SA 71; my italics).

According to Allan Hunter, the novel's representation of Winnie's and her mother's sacrifices for Stevie also suggests a Darwinian reading of what he calls their "curious altruism" (176):

> [Both of them] are willing to compromise every other standard of honesty and decency for Stevie. It seems they are inherently – genetically – predisposed towards acts of abnegation that Conrad saw as typical of women [...]. If natural selection has made sure that the two women are likely to act that way, then their altruism is instinctive, not really conscious. Can it therefore *be* altruism? (176)

Although, as we have seen, Winnie and her mother are forced into their "acts of abnegation" at least as much by economic necessity as by genetic predisposition, it is certainly true that Winnie's devotion to Stevie is frequently described in instinctual terms. What is, however, even more troubling than the idea that Winnie's and her mother's love for Stevie might be 'mere' instinct is that their sacrifices initiate a tragic chain of cause and effect which inexorably leads to the destruction of the very person they were meant to save. As Aaron Fogel has pointed out it is "sympathy itself [that] causes the tragedy: it is the effective cause and not only the permeating affect. As maenads of pity and charity, Winnie and her mother involuntarily help to kill Stevie, driven not by intoxication but by pity" (188). Even more so than in his other novels Conrad seems to be intent on showing how altruism in a society thus constituted may be an ambiguous moral concept and may even have destructive results.

The status of moral responsibility in the novel is similarly complex. On the one hand the insistence on the characters' lack of freedom throws doubt on whether the figures can be held genuinely responsible for their deeds. On the other hand the novel shows that characters, such as Winnie, Verloc, or Ossipon, who try to evade taking responsibility for their actions, are nevertheless destroyed by their consequences. As regards Winnie, Ruth Kolani has noted that the murder of her husband is the most important of a "series of 'agentless acts' (87) which foreground '[u]naccountability, [...] the evasion of responsibility as a function of the dissociation between character and action" (87). When carrying out her deed Winnie is controlled by her instincts and hardly aware of what she is doing. Stylistically this is underlined by the separation between agent and weapon used: "Her right hand skimmed lightly the end of the table, and when she had passed on towards the sofa the carving knife had vanished without the slightest sound from the side of the dish" (SA 197). The actual killing is described from Verloc's perspective. His slow decoding of what is happening to him is once again rendered in terms which suggest agentless action: Verloc only sees "the moving shadow of an arm with a clenched hand holding a carving knife [which] flicker[s] up and down" (SA 197). Before Verloc can "move either hand or foot" the knife is "already planted in his breast" (SA 197). The knife seems to have a murderous life of its own. It is consistent with the evasion of agency that it takes Winnie until the end of the chapter to realize what has happened. Although it is clear to her that it is *she* who has committed the murder, she does not seem to accept full *moral* responsibility for it. She knows that she has done something which in her society is punished by death but she has no feelings of guilt, or believes that she has done something wrong: "Mrs Verloc […] was compelled to look into the very bottom of this thing. She saw there no haunting face, no reproachful shade, no vision of remorse, no sort of ideal conception. She saw there an object. That object was the gallows" (SA 201). As Nic Panagopoulos interprets the passage, "[t]he 'Furies' that [start to] torment her are not those of divine law or personal guilt but impersonal social justice" (127). Later on, when Winnie commits suicide by throwing herself into the Channel, she is not driven by feelings of moral accountability but because she knows that she will not be able to escape the consequences of her action: without friends and money, and on the run from the law she cannot survive.

Ossipon, who triggers Winnie's desperate act by his betrayal, does not openly admit to any kind of moral responsibility either. As has been shown earlier, he distances himself from Winnie by employing Lombroso's typology and reducing her to a scientific specimen. Nevertheless, the consequences of his deed come back to haunt him in the shape of newspaper phrases describing Winnie's death in the Channel. Although he laments his "cursed knowledge" (SA 229) of the affair and even offers the Professor the "legacy" (SA 230) he has stolen from Winnie, he does not openly admit to moral accountability. Characteristically, rather than accepting his guilt, he resorts to scientific diagnosis: ""I am seriously ill," he muttered to himself with scientific insight" (SA 213). There is, however, no doubt that it is his unacknowledged complicity in Winnie's death that is driving him into alcoholism and an early grave.

Verloc's violent end, too, is partly due to his refusal to accept full moral responsibility for Stevie's death. One reason for this is Verloc's belief that "the value of individuals consists in what they are in themselves" (SA 177). As, according to this reasoning, Stevie has little worth as a human being, Verloc thinks he can use him with impunity to carry out the bomb plot. Although he later on assures his wife that he "never meant any harm to come to that boy" (SA 175), it is obvious that he regrets his death not for Stevie's but for his own sake. He realizes that "Stevie dead was a much greater nuisance than ever he had been when alive" (SA 174). In his attempts to justify himself to his wife, his strategy is to play down the extent of his responsibility for Stevie's annihilation. First of all, he blames the "silly, jeering, dangerous brute" (SA 180) that ordered him to commit the outrage. Then he argues that if he had not thought of his wife, he "would have taken the bullying brute by the throat and rammed his head into the fireplace" (SA 181). He implies that by carrying out Vladimir's order and trying to save his job he actually acted on Winnie's behalf. He then goes so far as to accuse Winnie of having "brought the police about our ears" (SA 187) because of the address she sewed into Stevie's coat. The climax is reached when he claims that it was Winnie who gave him the idea of using Stevie to carry the bomb by constantly praising her brother up to him. His conclusion is that Winnie is complicit in his death: "Don't you make any mistake about it: if you will have it that I killed the boy, then you've killed him as much as I" (SA 194). Although there is an element of tragic truth in Verloc's accusations, the assertion that Winnie intentionally contributed to the killing of her beloved brother is perverse and merely indicative of Verloc's fatal ignorance of the true state of his domestic situation. The consequences of his deed engulf him just as he makes himself comfortable on the sofa and ironically wishes "for a more perfect rest – for sleep – for a few hours of delicious forgetfulness" (SA 195). Similarly to *Heart of Darkness* and *Nostromo*, *The Secret Agent*, therefore, also seems to argue that it is impossible to avoid responsibility for our actions even if we have not freely willed them.

A final question that needs to be addressed is the role of the narrator with regard to what Kolani has termed the "moral 'anarchy'" (87) of the novel. Because of the lack of a character with true moral integrity, the question arises whether the narrator might provide a source of moral affirmation. Certainly, he is more overtly present in *The Secret Agent* than in *Nostromo*. With the help of his heavily ironic detachment he constantly makes the reader aware of his total control over the action and characters. Many critics have interpreted this narratorial stance negatively. Irving Howe is representative when he claims that "the novel resembles, at times, a relentless mill in which character after character is being ground to dust" (95). Hillis Miller takes a more nuanced view and explains the function of the narrator's traits as follows:

> To describe this town [London] from the point of view of someone blindly enclosed in it would be no way out of the darkness. The nature of the collective dream is invisible to the dreamers because it determines what is seen and how it is judged. If society is to be exposed there must be a withdrawal to some vantage point outside it. (*Poets*, 44)

This is why the detachment of an ironic point of view becomes necessary. The terms Hillis Miller uses invite a comparison between the effects of Conrad's narrator and those of Schopenhauer's moments of contemplation during which the "miserable pressure of the will" is lifted and we become free to view "the universal spectacle of the will" (Safranski 216). As we have seen, Conrad's characters, such as Monygham and Mrs Gould, Marlow, and Stevie, experience such moments of insight. They are of great moral value and related to how Conrad defines the task of the writer in the "Preface" to *The Nigger of the 'Narcissus'*: "[B]y the power of the written word, to make you hear, to make you feel – [...] before all, to make you *see*" ("Preface" x). In *The Secret Agent* the narrator's perspective might be regarded as the extended realization of such a Schopenhaueran moment, giving insight not just into the workings of a specific society but also into the human condition. The ironic and often comic manner in which this is done is another parallel to Shopenhauer, whose moments of contemplation are characterized by "non-participatory viewing, without being involved in blinding seriousness" (Safranski 339). In his "Author's Note" to the novel Conrad indeed reveals that he wanted to create a narrator who would "enable [him] to say all [he] felt [he] would have to say *in scorn as well as in pity*" (7; my italics). The complex ways in which the latter effect is achieved – despite or even because of this scorn – has been subject to debate. John Lyon, for instance, argues that "[t]he security of ironic withdrawal is itself ironically unmasked for the reader: it dissolves in the face of the absorbing, if melodramatic, immediacy of the 'scenic present' [...]" (Introduction, *The Secret Agent* xxxvi). Hugh Epstein similarly claims that "the novel does retrieve moments in which words are held to express a significance that resists the irony that crowds upon them" (Introduction xiii). Such instants occur in particular during the scenes featuring Winnie, her mother, and Stevie. Due to the unchronological structure of the narrative we know in advance that the two women's attempts to secure Stevie's future are doomed and futile. However, because of the masterly precision with which the characters' suffering is rendered we are made to experience a kind of pity that, in Berthoud's words, "constitutes a rebuttal of the sentimentalism and patronage that characterizes well-bred sympathy" (*"The Secret Agent"* 114). Similarly, if taken out of context, remarks such as Stevie's about the nature of his society – ""Bad world for poor people"" (SA 132) – appear banal and trivial. However, as Epstein has noted, the effort it costs Stevie to reach this conclusion and put into words "stands as the index of a moral responsiveness greater than the words themselves and remains active in unresolved opposition to the almost excessive authority of the narration" (Introduction xiii). This analysis also holds true for Winnie's reply to Stevie that ""Nobody can help that"" (SA 132), or for the cabman's statement that ""This ain't an easy world"" (SA 129). As the narrator phrases it, these utterances express "the lament of poor humanity, rich in suffering and indigent in words" (SA 223) and contain "the truth – the very cry of truth – [which is] found in a worn and artificial shape picked up somewhere among the phrases of sham sentiment" (SA 223). Some critics have argued that the narrator's perspective not only includes a moral component but that the negativity of his portrait of society also prepares a way beyond it. Allan Hunter, for instance, claims that the narrator is only able to "demonstrate the short-comings of humanity" *because* he "tacitly assumes that there are values worth preserving" (175). Cedric Watts similarly asserts that in the novel "we witness a largely debased world from a perspective implying an alternative world, sometimes ruthlessly patrician but generally more civilised and more rational" (Introduction, *The Secret Agent* xxiv). The moral affirmation implied in the narrator's perspective is, however, more vague than these critics suggest. Especially because the novel insists that it is not just a particular social or economic system that is flawed but the human condition as such, it is difficult to imagine that, as readers, we are meant to believe in a true alternative. It is worthwhile recalling Conrad's essay "Autocracy and War," in which he expresses hope for moral progress in world politics due to "a common conservative principle" (111). Quite characteristically, Conrad cannot or will not define this principle in detail and seems to doubt its very existence in the next sentences: "Whether such a principle exists – who can say? If it does not, then it ought to be invented" (111). The hope implied in the narrator's stance in *The Secret Agent* for a different world, in which moral notions and human freedom enjoy unambiguous validity, is certainly not any more concrete than that.

8. Conclusion

My hypothesis regarding Conrad's position in the free will and determinism debate was that his fiction addresses issues directly connected to the freedom-of-the-will-problem, even though it is not informed by one particular theory. By taking recourse to the philosophical, cultural, and historical background, it was possible to establish that Conrad was certainly not a compatibilist. This position would have been typical of a Victorian author such as George Eliot who reconciled free will and determinism by holding that as long as our actions are not coerced they are free. Conrad's stance, in contrast, is without doubt incompatibilist, which is characteristic of a Late Victorian/Early Modernist writer. In his works there is an unresolved tension between the insistence on moral responsibility for our actions, which presupposes the existence of free will, and the recognition of all-powerful external and internal forces that deny it. Within incompatibilism we can distinguish between three positions which, according to my hypothesis, are reflected in Conrad's fiction. Firstly, hard determinism combined with scepticism as regards human beings' ability to discover the truth about themselves and the universe. Secondly, near-determinism as exemplified by the theories of late nineteenth century evolutionists, such as T.H. Huxley, and early twentieth century physicists, such as Heisenberg and Bohr. Near-determinism accepts an element of chance or indeterminism in an otherwise strictly deterministic world. Conrad does not, like the libertarians in the philosophical debate, regard this as an opening for free will but rather as further evidence of loss of control: if randomness is accepted as part of the world, it becomes unknowable and capricious. These implications lead Conrad to occasionally resort to radical indeterminism or solipsism, which is the third position we find in his novels: no order is visible in the world outside us; universal causation is denied; our actions are purposeless and human existence therefore absurd; the only remaining source of knowledge is our solitary consciousness. The paradigmatic analysis of Conrad's *Heart of Darkness*, *Nostromo*, and *The Secret Agent* has substantiated my hypothesis by showing how these three positions are reflected in recurring themes, such as the concern with how impersonal forces impinge on the individual and with the problem of morality and moral responsibility in a materialist-Darwinian universe.

In my analysis of *Nostromo* the focus was on the representation of the historical process and the relationship between the individual and history. The novel, as we have seen, takes a pessimistic view of possibilities of influencing the course of history and reveals human beings to be subject to various deterministic forces that severely limit their scope of action. This is explored in particular with regard to Charles Gould and his hope that with the help of the exploitation of the silver mine and the concomitant industrialisation of the country he will be able to break the vicious circle of revolutions and counter-revolutions and bring stability, justice, and progress to the country. In the course of developments he sees himself forced to finance a coup d'état and later on a counter-revolution to bring about the secession of Sulaco so that, at the novel's conclusion, he seems to be just another example of the long line of adventurers, revolutionists, and ruthless imperialist exploiters that make up the country's tragic history. Far from being able to channel the materialist forces he has unleashed towards a non-materialist end, they have become an end in themselves and seem to control him completely. On a more abstract level Gould's fate suggests that the so-called 'Whig view of history' cannot be used as an interpretative model to grasp the representation of history in the novel. After all, it regards history as an ordered, progressive process and advocates a compatibilist attitude towards the freedom-of-the-will-problem, namely that there is a balance between impersonal forces on the one hand and the possibilities of individual human beings on the other to shape not just their own lives but also history. The novel seems to mock Victorian bourgeois historiography and its grand narratives of progress explicitly by showing how inadequate the accounts of historical events by Don José Avellanos and Captain Mitchell are. As regards the freedom-of-the-will-problem *Nostromo* seems to favour incompatibilism in general and hard determinism in particular.

Because the determinist force on which *Nostromo* puts most emphasis is economics, the question arises in how far Marxism offers a more adequate model to describe the workings of history as presented in the novel. Certainly, the prime mover of the main events is Charles's decision to exploit the San Tomé mine, which precipitates the industrialisation of Sulaco, the installation of the Ribiera government, the Monterist revolution, and the foundation of the Occidental Republic. At the conclusion of the novel there are even hints that new revolutions are in the offing. Although the historical events are initiated by individual human beings, the novel stresses that it is the dynamics of material interests which dictate their actions and not the other way round. The narrative emphasises the divisiveness of capitalism, describes the industrialisation of Sulaco in negative terms, and shows how the worship of the silver corrupts the country's society. An exploration of the latter, however, also makes us aware of the limits of Marxist interpretations of *Nostromo*. Especially the novel's insistence on the mutual influence between the development of material interests and our animal instincts of egoism and greed draws our attention to the presence of Darwinian determinism and prompts a reading of the representation of history in terms of contemporary evolutionary theories that foreground the importance of chance. A close look at the participation of Hirsch, Monygham, and Decoud in the "War of Separation" shows that, viewed from the perspective of the micro-level of events, the secession appears to be as much the result of chance as of particular deterministic forces working in the background. The protagonists involved are motivated primarily by egoistic reasons and the establishment of an independent Sulaco is at best a secondary consideration. It seems completely arbitrary that the result of their actions is some kind of unintentional cooperation that leads to the realization of the 'master plan', the foundation of the Occidental Republic. Such a view of how history is made and its implications for free will and determinism largely correspond to T.H. Huxley's theory of evolution and his version of near-determinism: although the workings of the universe can broadly be described along deterministic lines, we also have to recognize randomness as an essential element. One consequence of this view is that we have to abandon the belief that we can discover the absolute truth about the workings of history. Another is that the possibilities of the individual to influence the historical process meaningfully are reduced towards zero. In moments of crisis such a deterministic viewpoint can transform itself into solipsism as it is, for instance, illustrated by Martin Decoud's experience during his night journey on the Golfo Placido and his stay on the Great Isabel. This analysis of *Nostromo*'s representation of history in general and of the relationship between the individual and the historical process in particular is underlined by the novel's narrative strategies, in particular the use of unchronological time-structures, of perspectival mobility, and of delayed decoding.

Due to its different narrative situation and its narrower canvas the nature of the historical process is not such an explicit topic in *Heart of Darkness* as in *Nostromo*. Nevertheless, as the idea of history as progress is central to imperialist ideology, it is implicitly at issue in Conrad's 1899 tale as well. In the discussion of *Heart of Darkness* I employed the term 'empire machine' as a metaphor for the coalescence of various historical, economic, and ideological forces that condition the existence of the characters in the tale. The economic aspects of imperialism are foregrounded especially in the early parts of *Heart of Darkness*. When Marlow, for instance, describes the landing of soldiers and custom-house officers or the French man-of-war shelling the coast, he emphasizes the impersonal and mechanical repetitiveness of a process which is totally indifferent to individual lives. The suggestion that human beings function like cog-wheels in a huge machine whose allegiance is only to material interests is reminiscent of Emilia Gould's description of the San Tomé mine but also of Conrad's famous letter to Cunninghame Graham in which he refers to the universe as a 'knitting machine' which is in complete control of our lives. The metaphor also resurfaces in the *Secret Agent*, where policemen and criminals are described as "[p]roducts of the same machine, one classed as useful and the other as noxious" (SA 74). In *Heart of Darkness* Marlow is shocked at the kind of 'economic activities' he observes at the Outer and Central Stations. Instead of economic efficiency, regeneration, and progress he encounters "inhabited devastation" (HD 32) and "a wanton smash-up" (HD 34). Instead of being elevated to a higher level of civilization as claimed by imperialist ideology, Marlow finds that the Africnas are reduced to 'beasts of burden', are put into chain-gangs, or are left to die in the 'grove of death'. The white 'empire builders' Marlow encounters seem hardly human. Some of them, such as the chief accountant at the Outer Station, appear to be conscious automata. The 'pilgrims' at the Central Station have made the Company's economic aim their exclusive desire: to get as much ivory as possible in order to earn percentages. Just as the Costaguaneros worship the silver, the pilgrims seem to pray to ivory. In this respect Kurtz is in no way different from the other whites. A primary motive for him to go to Africa is his lack of money and he establishes his reputation by amassing more ivory than all the other traders. At the Inner Station he even gets the native tribes to assist him in his brutal ivory raids across the country. Although Kurtz's behaviour has taken him, in Marlow's judgement, "beyond the bounds of permitted aspirations" (HD 107), he has been encouraged by the economic system he is part of. To some extent Kurtz has therefore fallen prey to the immoral and inhuman values of a system over which he has no control.

Just as in *Nostromo* Conrad also emphasises in *Heart of Darkness* how the values of capitalism are fatefully intertwined with our animal instincts so that the latter are blown out of all proportion. The pilgrims, the members of the Eldorado Exploring Expedition, the General Manager, and the brickmaker are all characterized by insatiable greed for material advantage, by an obsession with their careers within the Company hierarchy, and by a sadistic lust in exploiting, humiliating, and torturing the natives. Kurtz takes pride of place among these 'hollow men' and in his destructive voracity often resembles Freud's concept of the 'id'. Kurtz's atavistic regression from a paragon of European civilization to a beast crawling on all fours also suggests a reading in terms of contemporary pseudo-Darwinian theories of degeneration as propounded by Cesare Lombroso and his disciple Max Nordau. Another aspect of *Heart of Darkness* that invokes Darwinism is Marlow's emphasis on the unconquerable might of African nature. Although in *Nostromo* we also come across a timeless, majestic landscape from whose perspective mankind's struggles appear futile and insignificant, nature is not anthropomorphised to such an extent as in *Heart of Darkness*. In the latter novel nature appears to be an omnipotent, hostile force constantly ready to move in for the kill.

Another deterministic force that Marlow contends with in the course of his journey is imperialist ideology, which not only manifests itself in particular rhetoric but also epistemology. Marlow's thoughts, perceptions, and utterances are sometimes clearly informed by imperialism, whereas at other times, due to his sceptical and moral imagination, he manages to distance himself from it. A case in point is his view of the Africans. He is appalled at their brutal treatment at the Outer and Central Stations and feels pity for them. Furthermore, he is curious as to the meaning of African behaviour and culture and therefore engages in a limited and largely unspoken dialogue with 'the other', thus building bridges across the gulf between Europeans and Africans generated by imperialist ideology. On the other hand we also come across instances in Marlow's narration where he cannot resist the pressures of imperialist epistemology and indulges in descriptions of Africans that today would be regarded as racist. Marlow's actions to protect Kurtz's image on his return to Europe are particularly significant with regard to his shifting attitude towards imperialist ideology: he passes on a censored version of Kurtz's report to the press. Marlow thus actively contributes to the proliferation of imperialist propaganda and to the suppression of evidence as to the genocidal dimensions of the colonisation of the Congo. However, the political and ideological meaning of his deed dawns on him later on and his guilt at having suppressed the truth is one of the main motives for telling his tale in the first place. Kurtz himself can be seen as both purveyor and victim of imperialist ideology. Revealingly, his most salient characteristic is his gift of expression, which he uses to produce the grandiloquent imperialist propaganda typical of the time. Unlike Marlow, Kurtz is not able distance himself from this kind of rhetoric but believes in its literal truth. He, for instance, succumbs to imperialism's promise of self-deification and freedom for the white man in the colonies, which was based on pseudo-scientific theories that seemingly proved the superiority of the white 'master race'. Consequently, Kurtz sets himself up as a kind of savage god at the Inner Station and wields absolute, arbitrary power over his followers. However, far from being free, Kurtz appears to be completely controlled by his most basic instincts.

The deterministic forces mentioned above have a formidable influence on Marlow's freedom of choice and the constitution of his identity. From the start of his African adventure when the idea of going to the Congo takes hold of him, he has little control over what happens to him. His initiation into the imperialist 'conspiracy' already begins in Europe with his interview at the Company headquarters and the examination by the doctor. His naïve and enthusiastic aunt also makes him aware that in terms of imperialist ideology he has now been turned into a quasi-divine being. Marlow's feeling of being an impostor is reinforced when he arrives in Africa and has various identities thrust upon him. At the Central Station, for instance, Marlow is astonished to find out that he is associated with the Kurtz faction in the latter's quarrel with the General Manager. Although at that time Marlow hardly knows who Kurtz is he accepts the identity thrust upon him. In the course of his up-river journey Marlow becomes obsessed with meeting Kurtz and is distraught when it seems that he might already have died. Frequently Marlow perceives Kurtz as part of larger deterministic forces over which he has no control. When Kurtz entrusts him with his infamous report and other papers, he turns Marlow into the keeper of his memory. Back in the 'sepulchral city' Kurtz still seems to dictate Marlow's actions. His presence as Marlow's sinister double is almost palpable during the visit to the Intended. She automatically assumes that Marlow is an admirer of her late fiancé and leaves him no choice but to tell her what *she* wants to hear about Kurtz's end. Given Marlow's lack of power over what happens to him, it is not surprising that he defines the human condition as a "mysterious arrangement of merciless logic for a futile purpose" (HD 112). Indeed, he sometimes feels so oppressed by the forces he is exposed to that he resorts to solipsism. Thus he frequently insists on the unreal, dream-like nature of his African experience and doubts his ability to perceive reality clearly. Kurtz, too, remains an indistinct and ambiguous figure throughout the narrative and Marlow's evaluation of him is contradictory and fraught with paradoxes. Marlow frequently couples the solipsistic perspective with linguistic scepticism and at one point even wonders whether he is able to convey any meaning to his audience.

Similar to *Nostromo* various techniques of presentation are employed in *Heart of Darkness* to express the deterministic and the solipsistic paradigm. For instance, Marlow's difficulties in decoding African reality are emphasised by the use of delayed decoding, which makes the reader almost literally experience Marlow's difficulties in comprehending the bewildering sense impressions he is bombarded with. In philosophical terms, delayed decoding undermines universal causation and presents the effect of an occurrence before revealing its cause. In this way the technique inserts a degree of indeterminism into the process of making sense of reality, which we conventionally imagine to take place in an ordered, rational, and cause-and-effect manner. Among the techniques used to reinforce determinism are, for instance, the evolutionary or "dwarfing perspective" (Watts, *Heart* 71) or the presentation of the animate as though it were inanimate or of the organic as though it were mechanical.

In *The Secret Agent* London fulfils a similar function to that of nature in *Nostromo* and *Heart of Darkness*. It is certainly more than mere setting but a character or force in its own right. That its most salient characteristic is interminable darkness provides a direct link to the frame-tale of *Heart of Darkness*, in which the primary narrator repeatedly notes the brooding gloom over "the place of the monstrous town" (HD 17-18) in the vicinity. The implication is, of course, that 'the heart of darkness' is not located in the so-called 'Dark Continent' but in the British capital, the hub of European civilization. It is highly ironic that when in *The Secret Agent* we move directly into "the very centre of the Empire on which the sun never sets" (SA 162) it appears to be a place of perpetual darkness. The urban environment in *The Secret Agent* is anthropomorphised to a similar degree as the African wilderness in *Heart of Darkness*. Although it is man-made, the city seems to have slipped from human beings' control and exercises a mysterious power over them. Sometimes the town is likened to an inhuman monster that swallows up its inhabitants; sometimes it appears as an oppressive accumulation of timeless dead matter which is equally alien to the teeming millions that live in its midst. This entity, therefore, is made up of contradictory elements: it is organic and inorganic, static and constantly changing, deterministic and indeterministic.

Similar to *Heart of Darkness* and *Nostromo*, *The Secret Agent* exposes the insincerity and hypocrisy of political rhetoric. The anarchists, for instance, vociferously attack the political and social status quo and indulge in grandiose speeches about changing the world. However, they are not prepared to actively lift a finger towards realizing their goals. It is obvious that they are quite happy to live safely within society's conventions. *The Secret Agent* does not, like *Heart of Darkness*, explicitly explore ideology as a deterministic force that informs our ways of perceiving and decoding reality. Nevertheless, the novel is concerned with 'repressive structures', such as the police and the penal system, which ensure that individuals conform to a certain kind of behaviour. The police in the novel do not just aim at omnipresence in the streets of London but also at omniscience via a sophisticated and surprisingly comprehensive system of surveillance. What is particularly disconcerting about the police apparatus portrayed in *The Secret Agent* is its latent corruption. Chief Inspector Heat, for instance, proposes turning Michaelis into the scapegoat for the Greenwich bombing because he wants to revenge himself on him. His official reason – that the anarchist's arrest would be the most convenient way for the department to proceed – is hardly less disturbing. Neither has the Assistant Commissioner's intercession in favour of Michaelis anything to do with ideas of legality, the fear of a possible miscarriage of justice, or the need to save an innocent man from imprisonment: he wants to placate his difficult wife and safeguard his domestic peace.

Although silver and ivory are not to be had in the London of *The Secret Agent*, material interests are just as ubiquitous and just as powerful. The novel highlights the immense gap between the rich and the poor and shows how the latter's lives are completely determined by economic necessity. Mrs Neale, for instance, is transformed by poverty and hardship into a domestic animal; the cabdriver is forced to abuse his decrepit horse in order to feed his family; Winnie is compelled to marry Verloc and her mother feels obliged to retire to a dismal almshouse in order to provide for Stevie. More generally speaking, we can observe that, like in *Nostromo*, everyone seems to be *nostre uomo*, 'our man', to everyone else. Thus Vladimir uses Verloc to implement his bombing plan, while Verloc, in turn, uses Stevie to carry it out; Karl Yundt and Ossipon exploit their female companions to survive financially; the Assistant Commissioner uses his wife to gain access to the highest levels of society; Inspector Heat wants to use Michaelis as a scapegoat, while Michaelis himself uses the Lady Patroness to enable him to write his autobiography. Conrad thus emphasizes how basic human instincts, such as egoism and greed, are exacerbated by the mechanisms of capitalism, which seem similar to those of Natural Selection. Poignantly, it is the otherwise hypocritical and feckless anarchists who draw attention to this fateful combination by means of the extravagant, blood-curdling metaphors they employ to describe capitalist society. *The Secret Agent*, however, also shows that, quite apart from its entanglement in material interests, the instinctual, animalistic nature of human beings must be regarded as a deterministic force in its own right. The character portrayals, however, do not *only* invoke Darwinism proper. The fact that the figures are frequently compared to animals, display grotesque physical characteristics, and are prone to atavistic regression suggests that we also have to take pseudo-scientific theories of degeneration into account as a possible deterministic subtext. Whereas in

Heart of Darkness and *Nostromo* a reading of certain characters in degenerationist terms is merely hinted at, in *The Secret Agent* it is explicitly suggested by the frequent references to Cesare Lombroso.

Just as in Conrad's two earlier novels, the protagonists in *The Secret Agent* also find themselves subject to a number of determinist forces that leave hardly any room for free will. The characters' typical reaction to these unpropitious conditions is to ignore them and to follow Winnie's maxim that "things do not stand much looking into" (SA 136). In the course of the narrative most of the figures are confronted with the sudden intervention of the unexpected in their lives, which, however, makes their lack of freedom and choice even more apparent. After being ordered out of the blue to commit the Greenwich bomb outrage Vladimir finds himself caught in a nightmare from which he does not awake until his murder; the shock of her brother's death turns Winnie into a mindless killer; during his interview with his superior the complacent Inspector Heat feels that the floor is being pulled away beneath his feet; even Vladimir's arrogance is shaken when the Assistant Commissioner tells him more or less openly that he has been discovered as the instigator of the Greenwich bombing. On a narratological and structural level the sense of strict determinism is reinforced by an inexorable plot, and a narrator who has an iron grip on the fictional world and views his characters with scathing scorn and irony from a position of god-like aloofness.

The problem of morality and moral responsibility in Conrad's fiction has been a central concern of this study. It arises due to Conrad's incompatibilist stance regarding free will and determinism and his uncompromising allegiance to a non-theological and scientific-determinist world-picture, in which the concept of a 'pure' and 'undiluted' morality no longer exists after its divine sanction has vanished. For this reason my analysis of *Heart of Darkness* has, for instance, focused on the question why Marlow feels responsible for his actions even though he seems to have so little control over them and why Kurtz, the erstwhile paragon of European civilization, loses all vestiges of morality. One answer that Marlow himself gives is that some people like himself *do* possess a moral instinct whereas others like Kurtz do not. Characteristically, however, Marlow undermines this position by telling his listeners on board the *Nellie* that morality has not become an innate quality of Europeans but is merely externally enforced by the system of constraints that dominates our societies. Marlow suggests that, exposed to similar conditions as Kurtz, his friends would degenerate just as rapidly. If we apply this argumentation to Marlow's own behaviour, we could argue that he does not lose his restraint because, throughout his African journey, he clings to the confines of his ship, which for him functions as a remnant of European civilization. He supplements this strategy by a "deliberate belief" (HD 63), which he, however, does not define but which seems close to the work ethic as propounded, among others, by Thomas Carlyle. Marlow's two positions as regards the nature of morality are summed up in T.H. Huxley's definition of the individual's moral sense. Huxley argues that the latter is

> dependent in part upon associations of pleasure and pain, approbation and disapprobation formed by education in early youth, but in part also on an innate sense of moral beauty and ugliness [...] which is possessed by some people in great strength, while some are totally devoid of it. (quoted in Reed, "Huxley" 33)

Of course, if morality is just another word for restraint, which is, furthermore, imposed from the outside, then genuine moral responsibility and the possibility of free choice might not exist either. Although these doubts run through Marlow's narration, his response is not one of resignation but of affirmation. Marlow's behaviour suggests that to ensure that human beings do not lose their humanity, a "deliberate belief" in moral concepts and therefore also in limited human freedom is necessary despite the awareness of the possible illusory nature of this belief. Although Marlow is compromised by his participation in the imperialist exploitation of Africa, his feelings of guilt, which manifest themselves in his drive to narrate his story, show that he accepts responsibility for what he has seen and done, even if he has had little choice in the course of his actions. Similarly, even though he doubts whether he is able to convey the truth of his experience, he nevertheless doggedly persists in his narration, which can therefore be interpreted as an assertion of his will as against the determinist forces that dwarf him.

In *Nostromo* the ambiguity of moral action in a materialist-Darwinian world is explored in particular with regard to Emilia Gould and Dr Monygham. Similar to Marlow both of them base their actions on a "deliberate belief" in moral principles and in a humanitarian code of conduct, which distinguishes them from virtually all the other characters in the novel. Just as Marlow's moral stance enables him to view imperialism and its effects on Africa critically, it enables Mrs Gould and Monygham to question the benefits of the industrialization of Sulaco and to become aware of the costs in moral and human terms exacted by the exigencies of material interests. Monygham's moral principles, however, reveal paradoxical aspects when he becomes a participant in the 'War of Separation'. His motives for his involvement are his love for Emilia, his exacting code of conduct, and feelings of guilt about having informed on his friends under torture. In his determination to save Emilia by playing a hazardous cat-and-mouse game with Sotillo to keep him off the town, he becomes oblivious to all other concerns and regards everyone else that comes his way as a mere means to that end. Emilia's actions, too, may become suspect if we view them from a postcolonial or psychoanalytic perspective. They thus may appear either as a cover-up of her husband's imperialist exploits or as a substitute for her unfulfilled marriage. Thus even Emilia's altruism is not free from a certain degree of selfishness. Nevertheless, there is no doubt that the novel in general takes a positive view of characters such as Emilia Gould and Dr Monygham without being blind to the fact that in a non-theological, materialist world 'pure' morality no longer exists. Although from some perspectives, therefore, an insistence on moral principles may seem hypocritical, those characters that live by them appear freer and more human than those that do not. Without morality, we are reduced to the level of animals and are completely controlled by external forces and internal drives.

The Secret Agent is certainly Conrad's most pessimistic novel as regards moral affirmation in a materialist world. The novel does not contain characters such as Mrs Gould, Dr Monygham, or Marlow, who can be regarded as sustainers of humanity because of their "deliberate belief" in moral principles and a humanitarian code of conduct. The only character of comparable stature in *The Secret Agent* is the Assistant Commissioner, whose probity is, however, undermined by the way his ostensibly moral action not to arrest Michaelis is revealed to be motivated by petty private interests. Neither can Stevie, whom some critics view as a variant of the 'holy idiot' stock-type, be regarded as the moral centre of the novel. His compassion, after all, is not informed by the Christian principle of 'turning the other cheek' but is merely the result of a chain of instinctive, uncontrollable reflexes and inextricably linked to his fear of physical pain. The Darwinian and Nietzschean idea that altruism is egoism in disguise because it is informed, at least to some extent, by fear for one's own well-being is expressed explicitly in the scene where Chief Inspector Heat sympathetically contemplates Stevie's remains in the hospital (cf. SA 71). However, the most disconcerting point about morality made in the novel is that self-less, altruistic actions, such as Winnie and her mother's attempts to save Stevie, may set into motion a remorseless chain of cause-and-effect which leads to the destruction of the very person these sacrifices were supposed to protect. The question therefore arises whether the novel implies that in a Darwinian-materialist world conventional morality has become obsolete altogether. Certainly, *The Secret Agent* does not go as far as that. Showing that altruism is to some extent informed by egoism or that well-meant moral actions may sometimes have disastrous consequences, does not, in principle, invalidate morality as such. Nowhere is it implied in the narrative that Winnie and her mother should not have sacrificed themselves for Stevie or that the latter's compassion is worthless. Some critics have even argued that moral affirmation in the novel can be attributed to the narrator, whose ironical but clear-sighted stance evokes pity for the plight of the characters in the reader and may therefore have a cathartic effect.

In *The Secret Agent, Nostromo,* and *Heart of Darkness* Joseph Conrad shows that in a non-theological, deterministic world free will is more often than not reduced to an illusion. Although a belief in the latter may be life sustaining, we nevertheless have to readjust the way we view ourselves, our possibilities of actions, our relationships to others, and our conceptions of morality and moral responsibility. It is this unflinching view of the human condition in a materialist universe which distinguishes Conrad's novels from their Victorian forebears and turns them into landmarks of modernity.

9. Works Cited

With the exception of *The Secret Agent* all references to Joseph Conrad's works are to *Dent's Collected Edition of the Works of Joseph Conrad.*
References to Joseph Conrad's letters are, unless otherwise noted, to *The Cambridge Edition of the Letters of Joseph Conrad.*

Conrad, Joseph. *Dent's Collected Edition of the Works of Joseph Conrad.* 22 vols. London: J.M. Dent, 1946-55.
—. *The Secret Agent.* Ed. Bruce Harkness and S.W. Reid. The Cambridge Edition of the Works of Joseph Conrad. Cambridge: Cambridge University Press, 1990.
—. *The Cambridge Edition of the Letters of Joseph Conrad.* 9. vols. Cambridge: Cambridge University Press, 1983-2007.
—. *Joseph Conrad's Letters to R.B. Cunninghame Graham.* Ed. Cedric Watts. Cambridge: Cambridge University Press, 1969.

Achebe, Chinua. "An Image of Africa: Racism in Conrad's *Heart of Darkness.*" *Heart of Darkness.* By Joseph Conrad. Ed. Robert Kimbrough. 3rd ed. London: Norton, 1988. 251-262.
Adams, Richard. *Heart of Darkness.* Harmondsworth: Penguin, 1991.
Allen, Walter. *The English Novel: A Short Critical History.* Harmondsworth: Penguin, 1991.
Ayer, A.J., "Freedom and Necessity." *Free Will.* Ed. Gary Watson. Oxford: OUP, 1982. 15-23.
Bantock, G.H. "The Social and Intellectual Background." *From James to Eliot.* Ed. Boris Ford. Harmondsworth: Penguin, 1983. 13-57.
Barry, Peter. *Beginning Theory.* 2nd ed. Manchester: MUP, 2002.
Batchelor, John. *The Life of Joseph Conrad: A Critical Biography.* Oxford: Blackwell, 1996.
Bell, Michael. "The Metaphysics of Modernism." *The Cambridge Companion to Modernism.* Ed. Michael Levenson. Cambridge: CUP, 1999. 9-32.
Berthoud, Jacques. *Joseph Conrad: The Major Phase.* Cambridge: CUP, 1978.

—. "The Modernization of Sulaco." *Conrad Cities: Essays for Hans van Marle*. Ed. Gene M. Moore. Amsterdam: Rodopi, 1992. 139-157.

—. "*The Secret Agent.*" *Cambridge Companion to Joseph Conrad*. Ed. J.H. Stape. Cambridge: CUP, 1996. 100-121.

Bowler, Peter J. *Evolution: The History of an Idea*. Berkeley: California UP, 1989.

—. *Charles Darwin: The Man and His Influence*. Oxford: Blackwell, 1990.

Bradbury, Malcolm. *The Modern British Novel*. Penguin: Harmondsworth, 1994.

Brantlinger, Patrick. *Rule of Darkness: British Literature and Imperialism, 1830-1914*. Ithaca: Cornell UP, 1990.

—. "Thomas Henry Huxley and the Imperial Archive." *Thomas Henry Huxley's Place in Science and Letters: Centenary Essays*. Ed. Alan P. Barr. Athens: Georgia UP, 1997. 259-276.

—. "Victorians and Africans: The Genealogy of the Myth of the Dark Continent." *Joseph Conrad's* Heart of Darkness: *A Casebook*. Ed. Gene M. Moore. Oxford: Oxford University Press, 2004. 43-88.

Brooks, Peter. "An Unreadable Report: Conrad's *Heart of Darkness*." *Joseph Conrad: Contemporary Critical Essays*. New Casebooks. Ed. Elaine Jordan. Basingstoke: Macmillan, 1996. 67-86.

Bullock, Alan. "The Double Image." *Modernism: A Guide to European Literature 1890-1930*. Ed. Malcolm Bradbury and James McFarlane. Harmondsworth: Penguin, 1991. 58-70.

Campbell, C.A. "Has the Self 'Free Will'?" *Reason and Responsibility: Readings in Some Basic Problems of Philosophy*. Ed. Joel Feinberg and Russ Shafer-Landau. 10th ed. Belmot: Wadsworth, 1999. 441-451.

Carlyle, Thomas. "Signs of the Times." *Selected Writings*. Ed. Alan Shelston. Penguin: Harmondsworth, 1986. 61-85.

Carpenter, Rebecca. "From Naiveté to Knowledge: Emilia Gould and the "Kinder, Gentler" Imperialism." *Conradiana* 29 (1997): 83-100.

Childs, Peter. *Modernism*. London: Routledge, 2000.

Christmas, Peter. "Conrad's *Nostromo*: A Tale of Europe." *Joseph Conrad: Critical Assessments*. Vol.2. Ed. Keith Carabine. Mountfield: Helm Information, 1992. 608-630.

Clifford, James. *The Predicament of Culture: Twentieth-Century Ethnography, Literature, and Art*. Cambridge, Mass.: Harvard UP, 1988.

Conroy, Mark. "The Panoptical City: The Structure of Suspicion in *The Secret Agent*." *Conradiana* 15.3 (1983): 203-17.

Cunningham, Valentine. *In the Reading Gaol: Postmodernity, Texts, and History*. Oxford: Blackwell, 1994.

Desmond, Adrian. *Huxley: From Devil's Disciple to Evolution's High Priest*. Penguin: Harmondsworth, 1998.

Dilman, Ilham. *Free Will: An Historical and Philosophical Introduction.* London: Routledge, 1999.

Double, Richard. *Beginning Philosophy.* Oxford: OUP, 1999.

Drew, Philip. *The Meaning of Freedom.* Aberdeen: Aberdeen UP, 1982.

Epstein, Hugh. "A pier-glass in the cavern: The construction of London in *The Secret Agent.*" *Conrad's Cities: Essays for Hans van Marle.* Ed. Gene M. Moore. Amsterdam: Rodopi, 1992. 175-196.

—. Introduction. *The Secret Agent.* By Joseph Conrad. Ware: Wordsworth, 1993. vii-xxiii.

—. Notes. *The Secret Agent.* By Joseph Conrad. Ware: Wordsworth, 1993. 221-224.

—. "An Analogous Art: *The Secret Agent* and John Virtue's *London Paintings and Drawings.*" *Conradian* 32.1 (2007): 117-128.

Erdinast-Vulcan, Daphna. *Joseph Conrad and the Modern Temper.* Oxford: Claredon, 1991.

—. ""Heart of Darkness" and the Ends of Man." *Conradian* 28.1 (2003): 17-33.

—. "Some Millenial Footnotes on *Heart of Darkness.*" *Conrad in the Twenty-First Century: Contemporary Approaches and Perspectives.* Ed. Carola M. Kaplan, Peter Lancelot Mallios, and Andrea White. London: Routledge, 2005. 55-65.

Feinberg, Joel and Russ Shafer-Landau. *Reason and Responsibility: Readings in Some Basic Problems of Philosophy.* 10th ed. Belmont: Wadsworth, 1999.

Fleishman, Avrom. "The Symbolic World of *The Secret Agent.*" *English Literary History* 32 (1965): 196-219.

—. *Conrad's Politics: Community and Anarchy in the Fiction of Joseph Conrad.* Baltimore: Johns Hopkins Press, 1967.

Fogel, Aaron. "The Fragmentation of Sympathy in *The Secret Agent.*" *New Casebooks: Joseph Conrad.* Ed. Elaine Jordan. Basingstoke: Macmillan, 1996. 168-192.

Fothergill, Anthony. *Heart of Darkness. Open Guides to Literature.* Milton Keynes: Open University Press, 1989.

Forster, E.M. *Aspects of the Novel.* Harmondsworth: Penguin, 1990.

—. "The Pride of Mr Conrad." *Joseph Conrad: Critical Assessments.* Ed. Keith Carabine. Vol. 1. Mountfield: Helm Information, 1992. 396-399.

Funk-Rieselbach, Helen. *Conrad's Rebels.* Ann Arbor: UMI Research, 1985.

Gibson, Andrew. "Ethics and Unrepresentability in *Heart of Darkness.*" *Conrad and Theory.* Eds. Andrew Gibson and Robert Hampson. Amsterdam: Rodopi, 1998. 113-137.

Gill, David. "The Fascination of the Abomination: Conrad and Cannibalism." *Conradian* 24.2 (1999): 1-30.

Goonetilleke, D.C.R.A. *Joseph Conrad: Beyond Culture and Background.* Basingstoke: Macmillan, 1990.

Gribbin, John and Michael White. *Darwin: A Life in Science.* London: Touchstone, 2000.

Griffith, John W. *Joseph Conrad and the Anthropological Dilemma: 'Bewildered Traveller.'* Oxford: Clarendon, 1995.

Guerard, Albert. *Conrad the Novelist.* Cambridge, Mass.: Harvard UP, 1958.

Hama, Mark. "Time as Power: The Politics of Social Time in Conrad's *The Secret Agent.*" *Conradiana* 32.2 (2000): 123-143.

Hampson, Robert. ""If you read Lombroso": Conrad and Criminal Anthropology." *The Ugo Mursia Memorial Lectures.* Ed. Mario Curelli. Milano: Mursia International, 1988. 317-335.

—. *Joseph Conrad: Betrayal and Identity.* Basingstoke: Macmillan, 1992.

—. ""Topographical Mysteries": Conrad and London." *Conrad's Cities: Essays for Hans van Marle.* Ed. Gene M. Moore. Amsterdam: Rodopi, 1992. 160-174.

—. Introduction. *Heart of Darkness.* By Joseph Conrad. Harmondsworth: Penguin, 1995. ix-xliv.

—. Notes. *Heart of Darkness.* By Joseph Conrad. Harmondsworth: Penguin, 1995. 125-139.

Harkness, Bruce and S.W. Reid. Notes. *The Secret Agent.* By Joseph Conrad. Cambridge: CUP, 1990. 413-427.

Harrington, Ellen Burton. "The Female Offender, the New Woman, and Winnie Verloc in *The Secret Agent.*" *Conradian* 32 (2007): 57-69.

Harris, Jose. *Private Lives, Public Spirit: Britain 1870-1914.* Harmondsworth: Penguin, 1994.

Hawthorn, Jeremy. *Joseph Conrad: Language and Fictional Self-Consciousness.* London: Edward Arnold, 1979.

Hillis Miller, J. *Poets of Reality. Six Twentieth-Century Writers.* Cambridge, Mass.: Harvard UP, 1966.

—. "*Heart of Darkness* Revisited" *Joseph Conrad*: Heart of Darkness. Case Studies in Contemporary Criticism. Ed. Ross C. Murfin. 2nd ed. Boston: Bedford/St. Martin's, 1996. 206-220.

—. ""Material Interests": Conrad's *Nostromo* as a Critique of Global Capitalism." *Joseph Conrad: Voice, Sequence, History, Genre.* Ed. Jakob Lothe, Jeremy Hawthorn and James Phelan. Columbus: Ohio State UP, 2008. 160-177.

Hollingdale, R.J. *Nietzsche: The Man and his Philosophy.* Cambridge: CUP, 1999.

Hollis, Martin. *Invitation to Philosophy.* Oxford: OUP, 1997.

Holubetz, Margarete. "Bad World for Poor People": Social Criticism in *The Secret Agent.*" *Arbeiten aus Anglistik und Amerikanistik* 7 (1982): 13-22.

Honderich, Ted. *How Free Are You? The Determinism Problem.* 2nd ed. Oxford: OUP, 2002.

—. *The Consequences of Determinism.* Oxford: OUP, 1988.

Hospers, John. *An Introduction to Philosophical Analysis.* London: Routledge, 1997.

Houghton, Walter E. *The Victorian Frame of Mind, 1830-1870.* New Haven: Yale UP, 1957.

Howe, Irving. *Politics and the Novel.* New York: Meridian, 1957.

Hunter, Allan. *Joseph Conrad and the Ethics of Darwinism.* London: Croom Helm, 1983.

Huxley, Thomas Henry "Prolegomena." *The Major Prose of Thomas Henry Huxley.* Ed. Alan P. Barr. Athens: Georgia UP, 1997. 284-308.

—. "Evolution and Ethics." *The Major Prose of Thomas Henry Huxley.* Ed. Alan P. Barr. Athens: Georgia UP, 1997. 309-344.

James, William. "The Dilemma of Determinism." *The Will to Believe and Other Essays in Popular Philosophy.* New York: Longmans, 1927. 145-183.

Jenkins, Gareth. "Conrad's *Nostromo* and History." *Literature and History* 6 (1977): 138-178.

Kermode, Frank. *History and Value.* Oxford: Clarendon, 1988.

Knight, Diana. "Structuralism I: Narratology. Joseph Conrad, *Heart of Darkness.*" *Literary Theory at Work: Three Texts.* Ed. Douglas Tallack. London: Batsford, 1987. 9-28.

Knowles, Owen. "Conrad's Life." *The Cambridge Companion to Joseph Conrad.* Ed. J.H. Stape. Cambridge: CUP, 1996. 1-24.

—. Introduction. *Heart of Darkness.* By Joseph Conrad. London: Penguin, 2007. xiii-xxxiii.

Knowles, Owen and Gene Moore. *Oxford Reader's Companion to Conrad.* Oxford: OUP, 2000.

Kolani, Ruth. "Secret Agent, Absent Agent? Ethical-Stylistic Aspects of Anarchy in Conrad's *The Secret Agent.*" *The Ethics in Literature.* Ed. Andrew Hadfield, Dominic Rainsford, and Tim Woods. Basingstoke: Macmillan, 1999. 86-100.

Larkin, Maurice. *Man and Society in Nineteenth-Century Realism: Determinism and Literature.* London: Macmillan, 1977.

Leavis, F.R. *The Great Tradition.* Harmondsworth: Penguin, 1972.

Lester, John A. Jr. *Journey Through Despair 1880-1914: Transformations in British Literary Culture.* Princeton: Princeton UP, 1968.

Levenson, Michael. "The Value of Facts in the *Heart of Darkness.*" *Heart of Darkness.* By Joseph Conrad. Ed. Robert Kimbrough. 3rd ed. London: Norton, 1988. 391-405.

Lindqvist, Sven. *'Exterminate All the Brutes'.* London: Granta, 2002.

"Lombroso, Cesare." *Oxford Reader's Companion to Conrad.* Ed. Owen Knowles and Gene Moore. Oxford: OUP, 2000.

Lothe, Jakob. *Conrad's Narrative Method.* Oxford: Clarendon, 1991.

Lyon, John. Notes. *Youth/Heart of Darkness/The End of the Tether.* By Joseph Conrad. Harmondsworth: Penguin, 1995. 300-313.

—. Introduction. *Youth/Heart of Darkness/The End of the Tether.* By Joseph Conrad. Harmondsworth: Penguin, 1995. vii-xlv.

—. Introduction. *The Secret Agent.* By Joseph Conrad. Oxford: OUP, 2004. xi-xxxix.

Mallios, Peter Lancelot. "Reading *The Secret Agent* Now: The Press, the Police, the Premonition of Simulation." *Conrad in the Twenty-First Century: Contemporary Approaches and Perspectives.* Ed. Carola M. Kaplan, Peter Lancelot Mallios and Andrea White. London: Routledge, 2005. 155-172.

Marx, Karl and Friedrich Engels. *The Communist Manifesto.* Harmondsworth: Penguin, 1985.

McFarlane, James. "The Mind of Modernism." *Modernism: A Guide to European Literature 1890-1930.* Ed. Malcolm Bradbury and James McFarlane. Harmondsworth: Penguin, 1991. 71-93.

McFee, Graham. *Free Will.* Central Problems of Philosophy. Teddington: Acumen, 2000.

Moseley, William W. Jr. "The Vigilant Society: *The Secret Agent* and Victorian Panopticism." *Conradiana* 29 (1997): 59-78.

Nagel, Thomas. "Moral Luck." *Free Will.* Ed. Gary Watson. Oxford: OUP, 1982. 174-186.

Newsome, David. *The Victorian World Picture: Perceptions and Introspections in an Age of Change.* London: Fontana, 1998.

"Nordau, Max [Simon]." *Oxford Reader's Companion to Conrad.* Ed. Owen Knowles and Gene Moore. Oxford: OUP, 2000.

Oates, Joyce Carol. "The Immense Indifference of Things: The Tragedy of Conrad's *Nostromo.*" *Joseph Conrad: Critical Assessments.* Vol.2. Ed. Keith Carabine. Mountfield: Helm Information, 1992. 590-607.

O'Connor, D. J. *Free Will.* Basingstoke: Macmillan, 1972.

Panagopoulos, Nic. *The Fiction of Joseph Conrad: The Influence of Schopenhauer and Nietzsche.* Frankfurt am Main: Peter Lang, 1998.

Parry, Benita. *Conrad and Imperialism: Ideological Boundaries and Visionary Frontiers.* London: Macmillan, 1983.

Ray, Martin. "The Landscape of *The Secret Agent.*" *Conrad's Cities: Essays for Hans van Marle.* Ed. Gene M. Moore. Amsterdam: Rodopi, 1992. 197-206.

Reed, John R. *Victorian Will.* Athens: Ohio UP, 1989.

—. "Thomas Henry Huxley and the Question of Morality." *Thomas Henry Huxley's Place in Science and Letters: Centenary Essays.* Ed. Alan P. Barr. Athens: Georgia UP, 1997. 31-50.

Rose, Jonathan. *The Edwardian Temperament: 1895-1919.* Athens: Ohio UP, 1986.

Ross, Stephen. "Desire in *Heart of Darkness.*" *Conradiana* 36 (2004): 65-91.

Ryle, Gilbert. *Aspects of Mind.* Ed. René Meyer. Oxford: OUP, 1993.

Safranski, Rüdiger. *Schopenhauer and the Wild Years of Philosophy.* London: Weidenfeld and Nicolson, 1989.

Said, Edward W. *Culture and Imperialism.* London: Vintage, 1994.

Schacht, Richard. "Nietzsche, Friedrich Wilhelm." *The Oxford Companion to Philosophy.* Oxford: OUP, 1995. 619-623.

Seymour-Smith, Martin. Introduction. *The Secret Agent.* By Joseph Conrad. Harmondsworth: Penguin, 1984. 9-36.

Sherry, Norman. *Conrad's Western World.* Cambridge: CUP, 1971.

Smith, Steve. "Marxism and Ideology. Joseph Conrad, *Heart of Darkness.*" *Literary Theory at Work: Three Texts.* Ed. Douglas Tallack. London: Batsford, 1987.

Solomon, Robert C. "Sartre, Jean Paul." *The Cambridge Dictionary of Philosophy.* 2nd ed. Cambridge: CUP, 1999. 812-813.

Spittles, Brian. *Joseph Conrad: Text and Context.* London: Macmillan, 1992.

Stallman, R.W. "Time and *The Secret Agent.*" *Joseph Conrad: A Critical Symposium.* Ed. R.W. Stallman. Athens: Ohio UP, 1982. 234-254.

Stevenson, Randall. *Modernist Fiction: An Introduction.* London: Prentice Hall, 1998.

Storr, Anthony. *Freud.* Oxford: OUP, 1989.

Stott, Rebecca. "The Woman in Black: Unravelling Race and Gender in *The Secret Agent.*" *New Casebooks: Joseph Conrad.* Ed. Elaine Jordan. Basingstoke: Macmillan, 1996. 193-214.

Strawson, Peter. "Freedom and Resentment." *Free Will.* Ed. Gary Watson. Oxford: OUP, 1982. 59-80.

Taylor, A.J.P. Introduction. *The Communist Manifesto.* By Karl Marx and Friedrich Engels. Harmondsworth: Penguin, 1985. 7-47.

Tredell, Nicolas, ed. *Joseph Conrad: Heart of Darkness.* Icon Critical Guides. Cambridge: Icon Books, 1998.

Trusted, Jennifer. *Free Will and Responsibility.* Oxford: OUP, 1984.

Warren, Robert Penn. "*Nostromo.*" *Joseph Conrad: Critical Assessments.* Vol.2. Ed. Keith Carabine. Mountfield: Helm Information, 1992. 572-589.

Watson, Gary. "Introduction." *Free Will.* Ed. Gary Watson. Oxford: OUP, 1982. 1-14.

Watt, Ian. *Conrad in the Nineteenth Century.* London: Chatto and Windus, 1980.

Watts, Cedric. *Conrad's 'Heart of Darkness': A Critical and Contextual Discussion.* Milan: Mursia International, 1977.

—. *The Deceptive Text: An Introduction to Covert Plots.* Brighton: Harvester, 1984.

—. *Joseph Conrad: A Literary Life.* Basingstoke: Macmillan, 1989.

—. *Nostromo.* Harmondsworth: Penguin, 1990.

—. "Conrad and the Myth of the Monstrous Town." *Conrad's Cities: Essays for Hans van Marle.* Ed. Gene M. Moore. Amsterdam: Rodopi, 1992. 17-30.

—. *A Preface to Conrad.* 2nd ed. Longman: Harlow, 1993.

—. Introduction. *The Heart of Darkness.* By Joseph Conrad. London: Dent, 1995. xvii-xxxvi.

—. Notes. *Heart of Darkness and Other Tales.* By Joseph Conrad. Oxford: OUP, 1996. 253-277.

—. Introduction. *The Secret Agent.* By Joseph Conrad. London: Dent, 1997. xvii-xxvi.

—. Notes. *The Secret Agent.* By Joseph Conrad. London: Dent, 1997. 239-256.

—. "Jews and Degenerates in *The Secret Agent.*" *Conradian* 32.1 (2007): 70-82.

Weatherford, Roy. *The Implications of Determinism.* London: Routledge, 1991.

Westphal, Jonathan. *Philosophical Propositions: An Introduction to Philosophy.* London: Routledge, 1998.

Whitworth, Michael. "Inspector Heat Inspected: *The Secret Agent* and the Meaning of Entropy." *The Review of English Studies* 49 (1998): 40-59.

Wilding, Michael. "The Politics of *Nostromo.*" *Essays in Criticism* 16 (1966): 441-456.

Williams, Raymond. *The English Novel from Dickens to Lawrence.* London: Hogarth, 1970.

Wollaeger, Mark A. *Joseph Conrad and the Fictions of Skepticism.* Stanford: Stanford UP, 1990.

Lightning Source UK Ltd.
Milton Keynes UK
UKOW051227121011

180212UK00001B/180/P